Aristotle

FROM

NATURAL SCIENCE

THE METAPHYSICS

ZOOLOGY

PSYCHOLOGY

THE NICOMACHEAN ETHICS

ON STATECRAFT

THE ART OF POETRY

ARISTOTLE ใ∾ Containing Selections from Seven of the Most Important Books of *ARISTOTLE* ใ∾ Books which have set the pattern for the development of much of our Western Civilization ใ∾ Books that live today as fully as when they were written. These are *Natural Science, The Metaphysics, Zoology, Psychology, The Nicomachean Ethics, On Statecraft,* and *The Art of Poetry.* ใ∾ Selected and translated from the original Greek into the English of today by PHILIP WHEELWRIGHT.

Bobbs-Merrill Educational Publishing
Indianapolis

The Bobbs-Merrill Company, Inc.
4300 West 62nd Street
Indianapolis, Indiana 46268

First Edition

Eighteenth Printing—1977

ISBN 0-672-63010-9 (pbk)

Preface

THE PRESENT AUGMENTED and revised edition offers a translation of chosen passages from seven of Aristotle's most important works: *Natural Science* (commonly known as the *Physics*), *Metaphysics* (which Aristotle, had he entitled it himself, would doubtless have preferred to call *First* or *Basic Philosophy*), *Zoology* (comprising passages from the *Historia Animalium, De Partibus Animalium,* and *De Generatione Animalium*), *Psychology* (*De Anima*), *The Nicomachean Ethics, On Statecraft* (the so-called *Politics*), and *The Art of Poetry* (the *Poetics*). By this diversity the modern reader may become acquainted, in relatively brief space, with the breadth as well as the detailed penetration of the great Stagirite's researches, deductions, and speculations.

My purpose in retranslating has been to re-envisage Aristotle, as well as I could, in modern idiom. Accuracy and expressive communication have been my two principal and complementary concerns: an essential accuracy of idea and context rather than a petty accuracy of word and phrase. In order to vary the English rendering in accordance with the variant connotations of a Greek key-word in different instances of its use, and at the same time to preserve those general identities or at any rate continuities of meaning which are the warp of Aristotle's thinking, I have frequently inserted the transliterated Greek word in parentheses. This practice will enable the teacher to compare my renderings of key-words with the more traditional ones and to expand his interpretations of them where he thinks advisable. Where such transliteration is employed, Greek nouns and adjectives are regularly put in the nominative singular, Greek verbs in the present infinitive. Where more than one English word is employed to translate a Greek word or phrase, the related English words are enclosed in inverted commas. Latin spelling of Greek words has been adopted to the extent required by usage and propriety: one can hardly write 'Platon,' for example, but nothing is gained by exchanging the pleasant sound of 'Tyrannion' for 'Tyrannio.' The letters *êta* and *ômega* are distinguished from *epsilon* and *omikron* (except in proper names) by the circumflex accent.

The text here followed is that established by Immanuel Bekker, as published in the Royal Prussian Academy edition: *Aristotelis Opera edidit Academia Regia Borussica* (Berlin, 1831–1870). Occasional acceptance of variant readings, however, I have not usually thought it advisable, in view of the semi-popular character of this volume, to specify.

I have accepted many suggestions and even purloined an occasional phrase (never more than that) from other translators: from the several volumes of the Loeb Classical Library translations and from those of the Oxford University Press translations prepared under the general editorship of Sir David Ross; from Carteron's French translation of the *Natural Science*, Carlini's Italian translation of parts of the *Metaphysics*, translations of the *Psychology* by Hicks and Hammond, of the *Nicomachean Ethics* by Peters, Hatch, and Welldon, of *On Statecraft* by Barker, Jowett, and Welldon, of *The Art of Poetry* by Butcher, Bywater, Cooper, and Twining.

My sense of gratitude points chiefly toward Professor Fritz Kaufmann of the Department of Philosophy in the University of Buffalo, who has put his erudition and critical wisdom at my disposal, although he cannot, of course, be held responsible for any deficiencies in the result.

P. W.

January, 1951

Contents

BOOK VIII. *Motion and the Unmoved Mover*

THE METAPHYSICS

BOOK I. (Alpha Major). *On Philosophical Wisdom*

BOOK II. (Alpha Minor). *On Philosophical Wisdom (Continued)*

BOOK IV. (Gamma). *Being and 'Ousia'*

BOOK VI. (Epsilon). *Science and Its Objects*

BOOK IX. (Theta). *On the Actual and the Potential*

BOOK XII. (Lambda). *The Eternal Unmoved Mover*

ZOOLOGY

PSYCHOLOGY

BOOK I. *General Discussion of the Soul*

BOOK II. *The Soul and Its Faculties*

BOOK III. *Mind as Related to Sensation and Desire*

THE NICOMACHEAN ETHICS

CONTENTS

ON STATECRAFT

BOOK I. *The State*

CONTENTS

BOOK III. *Justice*

BOOK VIII. *Education*

THE ART OF POETRY

INDICES

Editor's Introduction

Editor's Introduction

ARISTOTLE'S LIFE AND WRITINGS

His Life

ARISTOTLE was born in 384 B. C. at Stagira, a town in Macedonia, colonized by Grecian emigrants. His father, Nicomachus, was a physician of some renown, who, like most members of his profession, claimed descent from Asclepius, god of medicine and son of Apollo. During Aristotle's boyhood the family moved to Pella, the Macedonian capital, where Nicomachus became court physician to King Amyntas II. Pella was at that time a rude and desolate town lying among swamps. Nothing is recorded of Aristotle's life there, but subsequent events indicate that he won the friendship of Amyntas' son Philip. When a few years later Nicomachus and his wife died—succumbing perhaps to the mephitic climate—Aristotle was sent back to Stagira and put under the guardianship of a relative.

He came to Athens in his eighteenth year. Plato's Academy was already celebrated; Aristotle entered, and stayed until Plato's death in 347. Then at length, with the accession of Speusippus, an abstract theoretician, to the academic directorship, he left Athens for the court of his friend Hermeias at Assos, in the Troad, Asia Minor. Hermeias was a remarkable man. Of lowly, perhaps servile birth, and made a eunuch by some childhood accident, he had attended Plato's Academy as a young man, and had afterwards contrived to secure dictatorial powers in the Trojan towns

Assos and Atarneus. As Plato's teachings had stimulated his interest in philosophy, especially in political philosophy, his court
became frequented by former disciples of Plato who, like Aristotle, found themselves out of sympathy with the metaphysical
extravagances of Speusippus. Most likely Aristotle gave lectures
there, expounding his criticisms of the Platonic doctrine of separate forms or archetypes, and laying the foundations of his own
philosophical system.[1] A niece of Hermeias', who was also his
adopted daughter, became Aristotle's wife.

Meanwhile Philip, who had succeeded Amyntas as King of
Macedon, was plotting an empire. Entertaining designs against
Persia, he formed a secret alliance with Hermeias permitting
himself to use Assos and Atarneus as bases of operations in case
of war. These diplomatic maneuvers appear to have revived his
boyhood friendship with Aristotle, whom, admiring also his vast
erudition, he invited to return to Macedon as tutor to the thirteen-
year-old Prince Alexander. Aristotle went.

The next two decades were marked by the rise of the Macedonian Empire: first the subjection of the Greek free cities by
Philip, and after his assassination in 336 the conquest of the East
by Alexander. Aristotle, who apparently had left Macedon and
was pursuing scientific researches in his native town of Stagira
at the time of Alexander's coronation, was by now the acknowledged leader of those former Platonists who had drifted away
from the Academy after Plato's death. Hermeias was dead, having
been captured by the Persians and, on refusing to betray Philip,
crucified. Accordingly, in the spring of 334 B. C., when Alexander
was crossing into Asia, Aristotle sailed again to Athens, no longer
as a disciple but to found a school of his own. He chose as its
site a park in a suburb of the city, dedicated to the Muses and
to Apollo 'Lyceus' (i.e., enlightener, or possibly wolf-slayer),
hence known as the Lyceum. For the next eleven years he taught

[1] Werner Jaeger's evidence on this point (*Aristotle, Fundamentals of the
History of his Development*, pp. 171 ff.) appears fairly conclusive.

there. Mornings were devoted to 'acroamatic discourses' (relatively technical and advanced, for members of the school only) on philosophy and the sciences, delivered while teacher and pupils strolled about the lawns and colonnades of the Lyceum—for which reason the school received the name peripatetic (*peripatein*, 'to walk about'). Afternoons were devoted to 'exoteric discourses' (for the general public) on rhetoric and oratory together with sundry matters of a popular sort. At these afternoon conferences, because of the multitude of auditors, Aristotle did not walk but sat while lecturing. Much of the remainder of the day must have been devoted to writing up, possibly with the aid of chosen students, the substance of his lectures for permanent record—i.e., in nearly the same form as we possess them today.[2] Research, too, kept him busy, thanks largely to the generosity of Alexander, who sent gifts of money and specimens of fauna and flora from the East. Nor was the social life of the school neglected. Common meals were held, for which Aristotle wrote regulations which appear to have covered, among other matters, the rules for gentlemanly drinking.[3]

When Alexander died in 323, a wave of long pent up anti-Macedonian feeling swept over Greece. A charge of irreligion was trumped up against Aristotle. Recalling the fate of Socrates and declaring that he would not give the Athenians a second chance to sin against philosophy, he turned over the direction of the Lyceum to his pupil Theophrastus and retired to his country estate in Euboea. There, one year later, in 322 B. C., he died.

His Writings

The writings of Aristotle offer a peculiar problem, in that we cannot be sure whether or not, in the form we have them today, Aristotle really wrote them. The prose style is unfinished, loose,

---

[2] See pp. xxi–xxv for evidence on this point.
[3] According to evidence as furnished and interpreted by Eduard Zeller, in *Aristotle and the Earlier Peripatetics*, Vol. I, p. 29, n. 2.

and choppy; in marked contrast to the conscientious precision with which key words are employed. There are redundancies and elaborations sometimes painful in their obviousness, contrasting with an elsewhere almost unintelligible brevity. Loosely connected clauses are often inserted in the middle of a sentence, upsetting an otherwise orderly movement of thought—a practice expressly interdicted by Aristotle in his treatise on oratory.[4] In short, that "incredible flow and sweetness of diction" for which Aristotle is praised by Cicero,[5] is nowhere evident in the surviving corpus of Aristotle's works.[6] How are we to account for these discrepancies? Interpolations by copyists, although doubtless some have been made, afford no sufficient explanation for stylistic peculiarities that are not scattered accidents but characteristic of the very fibre of the writings as we have them. Three principal explanations have been advanced: (1) that the Aristotelian Corpus (i.e., the body of extant writings which, irrespective of the present controversy as to their original function and subsequent history, are accepted today as authentic) was not written by Aristotle but represents the notes taken by students at his lectures and afterwards written up by them; (2) that it represents Aristotle's own notes for projected lecture-courses; (3) that the original Aristotelian writings were lost, recovered in a damaged condition, and pieced together by incompetent editors. Clearly the student of Aristotle cannot be indifferent to the claims of these alternative hypotheses; for if either the first or third of them is true, it means that in reading 'Aristotle' we are not getting Aris-

---

[4] In *The Art of Oratory* (*Rhetoric*), Bk. III, Chap. v, Aristotle offers the following sentence as an example of what to avoid: "But I, when he told me— for Cleon came begging and praying—set forth, taking them with me." The fault, he explains, is that a logical connection is broken up by the introduction of a merely casual connection; thus separating subject and predicate so as to strain the hearer's memory, and produce obscurity. Yet this very fault occurs frequently throughout the corpus of Aristotle's extant 'writings.'

[5] Cicero, *Topics*, Bk. I, Chap. i.

[6] The treatise on the *Athenian Constitution* falls under a separate category, in that it was written independently of Aristotle's lectures at the Lyceum.

totle's own words, and frequently perhaps not even the exact substance of his thought; while on the remaining supposition, the language, although perhaps truly Aristotle's, was intended only for his own use. Let us therefore examine briefly the evidence for and against each of the proposed hypotheses.

(1) The student note-taking hypothesis was first brought into prominence by Wilhelm Oncken, an acute Aristotelian scholar of the nineteenth century. The principal grounds on which Oncken bases his hypothesis are: (a) the defects of style already noted, which he declares are such as might be expected of a "peripatetic monologue hastily transcribed and carelessly written up from the notes of the listeners"; [7] and (b) the apparent references in the *Ethics* to an audience.[8] The second of these considerations establishes, no doubt, a close connection between the writings and Aristotle's lectures at the Lyceum, but it can be explained almost as satisfactorily by an alternative hypothesis presently to be advanced. As for the defects of style, their significance need not be what Oncken supposes. For, as Zeller remarks, "it is not here a question of any such defects as commonly arise in the redaction of well-ordered lectures badly reported, through omissions and repetitions and the erroneous piecing together of the broken argument. It is more a question of peculiarities of style not restrained by the writer, which are too characteristic and too constant in their character to allow us to make chance and the errors of third persons answerable for them." [9]

There are positive difficulties, too, in the note-taking hypothesis; the most prominent of which follow. (a) Since the notes covering the various phases of Aristotle's teachings must presumably have been taken down by more students than one, how are we to account for the comparative uniformity of style throughout? The

[7] Wilhelm Oncken, *Die Staatslehre des Aristoteles in historisch-politischen Umrissen*, esp. pp. 48–63.
[8] Oncken considered that he had established his theory with higher probability for the *Ethics* and *On Statecraft* (*Politics*) than for the other works.
[9] Zeller, *op. cit.*, Vol. I, p. 134.

style of the several treatises, whatever its defects, and although it shows evidences of more hasty writing in some parts than in others,[10] contains on the whole no greater variation than might plausibly be found within the writings of a single individual. (*b*) It is a little hard to see how students could have taken down, *while walking*, such detailed notes on such complicated and difficult subjects as, e.g., the *Metaphysics* and the middle books of the *Natural Science* (*Physics*). (*c*) Finally, the manner in which Aristotle's immediate followers clung to the letter of his writings suggests that they were dealing, or assumed that they were dealing, with his own words.[11] These considerations, while they do not gainsay the note-taking character of the Aristotelian writings, establish a strong improbability that those writings are the bare products of students acting on their own initiative, and unsupervised by the head of the School.

(2) Does the Corpus, then, represent Aristotle's own notes, from which he was to lecture? This hypothesis, like the first, has been advanced in order to account for the extreme, sometimes almost unintelligible conciseness of the style; and is apparently supported by Cicero's description of the acroamatic writings of Aristotle and Theophrastus as *commentaria*—i.e., memoranda, or notebooks.[12] But surely, even recognizing the stylistic defects and abbreviations already noted, the exposition as well as the sentence structure is in general (particularly in the *Ethics*) far more elaborate than would have been necessary if intended only as Aristotle's private memoranda. The cross references, too (as Zeller points out) are more numerous than Aristotle would have been likely

---

[10] Book III of the *Psychology* (*On the Soul*) is more abbreviated and hurried in its style than Books I and II. Many passages in the *Ethics* are over explicit and redundant as compared with, e.g., the *Natural Science*.

[11] This point is established by Christian A. Brandis, *Aristoteles, seine akademischen Zeitgenossen und nächsten Nachfolger*, p. 114, on the basis, for instance, of letters quoted by Simplicius (*Physics*, 216a, and elsewhere) in which Eudemus requests and receives from Theophrastus the exact text of a particular passage.

[12] *De Finibus*, Bk. V, Chap. v.

to require for his own use. Cicero's designation of the writings as *commentaria* need not be disputed: they are admittedly *commentaria*, but we have yet to discover in what sense.

(3) Finally, there is the hypothesis based on the following story told three centuries later by the geographer Strabo.[13] Aristotle bequeathed his library (so the story runs) to his successor Theophrastus, who in turn bequeathed it, together with his own, to a pupil named Neleus. Neleus took this collection of manuscripts to his home at Skepsis in the Troad, Asia Minor. A generation later, when the kings of the house of Attalos were marauding the district to collect books for the royal library at Pergamon, the heirs of Neleus hid the collection in an underground tunnel. Almost a century and a half later (c. 100 B. C.), after the Attalid kingdom had been taken over by Rome, the scrolls, now in a half-ruined condition as a result of 'moths' (worms?) and damp, were retrieved and sold to Apellicon of Teos, a wealthy resident of Athens. "Apellicon," according to Strabo, "was more of a bibliophile than a philosopher. With the idea of restoring what had been eaten away he had the writing recopied, but the gaps were not rightly filled, and the works were published full of errors. The result was that while the earlier Peripatetics who came after Theophrastus possessed scarcely any books at all (the few that they did possess being chiefly of a popular sort), so that they had no definite basis for their philosophy, and had to content themselves with rhetorical essay-making; on the other hand, the later school, although the publication of the books enabled them to become better philosophers as well as better Aristotelians, had to resort to conjecture on a great number of points, owing to the abundance of errors that had crept into the manuscripts." Finally (Strabo goes on to say) Sulla, after his capture of Athens, carried off Apellicon's library to Rome, where Tyrannion, a grammarian and enthusiastic Aristotelian scholar, obtained permission from the custodian to arrange the manuscripts. Here Strabo's account ends. We know

[13] Strabo, *Geography,* Bk. XIII, Chap. i, Sec. 54.

from other sources, however, that Andronicus of Rhodes devoted himself to the task of publishing an authentic and complete edition of Aristotle's works, grouping the various treatises and fragments under suitable headings.[14]

Now, clearly it is important to decide whether or not this story, with all its implications, is likely to be true. The point at issue, of course, is not whether one set of manuscripts containing the Aristotelian writings underwent the adventures thus described; we know on external evidence, as a matter of fact, that Aristotle left his own personal library to Theophrastus, who in turn left his to Neleus of Skepsis.[15] The real question is whether this library which was thus passed on by the first two heads of the School contained the only copies of the Aristotelian writings in existence —as Strabo plainly implies by his reference to the Peripatetics' lack of authentic documents. If we must answer this question affirmatively, it is a probable corollary that the Corpus as we possess it is hardly, in any exact sense, the work of Aristotle or even of his immediate disciples, but is the product of half-legible shreds of manuscript [16] patched together and supplemented by Apellicon, and later by Tyrannion and Andronicus, with hearsay accounts of the Peripatetic doctrines.

The unwelcomeness of this consequence is, of course, nothing against the hypothesis in question; but there is strong reason to challenge that hypothesis on other grounds. Briefly, (a) Despite all its defects of exposition and of style, the Corpus is still too magnificent a record of doctrine and of insight to have had the

[14] Andronicus' recension is first mentioned by Plutarch, in his *Life of Sulla*. The topical rearrangement of the treatises is told by Porphyry, in his *Life of Plotinus*.

[15] Diogenes Laertius, *Lives of the Philosophers:* chapters on Aristotle and Theophrastus.

[16] Professor Floyd A. Spencer, whom I consulted on this matter, has given it as his opinion that papyrus could probably not have been preserved in legible condition for one hundred and fifty years underground in the Troad; although in Egypt much longer preservations were possible both on account of the drier climate and because the Egyptians were more skilled in the art of embalmment.

synthetic origin here suggested. (*b*) The original writings were of course the most valuable tangible possession of the Peripatetic School after Aristotle's death. The Peripatetics were industrious scholars and presumably, like most scholars before the invention of printing, assiduous copyists. Are we to suppose that in the thirty-five years at their disposal between Aristotle's and Theophrastus' death they would have made no copies of the more important treatises of their late teacher? Or that Theophrastus, who in his will [17] shows the greatest solicitude for the future of the School, would have made no provision for their doing so? Or that he would have bequeathed the School's most priceless treasure to an individual unless there were other copies? (*c*) Cicero was a friend of Tyrannion, and was interested (though but superficially) in the Peripatetic philosophy; yet nowhere in his writings does he mention the presumably epoch-making discovery of the lost works of Aristotle, buried for over one hundred and fifty years. Nor is the supposed discovery mentioned by anyone else of that period except Strabo—not even by the Greek commentators, who appear to have used the edition of Andronicus either at first or second hand. (*d*) Finally, Zeller has assembled conclusive evidence to show that with the possible (but not certain) exception of the *Parts, Genesis,* and *Movements of Animals,* and the minor anthropological tracts, there is "either express proof or high probability" for the assertion that all the genuine portions of the Aristotelian Corpus were in use among scholars after the disappearance of Theophrastus' library from Athens.[18]

The strong objections to the three hypotheses just examined suggest an alternative hypothesis, which may be summarized as follows. We have referred to the fact that the lectures were given during morning strolls as evidence against the note-taking theory. The same fact furnishes also presumptive evidence that Aristotle would have wished to put the substance of his lectures into a

---

[17] Diogenes Laertius, *op. cit.*
[18] Zeller, *op. cit.*, Vol. I, pp. 143–153.

form that his disciples could retain. There was no time for literary elaboration: he was getting old, suffering from chronic dyspepsia, and in the few years ahead of him there loomed the task of systematizing for his students the greatest synthesis of human thought and knowledge the world has ever known, before or since.[19] Remember too that Aristotle was probably aiming to reach only a limited audience with these acroamatic discourses. Pressed for time and assured that his students, with whom he was in daily contact, could be trusted to grasp his thought with a minimum of elaboration, it is understandable that while he would have wished to leave with the School a record of his discourses, he should not have bothered to write them up with finished care. Doubtless as lectures or courses of lectures were repeated, new ideas developed, which would be set down or expanded at their proper place in the notes. As the process of emendation went on, the emended manuscripts would require recopying, which would be done by chosen disciples. Thus there might arise several recensions of a given course of lectures, particular examples of which, in fact, survive.[20] After Aristotle's death there would be the task of collating the various recensions and deciding upon an authentic text. It may be that Theophrastus assigned this task to scholars who had specialized in different branches of the Peripatetic teaching. This is conjectural, but it would serve to account for the decidedly more mature and concise thought-texture of, e.g., the *Metaphysics* than of the *Ethics*.

On the hypothesis here advanced, then, the Aristotelian writings are indeed notes, or '*commentaria*': not, however, notes taken by individual students, and not Aristotle's personal notes for projected lectures; but communal notes, intended as permanent records for the members of the Lyceum, written by Aristotle or under his direct supervision, and copied by students with probably no

[19] Not excepting that other stupendous synthesis, the *Summa* of St. Thomas; for it was upon Aristotle that Thomas built.

[20] The outstanding example is the two frequently overlapping bodies of ethical doctrine, the *Nicomachean* and the *Eudemian Ethics*.

other alterations than such as might be entailed by discrepancies between separate recensions. It may be that when Theophrastus' private manuscripts were carried off by Neleus to the Troad, there was no absolutely word-for-word copy of them in the possession of the School, but it is almost certain that there were other copies closely similar and no less authentic as records of what Aristotle had taught. This means that the work of Apellicon and more particularly of Andronicus, in the first century B. C., consisted not in drawing on their imaginations nor on hearsay to patch together the shreds of a well-nigh ruined collection of manuscripts, but in collating the ruined manuscripts retrieved from the cellar at Skepsis with other manuscripts possessed by the Peripatetic School at Athens, by the Alexandrian Library, and possibly by certain wealthy individual book-collectors. On this basis we may conclude, with Sir Alexander Grant, that "a general consensus ratifies, and nothing seriously impugns, the belief that in the leading portions of the great treatises which make up 'our edition' of Aristotle we possess the thought of the philosopher pretty nearly in the form under which it came from his own mind and was given originally either to his own disciples or to the world." [21]

Aristotle's principal extant works, commonly accepted as genuine, may be listed as follows. (Titles are given in English, Latin, or Greek forms, according to convenience and usage.)

(1) A group of six treatises on logic, designated by later editors the *Organon*, or 'instrument of thought.' It comprises the *Categories*, *De Interpretatione*, the *Prior Analytics*, the *Posterior Analytics*, the *Topics*, *De Sophisticis Elenchis*.

(2) On natural science: *Natural Science* (popularly known as the *Physics*), *De Generatione et Corruptione*, *Meteorology*.

(3) On zoology: *Historia Animalium*, *De Partibus Animalium*, *De Motu Animalium*, *De Incessu Animalium*, *De Generatione Animalium*.

[21] *The Ethics of Aristotle*, Vol. I, p. 2.

(4) On psychology: *De Anima*, here translated *Psychology;* also a collection of short treatises known as the *Parva Naturalia,* comprising: *De Sensu et Sensibili, De Memoria et Reminiscentia, De Somno, De Somniis, De Divinatione per Somnum, De Longitudine et Brevitate Vitae, De Vita et Morte, De Respiratione.*

(5) The treatise on *Basic Philosophy,* which has come to be called *Metaphysics* because in Andronicus' edition it was placed after the *Physics (meta ta physika).*

(6) Two versions of the ethical doctrine: the *Nicomachean Ethics,* the *Eudemian Ethics.*

(7) On political science: the treatise *On Statecraft* (the so-called *Politics*); and one surviving chapter from the *Constitutions,* on the *Constitution of Athens.*

(8) *The Art of Oratory (Technê Rhetorikê).*

(9) *The Art of Poetry (Peri Poiêtikês).*

ARISTOTLE'S PHILOSOPHY

As the foregoing catalogue of titles indicates, Aristotle's writings cover virtually every field of knowledge that was studied in his day. The various fields of 'knowledge, or science' (*epistêmê*) are classified according to the primary distinction between the contemplative (*theôrêtikos*) [22] sciences and the 'practical, or moral' (*praktikos*) sciences. Contemplative science deals with "what cannot be otherwise than it is." The formula does not mean that contemplative science is limited to a study of what happens by necessity, for it can also study what happens 'usually'—in other words, it is concerned too with the realm of probable occurrences. But its objects have a kind of independence that the objects of practical science lack, in that they are what they are independently of human volition. There are three contemplative sciences, or branches

[22] To speak of 'theoretical' reason and 'theoretical' science, as many interpreters of Aristotle do, can mislead the unwarned reader. *Theoria* does not mean theory, but *a viewing, a beholding*—particularly, in this context, by the eye of the mind.

of contemplative science: 'basic philosophy' (*protê philosophia*) or theology, i.e. what we today call metaphysics; mathematics, with particular reference to geometry; and 'natural science' (*physikê*), including what we now distinguish as physics, biology, and psychology. The objects of basic philosophy are separate from matter and devoid of 'motion and change' (*kinêsis*); the objects of mathematics, although still incapable of motion and change, "have no separate existence but are inherent in matter"; [23] while, finally, the objects of natural science are at once material and in motion. As distinguished from the contemplative there are the practical sciences, principally statecraft (*politikê*), the 'architectonic' science of this group, of which ethics is a part. A practical science has to do with what is somehow accessible, directly or indirectly, to human deliberation (*boulê*) and 'purposive choice' (*proairesis*). Besides the sciences there are the arts (*technê*), which have to do with making (*poiêsis*) and involve a productive (*poiêtikos*) use of reason. Poetics (*poiêtikê*) [24] and 'oratory or rhetoric' (*rhetorikê*) are the two species of art on which important treatises by Aristotle have been preserved.

Aristotle's Relation to his Predecessors

Conceiving philosophy as an organic development, to which each individual philosopher makes some partial contribution, Aristotle pays more systematic attention to the doctrines of his predecessors than had ever been done before. Two of those doctrines were of particular importance: Heraclitus' doctrine of universal flux, and the Platonic doctrine of Forms as taught in the

[23] The description of the objects of mathematics as inherent in matter becomes intelligible if we keep in mind that with the Greeks mathematics was grasped in more directly visual terms than with us.

[24] I.e., the theory of *poiêsis* in the narrower sense, as poetry, or poetic creation. The double meaning is brought out in Diotima's statement: "You are aware that *poiêsis* is a term of broad application. In all cases where anything whatever passes from not-being into being, the cause is *poiêsis*; so that [in a sense] the works produced by all the arts are acts of *poiêsis* and the makers of them are poets." (Plato, *Symposium*, 205 B.C.)

Academy by Speusippus and Xenocrates after Plato's death.

(1) *Heraclitus' doctrine of Flux*. The early Greeks, to a much greater extent than is habitual with us today, tended to think in terms of qualities and qualitative antitheses. Whereas we have become accustomed, in theory at least, to interpret cold as nothing positive but merely an absence of heat, and both hot and cold as attributes of things rather than things in themselves, perhaps indeed even as mere appearances whose underlying reality is molecular movement or electrical energy; the Greeks took hot and cold, like moist and dry, dense and rare, etc., as pairs of equally real entities. We ourselves would admit that it is just as real an *experience* to suffer from cold as to suffer from heat, and that on occasion both heat and cold may *seem* more real than the objects from which they are supposed to emanate. The Greeks accepted a more direct realism than we in this respect: "what universally seems," as Aristotle remarks, "may be said to *be*."

When opposite qualities are regarded as having real membership in the universe, the problem of motion (*kinêsis*) takes on a different aspect. How to explain, for example, the cooling of a warm liquid? In the earliest examples of Greek speculative thinking this question took the form: what has become of the quality hot, which was but no longer is; and whence has come the quality cold, which was not but now is? So with all other cases of change: whence do qualities come and whither do they go? One of the first answers proposed was that of Anaximander of Miletus, in the middle of the sixth century B. C.: a quality, he declared, is evidently *displaced* by its opposite; so that when a liquid cools we must think of the quality cold as coming in from somewhere, and the quality hot as being pushed away. In order to explain the advent of the second quality, the cold,[25] Anaximander was obliged to postulate an infinite reservoir of qualities, rather like the mythical Chaos out

[25] In the few extant fragments of Anaximander he deals only with the question of how qualities arrive, not with their disappearance. Very likely the Greeks did not feel that passing out of existence was as much of a mystery or stood as much in need of explanation as coming into existence did.

of which the poets had told that all things originally came; save that its existence was present as well as past, and had no very definite relation to the perceived spatial world.

The difficulties of Anaximander's naïvely spatial way of thinking elicited, early in the next century, a radically different explanation of qualitative change. Heraclitus of Ephesus (the Dark, or Obscure, as he came to be called on account of his paradoxes) announced the startling doctrine that qualitative change is exactly what it seems to be: that the cold does not come from anywhere nor the hot go anywhere, but that the hot actually 'turns into' the cold— i.e., that the quality hot (not merely the object in which the heat resides) ceases to be hot and becomes cold. But if this is the case it evidently follows that hot and cold cannot be as uncompromisingly opposite and 'inimical' as they were popularly supposed to be. Hence Heraclitus' bizarre paradox that hot and cold, and in general any two opposite qualities, are one and the same.

(2) *The Platonic doctrine of Forms.* The doctrine of forms (*eidos*) or archetypes (*idea*),[26] frequently discussed by Plato in his Dialogues and probably taught by him at the Academy, although offered in part as a refutation of Heraclitus' extreme relativism, was nevertheless based upon an acceptance of his fundamental paradox. Of the world of sense it is true, Plato admits, that opposites intermingle. The same object may appear simultaneously as hot and cold, the same experience as pleasant and painful, the same amount as double and half. But this signifies only that sense-experience is evidently not a valid medium of truth. For truth, together with its object, Real Being, must be rational, i.e. char-

---

[26] The Greek word *idea* (ἰδέα) is customarily translated 'idea,' and the Platonic doctrine referred to as the Doctrine of Ideas. Properly speaking, ἰδέα does not mean what is usually connoted by our word 'idea.' It means: (1) the look or appearance of a thing, the immediate object of 'seeing' (*idein*); (2) a nature, kind, or sort. In Plato's writings the word carries both sets of connotations: it is the essential character belonging to a given class of objects, directly apprehensible by the spiritual vision as something distinct from the particulars that 'participate' in it. The English word 'archetype' seems best suited to convey this total meaning.

acterized by perfect self-consistency; whence it follows from the contradictions discoverable in sense-experience, that sense-experience does not reveal Real Being but only Appearance, and thus does not give truth but only opinion. Its findings, to be sure, are not completely false, nor its objects completely non-existent, as the Eleatic philosophers—Parmenides, Zeno, and Melissus—had taught. In an individual wisely nurtured by the State the experiences of sense will give rise to 'sound opinion' (*orthê doxa*), which must serve as our starting-point in any subsequent investigation of truth. But the reason why sound opinions are thus aroused by the data of perception is that each particular object of sense bears a certain likeness to the archetype in which it participates, and thereby serves as a reminder to the soul, which before its entrance into the body had directly envisioned the archetype and afterwards, owing to the continual impingement of bodily needs and impressions, forgotten it. All learning is thus reminiscence: it is the soul's inspired recollection of the divine archetypes of things, once clearly seen, now apprehended dimly through the veil of sensuous phenomena.

The Logical Basis of Being

Aristotle's problem was to formulate a theory of *being* and a theory of *change* that while avoiding the pure relativism of Heraclitus (which Aristotle interprets as an impossible denial of the law of contradiction) on the one hand, should at the same time avoid the metaphysical extravagance of the Platonic theory of archetypes. Although Aristotle had been a Platonist during the period of his connection with the Academy,[27] he had later abandoned the notion of a Form separable from the class of objects that it characterizes. The form (*eidos*) is not anything apart from particular objects, it is inherent in their very matter (*hylê*). Correspondingly, the process of learning to know a thing's form—i.e., the universal principles implicit in it—is not a process of remem-

[27] See Jaeger, *op. cit.*, especially Chaps. III, IV.

bering a pure archetype formerly beheld by the soul. The process of learning has a natural explanation. Man is an animal, and along with all other animals he possesses a 'power of sense-discrimination' (*aesthêsis*). But whereas in the case of most animals the perceptions are transient, in man and certain of the other more developed species they are preserved by a power of memory. When by means of memory the perceptions are long preserved and (as happens in the case of man alone) multiplied and compounded to a considerable degree, there grows up a rational order of thought, which, viewing each new experience in the light of previous experiences thus preserved, multiplied, and compounded in memory, discerns the universal characteristics shared by them. This is the original inductive or abstractive process referred to above; by which, as we carry it forward to embrace still wider classes of particulars, we come to apprehend the general characteristics or 'forms' (*eidos*) of things, which serve as the 'first principles' (*archê*) of our subsequent demonstrations.

Now, what are the general characteristics of things, which we come to know by the abstractive process just described? The first phase of Aristotle's answer is expressed in terms of his doctrine of the categories. To know a thing is to grasp its 'articulable meaning' (*logos*)—i.e., what can be *said* about it. Aristotle distinguishes ten types of articulable meaning, which, generally speaking, may be predicated of a subject (*hypokeimenon*): (1) its 'specific thinghood' (*ousia*), (2) its quantity, (3) its quality, (4) its relatedness, (5) its place, (6) its time, (7) its position or posture, (8) what it possesses, (9) in what way it is active, and (10) in what way it is being passively affected. These are the categories: the ten ways in which anything can be said to *be*.

The most crucial of them is *ousia*, which has a twofold significance. *Ousia* is, in the first place, the *hypokeimenon*, the logical subject, about which any of the ten types of assertion can be made: considered in this aspect it is what Aristotle calls 'primary *ousia*.' But suppose we ask what the subject that we are thus talking about *essentially is*. The fact that we can significantly ask this question indicates the second logical aspect of *ousia*. 'This' (*ousia* in the primary sense, or substance) is a man, a horse, an olive: in such a predication we specify the 'what' of 'this'—*ousia* in the secondary sense, the essence. Thinghood in the sense of essence, of what a thing most specifically *is*, thus falls naturally into the predicate of a sentence. In that sense it can be handled by the techniques of logic: it can be defined, and it can be employed as the middle term of a syllogism. But in the primary sense, as the natural subject of predication—the 'this' of which other concepts are predicated—it cannot be used logically, nor predicated of anything further, but must be directly grasped as a brute fact of sense-perception.

Physical Reality and Change

So far we have been regarding thinghood (*ousia*) from a purely logical point of view. 'Things,' however, are not merely logical subjects of discourse; they are also real entities having membership in the world of nature (*physis*). As such, they fall within the province not of logic but of 'natural science' (*physikê*): it is no longer their definition alone that is to be considered, but also their actual observable character and activities, together with the 'factors that determine' (*aitia*, or *aition*) these. Our point of view shifts, from considering a thing as a 'logical subject' of which certain meanings may be predicated, to considering it as a 'material basis' (*hylê*) of actual events—as a 'specific thing' (*ousia*) possessing certain capabilities (*dynamis*) of 'motion or change' (*kinêsis*).

If a thing's actual character fulfilled all the implications of its definition—e.g., if man, defined as a rational animal, were in the fullest measure to realize everything that both 'animal' and 'rational' connote—it would be 'complete and perfect' (*teleios*) of its kind, and hence divine. But, among mortals at any rate, perfect completeness or complete perfection is never found. In each actual embodiment there is always, to a greater or less degree, a 'falling short' (*sterêsis*) of what the thing ideally (i.e., by definition) is. The definition of a thing does not state the thing's 'full actual character' (*entelecheia*)—i.e., all that it happens to be at any moment and in any circumstances, so far as this represents an actualization of what it is implicitly by definition—but merely its 'general, formal character' (*eidos*). This formal character of a thing indicates, from a purely logical standpoint, the species under which the thing immediately falls; while from a 'natural' (*physikos*) standpoint it indicates the goal (*telos*) toward which all members of that species tend naturally to move. Form, then, is not, for Aristotle, a Platonic archetype existing independently of and apart from the matter that it shapes. Form is implicit in matter; or, from a converse standpoint, the matter of anything is its potentiality (*dynamis*) of receiving or becoming a certain form. Matter and form are thus mutually relative: every particular thing is in some sense both. Any specific thing is matter to the extent that it is potentially but not yet actually of this or that character, form to the extent that its potential character has already been specifically realized.

On the basis of the foregoing analysis it is plain that change cannot be, as Heraclitus had supposed, a bare ceasing-to-exist of one quality (or quantity, position, relation, etc.) and a simultaneous starting-to-exist of some opposite or intermediate quality or state. This, as Aristotle demonstrates, is only one isolated aspect of the process of becoming. "It is only an *ousia*—a substance, or 'specific thing as such'—that can be said without qualification to come into existence. Where the becoming is of something other than a concrete thing—where it is a quantity, for example, or a quality, or a relation, or a moment of time, or a being located—a subject (*hypokeimenon*) is evidently presupposed, and this will be a 'concrete thing' (*ousia*). For it is 'concrete thinghood' (*ousia*) alone that is never predicated of anything, being always the subject to which predications refer." Thus we might perhaps say, in reply to Heraclitus, that there is no absolute becoming—except in a relative sense. It is true, in a relative sense, that the hot becomes the cold; but the same process can be more fully and more adequately described by saying either (1) *this hot substance* becomes a cold substance, or (2) *this substance,* which was hot, becomes cold. On either interpretation we recognize, or at least postulate, the existence of an entity that persists throughout the change and whose persistence makes the change intelligible. We recognize, in other words, that the full significance of change is not exhausted in its perishing aspects; but that change implies an unchanging basis of reference, which, grammatically speaking, is the subject of which the change is predicated.

Change (*kinêsis*) is conceived by Aristotle as movement from a 'starting-point which is also a determining principle' (*arché*) to an 'end which is also a goal' (*telos*). To express this connotation the word *kinêsis* will, in what follows, usually be translated 'motion'; although it must be recognized as a much broader term than movement or motion in a purely local sense. Locomotion is, in fact, only one of the three or four types of motion that Aristotle recognizes; and motion (*kinêsis*) is in turn subsumed under the still broader term *metabolé,* which for want of a better word will have to be translated 'change.' There are as many types of 'change' as there are categories, or meanings of the verb 'to be'—in short, ten. The most important of these are (1) change in respect of thinghood—or coming-into-existence (*genesis*) and passing-out-of-existence (*phthora*); (2) change in respect of quantity—growth and decay; (3) 'change of quality' (*alloiôsis*); and (4) change of place, or locomotion (*phora*—lit., 'the state of being borne along'). Ordinarily Aristotle confines the word 'motion' to the last three of these types of change; although in at least one passage [28] he extends it to embrace the processes of coming into and going out of existence as well. At any rate, in each type of motion or change there are certain pairs of terms between which the change takes

[28] *Natural Science,* Bk. III, Chap. i. See particularly p. 43, n. 2.

place. An object may 'move,' for example, from white to not-white, or from small to large, or from up (light) to down (heavy). In change of thinghood, which is the most fundamental of the types of change, and is an important aspect of all organic growth, the opposites are: (*a*) the ideal character of a thing—i.e., the form (*eidos*), or 'final shape' (*morphê*), toward which it tends; and (*b*) the present lack (*sterêsis*), to some degree at least, of that final character.[29] At each stage of the process the form or proper nature of the thing is present largely as a potentiality (*dynamis*); the 'fulfillment, realization, or actuality' (*entelecheia*) of that ideal nature is progressive, and never quite complete so long as the process continues. The process of achieving such fulfillment Aristotle calls *energeia*. But from another point of view the process (*energeia*) itself is a fulfillment; for when a thing moves or changes it fulfills in that very act its nature as something movable or changeable: "to just the extent that the buildable in its buildable aspect is being built, to that extent it has attained fulfillment; and this fulfillment is what is called building." Similarly, "qualitative alteration is the fulfillment of a qualitatively alterable thing quâ qualitatively alterable"; and so in the case of the other types of movement and change. Accordingly Aristotle defines motion (*kinêsis*) in general as "the fulfillment of a potentiality quâ potentiality."

Causal Determination, Chance, and Luck

A further important question about motion remains: how is motion determined—i.e., how is it produced and how is its character maintained? There are, Aristotle finds, four types of 'determining factor' (*aitia*, or *aition*), i.e., four ways of being 'responsible' (*aitios*) for the existence or occurrence of anything. (1) There is the 'stuff, or material' (*hylê*), which is the first condition of anything existing or occurring at all—the material factor. (2) There is the implicit form (*eidos*) or meaning (*logos*) of the thing, which

[29] The 'not-yetness' of that character, as Wicksteed and Cornford have proposed calling it. (*Op. cit.*, in Bibliography.)

we state when we define it—the formal factor. (3) There is the actual impetus that produces the thing or that sets it in motion—the propelling factor (the so-called 'efficient cause'). (4) And finally there is the 'end or goal' (*telos*), i.e. the goal (*tou heneka*) toward which a thing tends naturally to strive—the telic factor. In a natural process, such as the development of an animal from embryo, the second and fourth types of determining factor are but two aspects—the logical and physical—of one and the same factor. Thus a given embryo develops into a pig rather than into a man because (1) certain limiting material possibilities are furnished by the mother's menstrual fluid (which Aristotle supposed to be the maternal contribution to the forming of the embryo), and because (2) the form of 'pig' is imprinted upon this material factor by (3) the action of the male semen.[20] The form, moreover, is, in temporal perspective, (4) the goal toward which the embryo tends to develop—in the same natural way as the roots of a plant tend to move toward water and its leaves toward light. In a human activity, on the other hand, the formal and telic determining factors may be quite distinct. For instance, when an architect builds a temple, the material determinant is the stone, marble, etc.; the formal determinant is the meaning of a temple, which is at the same time an idea in the architect's mind, by virtue of which he succeeds in building a temple and not an obelisk; the propelling determinant is the actual work done by the architect, the builders, and their instruments; while the telic determinant is the purpose in view—which for the architect, perhaps, is to gain public recognition, and for the populace, to have a place for worship and sacrifice.

There is also another factor involved in all motion, or rather an aspect of all motion; and that is 'pure spontaneous chance' (*auto-*

---

[20] The paternal semen "is no part (*morion*) of the resulting embryo, any more than the carpenter's contribution to a building becomes the actual material (*hylê*) of the timber with which he works. . . . What [each] contributes to the material is shape (*morphê*) and form (*eidos*) through the motion (*kinêsis*) [which he sets going] in the material."—*De Generatione Animalium*, Bk. I, Chap. xxii.

maton) or luck (*tychê*). Nothing exists or occurs, as we have seen, without certain factors that determine its existence or occurrence. Nevertheless a given thing or occurrence does not embrace the whole universe: there will be other things or occurrences that do not determine it and are not determined by it. Its relation to them, and their relation to it, is 'incidental, or accidental' (*kata sym-bebêkos*). A relation may be incidental with respect to any of the four types of determining factor. Consider the formal factor, for example. If we affirm that Socrates is a man and that Socrates is rational, the two predicates are related to each other essentially and necessarily, inasmuch as 'man' is the genus to which Socrates belongs, and 'rational' is a part of its definition. But suppose we affirm that Socrates is wise and that Socrates is snub-nosed. Both of these predicates express true facts about Socrates, but as neither of them expresses qualities that are 'essential' to him as a man, their relation to each other is accidental. We cannot say that to be snub-nosed is to be wise, nor that to be wise is to be snub-nosed; for the meaning of either one does not imply the meaning of the other. We can say only that *in this instance,* i.e. in the case of Socrates, the two qualities happen to be conjoined.

When an incidental relation subsists with respect to the telic determining factor, Aristotle calls it 'spontaneous chance' (*auto-maton*), or, in certain cases, luck (*tychê*). Honey-water (to use one of his own examples) has the property of curing fever. The curing of fever, in other words, is a part of the telic determinant of the action of honey-water. Now, occasionally honey-water will fail to cure a fever. Such a failure, of course, never occurs for no reason at all: there are always certain factors present that determine it— chief of which is perhaps the bodily disposition of the individual patient. But suppose such a failure occurs on the day of the new moon. The new moon has of course come about on schedule; there is nothing fortuitous about its occurrence. But the two events—the failure of honey-water to cure and the appearance of the new moon—although each is determined by factors pertinent to itself, are not in any way determined by, or determinative of, each other. They are related 'incidentally' to a particular occasion, just as the qualities wise and snub-nosed, in our former illustration, were related incidentally to the particular man Socrates. But in the present case, since it is a question of actual occurrence and not of purely logical predication, they are said to be related 'by chance.' And when, as in the instance of honey-water failing to cure, a chance event has the further characteristics (1) of affecting a moral agent capable of choice, and (2) of being the kind of thing that (although he did not actually choose it on this occasion) he would have chosen if he had been in a position to choose, the chance event is called a matter of luck.

Unmoved Movers

The importance of Aristotle's doctrine of the four types of determining factor, together with his related doctrine of chance, becomes manifest when we pass to his doctrine of the 'unmoved mover,' which is essential to his view both of God and of man, of divine and of human activities. What causes motion? In asking that question today we tend to frame our answer in terms of propelling determinants. Propelling determinants of motion are conceived as themselves in motion—i.e., we explain a given change by another change, whether observed or postulated, that has preceded it; whence the same question can be raised again regarding the moving cause of the motion: what has moved *it?* Can the process be extended back without limit? An infinite regress of particulars is for Aristotle an inadmissible supposition, if not, indeed, self-contradictory and meaningless. Every process must have its *archê*—i.e., its first step or temporal beginning, which serves also as its original explanatory principle. This *archê* cannot itself be in motion; for if it were we should have to ask by what agency it was moved, which would mean that the real starting-point of the series lay somewhere farther back. The real *archê*, then, causes motion without itself 'having' motion; it moves other things but does not itself (in the intransitive sense of the verb) move; in short, it produces events, but is not itself an event. This conclusion is essential alike to Aristotle's theology and to his ethics. The original unmoved, unchanging cause of all motion and change in the universe is called God (*theos*); while on a smaller scale each individual soul (*psyché*) is an unmoved mover of its own 'purposeful choices' (*proairesis*) and 'moral actions' (*praxis*).

But is the foregoing argument, after all, a mere game of words without any corresponding reality? Is Aristotle's demonstration of an 'unmoved mover' but an ingenious sophism, on a par with Zeno's denial of all motion whatever? No; for experience provides direct verification. In the phenomenon of desire an unmoved cause of motion is seen in operation. The object of desire, although productive of motion in the desiderative agent, is itself, quâ desired, something static. As an illustration, suppose that I am hit by a falling apple: the cause of this incident, and of the subsequent processes of anger or pain in me, is the apple quâ moving. The apple, in such a case, will have caused motion in me by virtue of the motion already existing in itself. Suppose, on the other hand, that I desire an apple: what is the cause of my desire? Not the apple quâ moving, for it is not the apple's motions that I desire, but the apple 'itself in its concrete thinghood' (*ousia*), i.e., the apple as an embodiment of a certain form that differentiates it from an orange, and the fulfillment of which differentiates a good apple from a bad. What causes desire, in short, is an object quâ desired, and an object quâ desired is an object in its unchanging aspect. Thus any 'object of desire' is an example of an unmoved mover.

Now, we distinguish between desires of a lower and of a higher order, between animal instinct and rational wish. Man is a creature with the faculty of reason; and in its practical as distinguished from its more contemplative function this faculty is an ability to subordinate desires of a lower order to 'rational principle' (*logos*). Such subordination is not a mechanical nor unconscious process: man as a rational creature has a 'natural' (i.e., living, and for him conscious) tendency to love reason and to bring his conduct into conformity with it. Rational principle thus plays a double role: (1) on the objective side, it is the ideal by which the rational soul desires to be guided—the unmoved mover of the rational soul; (2) on the subjective, it is the rational soul's own inherent power (*dynamis*) to act rationally. Rational principle, then, is at once: (2) an intimate part of a man's own rational nature, which he brings into active expression through the effort of 'moral choice'; and (1) a genuine *arché* of choice and of action, self-caused and not entirely dependent on anything external. There are, of course, material conditions of its exercise (e.g., the physical body must be alive and in tolerable health), but these conditions determine it merely 'in an incidental respect' (*kata symbebékos*). In short, man as a moral agent is not entirely determined by external conditions. He has within himself—or perhaps better, he *is* within himself— a power (*dynamis*) to become reasonable, i.e. to follow reason. His actualization of this power is precisely the effort of 'moral choice' (*proairesis*), which gives rise to 'moral action' (*praxis*). It is as an unmoved mover, then, that the soul performs, and is responsible for, moral action. Man has the power to steer his own course.

The Goal of Man

The goal at which he aims is his happiness (*eudaimonia*), real or imagined. But to different men happiness wears different guises. The majority take it to be pleasure, or in some cases money-making. To a smaller number it appears as a successful career—public offices, honors, renown. Each of these ideals is defective in that it requires for its realization too many extrinsic conditions: it lacks self-sufficiency (*autarkeia*). Only the life of mind in contemplation can be called self-sufficient; it alone, therefore, constitutes happiness in the true and full sense of the word. Even in this sense, of course, happiness presupposes a certain few external advantages: we should hardly call a man happy who was a victim of continuous pain, extreme poverty, or public disgrace. Nevertheless, granted the presence of normal external advantages (i.e., normal for a member of the Athenian aristocracy), the life of the mind is self-sufficient; and in any case it approximates more closely to self-sufficiency than any competing ideal. It, then, is the proper end of man—as is demonstrable also from the definition of man as an animal whose proper function is to think. Accordingly, the wise man will wish for such a life, will deliberate upon the means requisite for its attainment, and when a 'first step' of appropriate action has been discovered that lies within his power, will make that step an object of 'purposive choice' (*proairesis*).

Man's Political Nature

Self-sufficiency, however, does not mean isolation. Man is naturally political (*politikos*), and cannot lead the good life nor find happiness entirely apart from his fellows. By the very fact that he is a moral agent, a being capable of conscious purpose and choice, he becomes to that degree responsible to the society in which he lives. If bad conduct is excusable when caused by ignorance or by an external force, that is only because the agent does not then act willingly (*hekousios*), i.e. he is not, on that particular occasion, the real *archê* of his action: the relevant origin of his act is to be found in circumstances outside of the agent's own 'will' (*proairesis*). But where the agent's will can function freely—i.e., where there is a normal functioning of his 'practical reason' (*logos praktikos*) or 'moral sagacity' (*phronêsis*)—he is answerable for his conduct to society. Ethics thus leads us directly into statecraft (*politikê*), which concerns the details by which the 'government of a city-state' (*politeia*) is to be established and administered.

The city-state (*polis*)—conceived as having the size of a moderate city and the political autonomy of a state—is declared by Aristotle to be the most perfect form of human society (*koinônia*), being last in order of time but first in order of intrinsic nature and worth. Lesser and subordinate forms of social relationship are the 'household' (*oikia*), comprising the three relations of husband-wife, parents-children, and master-servants; and the village. Any combination of city-states into larger imperial powers appeared to Aristotle, and to most Athenians, as a movement toward barbarism, of which the Persian empire and the already threatening Macedonian conquest of the free Greek cities furnished uncongenial illustrations. The Greek sense of individuality was strong; and the full development of individuals seemed to require membership in a political unit small enough to permit some degree of active participation in the government and in deliberations respecting war and peace by all freeborn citizens. City-states may voluntarily enter into economic or military agreements with one another, but this in no way abrogates their autonomy: for (1) each side is free to terminate the agreement when its advantage so dictates, and (2) in such an agreement the motive is merely utilitarian and not the real good—i.e., the developed moral character—of all the citizens of *both* contracting states. The second consideration throws into relief Aristotle's conception of the essential aim and justification of a *polis:* "Whereas it comes into being for the sake of life, it exists for the sake of the good life."

Theory of Poetry

Aristotle, though by no means of a poetic temper, yet had the wit to see that a comprehensive philosophy such as he was undertaking to construct could not neglect the problem of poetry as an important element in the life of mankind. Plato, in whose speculations poetic imagination was a constant and effectively moving force, had resolutely banished poets from his ideal commonwealth on two grounds. First, he believed, they 'mimed' or 'imitated'—that is, gave a somewhat distorted account of—the actual world, which is itself a *mimêsis,* or somewhat distorted imitation of, the true reality. Poetry, with respect to its content, is thus two steps removed from reality, and so an impediment and distraction to the philosophic quest. Second, poetry, particularly as recited and enacted by the popular rhapsodists of the day, was alleged to stir men's emotions quite irresponsibly and without any governing consideration—much as the cinema, radio, and comics may be held to do today—and therefore to be socially injurious, because destructive of that temperance in men which is the psycho-moral foundation of political stability. It is not the least of the many evidences of Aristotle's large intelligence that he could so far overcome his temperamental limitations with respect to poetry as to correct and reconstruct Plato's misleading view both of what poetry essentially is and of what it does.

Now the kind of poetry in which Aristotle is chiefly interested is tragedy. He pays no attention to lyric poetry—an omission that is doubtless partly responsible for his inadequate view of metaphor; most of what he wrote on comedy has been lost; and the epic is treated briefly, for Aristotle considered that tragedy, as the more complex and developed poetic organism, had superseded it. His celebrated definition of tragedy, then, may properly be the focal point of a study of the *Poetics*. Tragedy, he declares, is (1) an 'imitation or representation' (*mimêsis*) of an action that is serious, entire, and of a proper magnitude; (2) using pleasurably embellished language; (3) proceeding not by narrative but by directly presented action; and (4) effecting through pity and fear a purgation (*katharsis*) of these emotions. The first of the four characteristics is shared by poetry with other arts; the second differentiates poetry proper; while the third and fourth differentiate tragedy from other species of poetry, particularly from epic. The first and fourth characteristics, moreover, are put forward by Aristotle in correction of the two above-mentioned elements in Plato's view of poetry, and as constituting his own answer to the basic questions of what poetry is and does. Tragic poetry is a *mimêsis*, and it effects a *katharsis*: this, in brief, is Aristotle's answer to the two primary questions.

Mimêsis as understood by Aristotle is at once a natural instinct in man, a direct response to its own proper object (not, as Plato supposed, always two steps away), and in its developed form the essential mode of being in which the arts of poetry, music, and dancing all share. Painting and sculpture involve *mimêsis* too, no doubt, but in another and purely static sense. Poetry, music, and dancing, as dynamic arts involving time and motion, are related not only by analogy but in origin. The Homeric minstrel played and recited, and helped out his performance by gesticulation and dance. All three of these elements can be regarded as mimetic, since they were employed interrelatedly to evoke an imagined situation in its full perceptual and emotive concreteness before the eyes, ears, and minds of the audience. *Mimêsis*, in short, comes close to what we might today call 'presentational symbolism,' [31] by which an object is not only referred to but is also brought vividly before the imagination in an act of re-presentation. The representation, in order to be of any aesthetic worth or significance, must have as its object something "serious, entire, and of a proper magnitude"; in other words its object—i.e., what is aesthetically emphasized in its object—will have what Clive Bell has called 'significant form.' In painting or sculpture the significant form is spatial; in poetry, music, and dancing it must develop through time. But inasmuch as a mere succession of events would not possess any aesthetic interest, the best object of these latter arts, and especially of tragic poetry, will be an action (*praxis*)—which is to say, it will involve or presuppose 'responsible human choice' (*proairesis*) at some point or other, and it will have, in Aristotle's terse formula, a beginning, middle, and end. A drama, or tragic poem, in miming a serious, complete, and substantial action, will likewise have a beginning, middle, and end; and the representation, so conceived, will constitute its plot (*mythos*).

Now it is the plot of a drama, aided by the five collaborative elements of diction (*lexis*), song (*melos*), staging (*opsis*), effective characterization (*êthos*), and 'intellectual content' (*dianoia*), that produces the effect of *katharsis* on the audience. *Katharsis*, or purgation, has a double background of usage, and correspondingly

[31] Cf. Susanne Langer, *Philosophy in a New Key*, Chap. IV, *passim*.

a double overtone of reference: medical and religious. In Greek medical theory health meant a right proportion and 'blending' (*krasis*) of bodily elements—whether these were conceived as 'humors, or bodily juices' (*chymos*) by the Hippocratic school, as the four primal elements (fire, air, water, earth) by the school of Empedocles, or as qualitative opposites by the Pythagorean and Coan schools. Sickness, therefore, meant some kind of disproportion, and *katharsis* meant the purgation of the excessive elements whereby right blending and health would be restored. That was one area of meaning. In a religious context *katharsis* meant spiritual purgation, a cleansing of the soul from guilt or defilement. Here, too, something like an expulsion of superfluous elements was involved: an aggressive man might have to eject some of the fiery elements, a slothful man some of the earthy elements of his psyche, in order to attain that happy ratio of psychic parts that constitutes health, harmony, and what we may call, in the broadest sense, spiritual integrity. Aristotle, having in mind the religious origin of tragedy,[32] and aware also of the religious interpretation of all excess as a kind of 'pride' (*hybris*) and usurpation, seems to have been on the verge of discovering the redemptive strain in tragedy; but the insight never becomes explicit. At all events, Aristotle's conception of *katharsis*, regardless of the precise weight we assign to its medical or religious overtones, is that by inducing a stylized and controlled discharge of certain excess emotions it results in a new psychic equilibrium, so that men depart from the theatre with more harmonious souls than when they entered. And the emotions chiefly catharated in this way are 'fear, or apprehension' (*phobos*)

[32] See p. 295 for his statement that tragedy grew out of the dithyramb, which (although he does not mention the fact) was a chant used in the worship of Dionysus. For fuller discussion see Margarete Bieber, *The History of the Greek and Roman Theatre* (Princeton University Press, 1939), Chaps. I, II, and IV; in which new evidences of the origins of Greek tragedy are drawn from recent excavations. Cf. William Ridgeway, *The Origin of Tragedy* (1910), Chaps. I, II; A. E. Haigh, *The Tragic Drama of the Greeks* (1896), Chap. I; A. W. Pickard-Cambridge, *Dithyramb, Tragedy and Comedy* (1927), Chaps. I, II.

and pity (*eleos.*) That is to say, there is the expectant tingling excitement, with an undercurrent of dread, as we await the tragic catastrophe, and there is the sympathetic pulling of our heartstrings when the blow has fallen and a 'reversal of situation' (*peripeteia*) followed by a 'scene of suffering' (*pathos*) is dramatically laid before us. By these and attendant devices a tragic drama purges men of two familiar kinds of emotional excess, and restores them to the 'due measure' and right balance of psychic elements that good citizenship requires. Thus Aristotle refutes Plato's allegation that poetry is necessarily hostile to political order, and establishes tragic drama, the most fully developed type of poetry, as an honorable contributor to the good life.

SELECTED BIBLIOGRAPHY

Translations of Aristotle

The Works of Aristotle, translated into English under the editorship of Sir David Ross, 11 vols. (Oxford University Press). T. W. Organ, *An Index to Aristotle in English Translation,* is a useful supplement to the Ross translation. (Princeton University Press, 1949).

Aristotle's writings are also available in the Loeb Classical Library, with Greek text and English translation facing each other (Harvard University Press). Especially recommended are: *The Physics,* translated by Philip H. Wicksteed and Francis M. Cornford (2 vols.); *The Metaphysics,* translated by Hugh Tredennick (2 vols.); *The Nicomachean Ethics* and *The Politics,* translated by H. Rackham (each in one volume); *The Poetics,* translated by W. Hamilton Fyfe.

De Anima (Greek and English on opposite pages), translated by R. D. Hicks (Cambridge University Press, 1907). William A. Hammond, *Aristotle's Psychology* (Macmillan, 1902), a translation of *De Anima* and *Parva Naturalia.*

A. E. Taylor, *Aristotle on his Predecessors* (Open Court, 1910). A translation of *Metaphysics*, Bk. I.

The Nicomachean Ethics. Translations by F. H. Peters (London, 1901), J. E. C. Welldon (Macmillan, 1897), and Walter M. Hatch (London, 1879) are among the best. The Hatch translation is accompanied by a translation of the ancient paraphrase sometimes attributed to Andronicus of Rhodes.

Politics (or *The Art of Statecraft*). Translations by Ernest Barker (Oxford University Press, 1946), J. E. C. Welldon (Macmillan, 1897), and Benjamin Jowett (Oxford, 1885).

Aristotle on Education, being extracts from the *Ethics* and *Politics*, translated and edited by John Burnet (Cambridge University Press, 1903).

Poetics (or *The Art of Poetry*). Translations by Preston H. Epps (University of North Carolina Press, 1942), Samuel H. Butcher (3rd edition, London, 1902), Ingram Bywater (Oxford University Press, 1920), Lane Cooper (Ginn & Co., 1913; a much amplified translation). An older but still very readable translation is by Thomas Twining (London, 1789; 2nd edition, 1812).

Exposition and Criticism

G. R. G. Mure, *Aristotle* (Oxford University Press, 1932).

Sir David Ross, *Aristotle* (2nd edition, Methuen, 1930).

A. E. Taylor, *Aristotle* (2nd edition, T. Nelson & Sons, 1944).

Fritz Maunthner, *Aristotle* (London and New York, 1907).

George Grote, *Aristotle*, 2 vols. (2nd edition, 1880). Contains a good exposition of Aristotle's logical doctrine.

Eduard Zeller, *Aristotle and the Earlier Peripatetics*, 2 vols. (Longmans, Green, 1897).

Werner Jaeger, *Aristotle, Fundamentals of the History of his Development* (Oxford University Press, 1934). An authoritative study of the evolution of Aristotle's thought.

William A. Heidel, *The Necessary and the Contingent in Aristotle* (University of Chicago Press, 1896).

James W. Miller, *The Structure of Aristotle's Logic* (Routledge, 1938).

Edith M. Johnson, *The Structure of Aristotle's Metaphysics* (New York, 1896).

Shute, Clarence W., *The Psychology of Aristotle* (Columbia University Press, 1941).

Spicer, Eulalie E., *Aristotle's Conception of the Soul* (University of London Press, 1934).

Arthur K. Griffin, *Aristotle's Psychology of Conduct* (Williams and Norgate, 1931).

Thomas Marshall, *Aristotle's Theory of Conduct* (T. Unwin, 1909).

Thomas Davidson, *Aristotle and Ancient ducational Ideals* (Scribner, 1912).

Ernest Barker, *The Political Thought of Plato and Aristotle* (New York, 1906).

Lane Cooper, *The Poetics of Aristotle; Its Meaning and Influence* (2nd edition, Longmans, Green, 1927).

Frank L. Lucas, *Tragedy in Relation to Aristotle's Poetics* (Harcourt, Brace, 1928).

Arthur O. Prickard, *Aristotle on the Art of Poetry* (Macmillan, 1891).

Frank Granger, "Aristotle's Theory of Reason" (*Mind,* 1893, vol. 18, pp. 307–318); "The Poetic Reason" (*Mind,* 1936, n.s. vol. 45, pp. 450–463).

Harold F. Cherniss, *Aristotle's Criticism of Presocratic Philosophy* (Johns Hopkins University Press, 1935); *Aristotle's Criticism of Plato and the Academy* (the same, Vol. I, 1944; a second volume announced).

Natural Science

Natural Science

BOOK I

BASIC PRINCIPLES OF NATURE

i. Starting point and method

IN EVERY FIELD of inquiry that has to do with 'initiating principles' (*archê*) or 'determining factors' (*aition*) or elements (*stoicheion*) it is through acquaintance with these that we attain knowledge— or, at any rate, 'scientific knowledge.' [1] For we can hardly be said to know a thing until we have become acquainted with its ultimate conditions (*aition*) and basic principles, and have analyzed it down to its elements. Clearly, then, in a scientific study of nature too, our first task will be to find out about its initiating principles.

The natural path of investigation starts from what is more readily knowable and more evident *to us* although intrinsically more obscure, and proceeds toward what is more *self*-evident and intrinsically more intelligible; for it is one thing to be knowable to us and quite another to be intelligible objectively.

The things that stand out as plain and obvious at first glance are confused mixtures, whose elements and initiating principles become known only on subsequent analysis. Accordingly we must proceed from the general character of a thing to its constituent factors; for what the senses discern most readily are concrete wholes, and a thing's general character is a kind of concrete whole,

[1] The verbal form of *epistêmê*.

embracing as it does a number of constituent factors or aspects. By way of analogy consider how names are related to their 'logical meaning' (*logos*). A name, such as 'circle,' gives a general indication of what is meant, while its definition (*horismos*) makes an explicit analysis of this meaning. Similarly, children begin by calling every man father and every woman mother, but as they grow older they learn to make suitable distinctions.

ii. Alternative possibilities to be considered

The initiating principles of things must be either one or more than one. If there is only one such principle it must be either changeless (*a-kinêton*), as Parmenides and Melissus have declared, or in motion, according to the doctrines of the physicists, some of whom take air, others water as the originating principle. If, on the contrary, there are more basic principles than one, they will be either finite or infinite in number. If more than one and finite they will be two, three, four, or some other specific number. If infinite, they must be either, as Democritus believed, all of the same essential kind and differentiated merely in respect of shape and form, or else opposed to one another in kind as well.

We are following here the same general procedure as those who seek to enumerate the 'things that really exist' (*onta, pl.*). Such thinkers ask first whether the basic constituents of things are one or more than one; next, if more than one, whether limited or unlimited. Thus they too are inquiring whether the elements and initiating principles of things are one or many.

As for the question whether all existence is one and unchanging, this falls outside the science of nature properly speaking. Just as the geometer cannot argue with a person who disputes the fundamental principles of geometry (for such questions belong not to geometry itself, but either to some special science or else to Science in general), so too there is no point in our arguing with those who dispute the basic principles of our present subject-matter. If everything were one, and an unchanging one at that, there could be no principles, for a principle must refer to a thing or things other than itself. To consider, therefore, whether everything is one in this fundamental sense would be like debating any other thesis upheld merely for the sake of argument—the thesis put forward by Heraclitus, for instance, or such a thesis as that a single man is the whole of existence. We should be refuting a mere 'quibble' (*logos eristikos*): an epithet that describes the arguments of Melissus and Parmenides alike; for their premises are false and their conclusions do not follow. Or rather, the argument of Melissus is so grossly false that it offers no difficulty: admit his one initial absurdity, and the rest is easy. But as physicists we must start from the assumption that natural objects, or at any rate some of them, do undergo change; and there is also inductive evidence for this. A scientist is not bound to solve every difficulty that can be raised against his science, but only such as represent an erroneous working out of his basic principles. . . .

v. The principle of antithesis

All of the earlier philosophers agree in taking pairs of opposite [qualities or forces] as basic principles. This is equally true of those who describe the universe as one and unchangeable (even Parmenides treats hot and cold as principles, calling them fire and earth), and of those who distinguish between the rare and the dense. It is also true of Democritus, who distinguishes solidity from vacuum, identifying the one with existence (*on*), the other with non-existence. Democritus furthermore admits distinctions and oppositions in respect of position, shape, and order: in respect of position there are the antitheses above vs. below, before vs. behind; in respect of shape, the angular, the straight and the curved.

Plainly, then, they all agree in somehow or other treating pairs of opposites as principles. And with good reason. For it is essential to first principles that they should be derived neither from one another nor from anything else, but that on the contrary everything else should be derived from them. A pair of primary opposites fulfills this condition: being primary they cannot be derived from anything else, and being opposites they cannot be derived from each other. Let us now proceed to a reasoned examination of what this statement means.

Our first step must be to recognize that one thing does not act upon nor become affected by nor turn into any other thing at random, except 'in an incidental sense' (*kata symbekêkos*). We could not describe a man's 'pallid whiteness' (*leukos,* adj.) as arising from his 'being cultured' (*mousikos*) unless this had been incidentally connected with a quality opposed to whiteness—i.e., 'swarthy blackness' (*melas*). White can arise only from 'not-white'; and by not-white I do not mean just any quality at random that happens to be other than white, but black or some intermediate color. 'Being cultured,' in turn, does not arise from anything at random, but from the '*un*cultured'—unless, of course, we postulate some quality intermediate between the two.

Qualities are restricted similarly in their disappearance. White does not pass into the quality of being cultured, except in an incidental sense; strictly speaking, it can pass only into the opposite of white—i.e., not into anything at all that happens to be other than white, but into black or some intermediate color. So too, 'being cultured' will not pass into anything at random, but only into the state of being uncultured, or else into some state intermediate between the two.

It is the same with everything else. Even composite structures, as distinguished from simple qualities, follow the same law; we overlook this aspect, however, because the corresponding lack of structure has received no name. Nevertheless, a particular harmony or arrangement of parts can only have arisen from a state in which that particular arrangement was lacking; and when it is destroyed it will pass not into anything at random, but into that state which is its specific opposite. Whether such an arrangement of parts is called a harmony or an order or a combination is immaterial: the rule holds good in any case. In fact, it holds good even of a house or a statue or any other such product. A house comes into existence out of materials previously unjoined; a statue, or anything else that has been moulded into shape, out of a material previously unwrought; all such constructions involving either a combination (*synthesis*) or an ordering (*taxis*) of parts.

This being so, we may conclude that whenever anything is created or destroyed it necessarily passes out of or into either its opposite or some intermediate state. And since each group of intermediates is derived from some pair of opposites (colors, for instance, from white and black), it follows that whatever comes into existence by a natural process is either itself one of a pair of opposites or a product of such a pair.

Up to this point, as I have had occasion to remark, we have been in agreement with most other writers on the subject; all of whom find the elements, or as they call them the 'principles' of things, in qualitative antitheses; although as they base their discovery on no rational grounds, it is as if they sensed the truth instinctively. Such writers, however, differ from one another in that some of them start from pairs of opposites that are comparatively fundamental, others from pairs that are less so; some choosing pairs that are logically more intelligible, others pairs that are more familiar to sense-experience. Some, for instance, posit hot and cold, or perhaps wet and dry, as the conditions of becoming, while others posit odd and even, or love and strife: which illustrates the difference just mentioned. But at the same time there is evidently one respect in which these thinkers agree, notwithstanding their obvious and acknowledged differences: all of them alike refer to the same table of opposites [2] for their basic

---

[2] This table, which is of Pythagorean origin, is reported by Aristotle (*Metaph.*, I. v) as follows: (1) limited vs. unlimited, (2) odd vs. even, (3) one vs. many, (4) right vs. left, (5) male vs. female, (6) at rest vs. in motion, (7) straight vs. curved, (8) light vs. darkness, (9) good vs. evil, (10) square vs. oblong. Not all the pairs of opposites used by early thinkers

principles, although the particular pair of opposites for which they assume priority may be wider or narrower in range. Some of them, as has already been observed, start from what is logically more intelligible, others from what is more familiar to the senses; these two starting-points being the universal and the particular respectively, inasmuch as 'logical explanation' (*logos*) deals with the universal and sense-perception (*aesthêsis*) with the particular. Great vs. small, for instance, is a logical distinction, while dense vs. rare is a distinction of sense.

Our general conclusion, then, is that basic principles will have the form of a pair of opposites.

vi. The primal triad

We come next to the question of whether the basic principles of nature are two or three or some greater number. Obviously they cannot be one, for there can be no such thing as a single opposite; nor infinite, otherwise nature could not be known. Theoretically a single pair of principles would suffice, because every genus is marked by one primary pair of opposites, and 'universal thinghood' (*ousia*) [3] is a kind of genus. In any case, a finite number of principles will be sufficient, and this being so it is better to suppose them finite than infinite; as we may see from the example of Empedocles, who claims to derive [from his four primary substances] all that Anaxagoras derives from an infinite number of them. Furthermore, some antitheses are more primary [4] than others, while some like sweet and bitter, white and black, arise from others; basic principles, however, must be permanent and unchanging. These considerations make it clear that the number of basic principles must be at once finite and greater than one.

Now granted that the basic principles are limited in number,

---

to explain natural phenomena are included in this list. The point of Aristotle's remark is that these thinkers all alike rest their doctrines upon the *general conception of antithesis*, of which the Pythagorean table is an embodiment.

[3] I.e., nature as a whole.

[4] Or what modern logicians call 'logically prior.'

there is good reason for supposing them to be more than two. In the first place, it is hard to conceive how density and rarity, for instance, each retaining its essential nature, could in any way act upon each other.[5] The same difficulty holds for every other pair of opposites: Love [in Empedocles' theory] is not to be thought of as gathering up Strife and creating something out of it, nor can Strife do this to Love, but rather both of them must operate on some third thing. This need of more than two principles to explain the world of nature has been recognized by a number of philosophers.

There is, moreover, a further difficulty in failing to postulate the existence of something underlying the basic pair of opposites. Opposites never appear as the substance (*ousia*) of a thing. But we cannot take as a basic principle what is merely a predicate of some underlying subject; otherwise (since a subject is evidently a principle in the sense of being prior to what is predicated of it) our supposed principle would be dependent upon a prior principle. Or putting the matter differently:[6] we agree that one substance cannot be the opposite of another substance; hence [if opposites were the basic principles from which all else is derived] it would follow that substance could be derived from something other than substance. But how could this be—i.e., how could non-substance be prior to substance?

Accordingly, if we accept both the previous argument [that opposites are in some way the basic principles of nature] and the present one [that opposites presuppose a substance in which

---

[5] The argument is cogent if we school ourselves to adopt that standpoint of 'direct realism' which accepts the qualities of density and rarity as equally real but opposed *states of being*.

[6] There is only one argument in this paragraph but it is stated in two forms: first as a syllogism of the second figure, then as a *reductio ad absurdum*. (1) Opposites are not substances; basic principles, since they are not attributes, must be substances; therefore opposites cannot be basic principles. (2) Substances are not opposites; therefore if opposites were basic principles the basic principles would be something other than substance—i.e., attributes; which however they cannot be.

they inhere, and of which they may.be predicated], must we not, in order to preserve the truth of both, postulate the existence of a third something [besides the pair of opposites, and on which they act]? It is this third principle which those thinkers have in mind who explain the entire universe in terms of some one natural substance such as water or fire or one of the intermediate elements. (In this connection it may be remarked that the intermediate elements furnish a sounder basis of explanation; for while the fact that fire, earth, air, and water are compounds formed out of certain pairs of opposites,[7] suggests that the underlying substance should be regarded as something different from any of these four, yet if it is to be identified with any of them the most logical choice would be air, which is least of all differentiated by sensible characteristics; and the second choice would be water.) At any rate, all of these thinkers agree in regarding their one underlying substance as taking shape by means of pairs of opposing principles, such as density and rarity, more and less; and all such principles are obviously, as has been said before, particular examples of excess and deficiency. As a matter of fact, this doctrine too (that the One and excess and deficiency are the basic principles of everything) is apparently of long standing. It is found, however, in a variety of forms; the earlier thinkers having regarded the Two as the active and the One as the passive principle, while certain more recent thinkers take a contrary position, regarding the One as the active principle and the Two as acted upon.

From these and similar considerations, then, we appear to have adequate grounds, as has already been remarked, for postulating three basic elements. Nor is there any reason to increase this number. For clearly one passive principle is enough. As for the opposites, suppose they were four in number, i.e., two pairs instead of one: then if the pairs were independent of each other,

---

[7] The Greeks thought of fire as essentially dry and hot, earth as dry and cold, air as wet (i.e., fluid) and hot, water as wet and cold.

we should have to assume a distinct neutral principle for each of them [making two passive principles, which has just been declared superfluous]; while if the pairs were not mutually independent, one of them could be derived from the other and would therein be superfluous as a principle. On another ground, too, it is clear that there cannot be more than one primary pair of opposites. The 'essential nature' (*ousia*) of everything that exists constitutes a single genus. Hence the [pairs of opposites which serve as] principles can only differ in the degree to which they are fundamental, not in essential kind; for in a single genus there is always a single pair of fundamental opposites, to which all other pairs of opposites may be reduced.

Thus we see that the elements in nature must be more than one but not more than two or three; whether specifically two or three, however, is, as I have said, a troublesome question.

vii. Explanation of becoming change

We pass now to a positive account of our own theory, starting with a general analysis of 'becoming, or change' (*genesis*); for it is the most natural mode of procedure to speak first of the general characteristics of things and afterwards to investigate the peculiarities of each detail.

When one thing is spoken of as 'coming to be' out of another thing, or out of another kind of thing, the process may be interpreted in both a simple and a compound sense. Here is what I mean. There is a sense in which (1) a man becomes cultured, another in which (2) his previous state of unculture passes into [8] a state of being cultured, and still another in which (3) an uncultured man becomes a cultured man. The terms that are regarded as undergoing change in the first two cases (i.e., man and the state of being cultured) as well as what each of them

---

[8] The same word, *gignesthai* or *ginesthai*, is translated 'become,' 'come to be,' 'come into existence,' or, 'pass into,' according to the requirements of English idiom.

'becomes' (i.e., cultured) I call simple; but when an uncultured man is regarded as becoming a cultured man both terms of the process are compound. In some cases of becoming, moreover, we can speak of something as coming into existence 'out of' some previously existing state—e.g., being cultured comes into existence 'out of' the state of unculture; while there are other cases where this mode of expression is inapplicable—e.g., we do not say that the state of being cultured comes into existence 'out of' a man, but simply that a man becomes cultured. Again, as regards the two ways in which a simple thing can be said to 'become something,' in the one case the thing persists through the process of becoming, in the other it does not: a man is still a man on becoming cultured; but his state of unculture, i.e., his not being cultured, does not persist either singly or in combination with the subject.

These distinctions and the several types of becoming that they reveal enable us to conclude that there must be in all cases a subject which, as we say, 'becomes something'—a subject which, though one numerically, is more than one in form. By its form I here mean the specific ways in which the subject is expressed; its two aspects, man and the state of unculture, being of course distinct. The one aspect, man, which has not the character of an opposite, survives the process of becoming; while the other aspect —the lacking culture, or the state of being uncultured, or the compound form 'uncultured man'—does not.

'Coming to be' (*gignesthai*) has several senses. In one sense of the word we do not speak of coming into existence but of becoming *something*. It is only 'substances, or concrete things as such' (*ousia*) that can be said without qualification to come into existence. Where the becoming is of something other than a concrete substance—a quantity, for example, or a quality, or a relation, or a moment of time, or a being located—a subject (*hypokeimenon*) is evidently presupposed, and this will be a substance (*ousia*). For it is substance alone that is never predicated of anything, being always the subject to which predications refer. Yet 'concrete substances' too—i.e., anything that can be said without qualification to exist—when they come into existence presuppose some kind of underlying substratum, as will be clear from the sequel. For in every case there is something already present, out of which the resultant thing is born; as animals and plants come from seed.

'Coming into existence' [9] takes place in several ways: (1) by change of shape, as a bronze statue; (2) by accretion, as things that grow; (3) by subduction, as a Hermes chiselled from a block of marble; (4) by combination, as a house; and (5) by 'qualitative alteration' (*alloiôsis*), where the material itself assumes different properties. In all of these cases it is evident that the process of coming into existence presupposes a substratum which is already existing.

Hence it appears that whatever 'becomes' is always composite: there is something [a new element of form] that comes into existence, and something else that becomes it. This 'something else' may be conceived in a double sense: as the enduring substratum, or as the original qualification which in the process is replaced by its opposite. In the example previously employed, 'uncultured' is the original qualification, 'man' is the subject; in the making of a statue the lack of form, shape, and order is the original qualification, while the bronze or stone or gold is the subject. If we grant, then, that all things are determined by causes and basic principles, of which they are the essential, not the accidental, result, it plainly follows that everything comes into existence at one and the same time from the subject and from a certain form. For 'cultured man' consists, so to speak, of both 'man' and 'cultured'; and the meaning of the composite term can be analyzed into these two component meanings. Elements like these, then, are the conditions of any becoming.

The subject of any change is numerically one, but with a duality

[9] I.e., *gignesthai* without the word 'something' (*tode ti*) attached.

of form. A man, or gold, or any other 'material susceptible of form' (*hylê*), can be regarded as a unit, and is the essential basis of the process that transpires; but the 'lack of form' (*sterêsis*) and its opposite are related to the process only incidentally. At the same time it is also possible to regard the acquired form— the order, or the state of culture attained—as something unitary. Thus we must recognize a sense in which the principles are two, and another sense in which they are three. From one point of view it seems enough to take as principles some pair of opposites such as cultured vs. uncultured, hot vs. cold, or joined vs. unjoined; but there is another point of view from which this interpretation is inadequate, inasmuch as opposites cannot be acted on by each other. We therefore solve the difficulty by postulating a substratum distinct from either of the opposites which successively inhere in it, and not itself the opposite of anything. So the principles appear to be, from one standpoint, two in number, corresponding to the two opposites of any pair; yet there is also a standpoint from which they must be regarded not as two but as three, owing to the essential difference of meaning between, e.g., being a man and being uncultured, or, in our other example, between being unshaped and being bronze.

We have now established and explained the number of principles required to account for the changes that take place in the natural world. It is clear that opposites are two, and also that they involve a third something underlying them, although from another point of view this third principle appears unnecessary, inasmuch as one of the opposites by its successive presence and absence will suffice to effect the change.

What the underlying substratum is, can be understood by analogy. As bronze is to a completed statue, wood to a bed, and still unformed materials to the objects fashioned from them, so the underlying substratum is to anything substantial (*ousia*), particular, and existent. . . .

viii. Correction of earlier natural philosophers

It remains to show that the conclusions here reached offer the only solution to the difficulties that beset the early philosophers.

The first of those who devoted themselves to philosophical speculations in an effort to discover the true nature of things were misled by their inexperience, which set them, as it were, on a wrong track. They declared that nothing either comes into or passes out of existence, because what comes into existence must come either from what exists or from what does not exist, neither of which alternatives is possible. What exists cannot become anything, because it already *is*; nor can anything come into existence out of what is non-existent, because in that case there would be nothing there for it to come out of. Developing the consequences of this argument these philosophers went so far as to declare of existence itself that it is not many but one. Such was their opinion and their reason for holding it.

In reply to this argument let it be said that when we speak of things as coming into existence 'either from what exists or from what does not exist,' or when we speak of the existent or of the non-existent as doing something or as being acted upon or as becoming something, our words are to be taken with the same qualification as when we speak of a doctor as doing something, being acted upon, or becoming something. Each of these expressions may be applied in a twofold sense both to the doctor and to existence. When a doctor builds a house he does so not in his proper capacity as doctor but quâ builder, nor is it as a doctor that he grows pallid but as one who has been dark-complexioned. When he cures or fails to cure a patient, on the other hand, he does so in his capacity as doctor. And as it is accurate to say of a doctor that he performs or suffers or becomes something only when this is true of him quâ doctor, so when we deny the possibility of generation out of the non-existent it is evidently the non-existent *as such* to which we have reference. It was through a failure to grasp this distinction that the philosophers in question erred, with the result that they even went to the length of supposing that nothing is generated or exists save bare undifferentiated existence; thereby denying the fact of becoming.

Now we ourselves agree that absolute non-existence cannot give rise to existence; we maintain, however, that everything arises from what is non-existent in some incidental respect. To come into existence implies a certain prior incompleteness (*sterêsis*) which is removed in the process of generation; and however surprising or paradoxical it may seem, any incompleteness is essentially a kind of non-being. In the same way we hold that existence, too, cannot be the source of existence, except incidentally. There is an incidental sense, however, in which existence does arise from existence; just as, supposing that a particular kind of animal, such as a dog, were to turn into another particular kind of animal, such as a horse, it would be incidentally true that animal had arisen from animal. The dog would have come into existence not only out of 'horse' but out of 'animal,' [and what it became would also be 'animal']; only in a secondary sense, however, for 'animal' persists through the process [and therefore cannot be identified with either of the opposed terms]. If, on the other hand, anything is to become 'animal' in an absolute and unqualified sense, it must have been something other than animal at the outset. Similarly it is true that 'existence' in an absolute sense cannot be generated either out of existence or out of non-existence; for when such a denial is made, 'non-existence,' as we have already said, signifies 'non-existence as such.' It should be noted, by the way, that this interpretation is perfectly consistent with the principle that everything either is or is not.

Here, then, is one manner of dealing with the problem; a second, resting on the distinction between potential and actual existence, is elaborated elsewhere.[10] Thus the difficulties are solved which have led men to deny the facts [of plurality and change] that

[10] *Metaph.*, Bk. IX. See pp. 86–96.

we have been discussing. Because of such difficulties our predecessors, when they sought to explain genesis and annihilation as well as the general phenomenon of change, got on a wrong track. Had they taken account of the constant nature which persists through any change, their misconception would have been cleared up.

ix. Matter, form, and becoming

Certain other philosophers, to be sure, have taken account of this constant factor in change, but their treatment of it has been unsatisfactory. In the first place they follow Parmenides in supposing that [if anything comes into existence at all] it must come out of absolute non-existence.[11] Secondly they suppose that because the subject which changes is numerically one, it can therefore have but a single potentiality—a quite inadmissible inference.

We ourselves, on the other hand, distinguish between the matter which undergoes change and the incompleteness (*sterêsis*) by which that matter is originally characterized. Matter, we say, partakes of non-existence only incidentally, while incompleteness is essentially a kind of non-existence. Matter, moreover, is more or less identical with the 'thing' (*ousia*) itself, while incompleteness is in no sense identical with it. . . .

The substratum which persists and the form that is imposed are jointly responsible for whatever is created—as in the impregnation of a womb. But there are some thinkers who fall into the error of regarding only the negative or defective aspect of matter, whereupon they identify matter with non-existence. For our part, we admit the existence not only of something divine and good and desirable [form] and of its simple opposite [lack of form, or incompleteness], but also of a third principle [matter, the subject] whose nature it is to strive [away from the incompleteness

---

[11] Parmenides, however, contraposed this argument, holding that since nothing can arise out of absolute non-existence, nothing therefore can ever come into existence at all—i.e., that no change is ever possible.

and] toward the form which it desires. Those who identify matter with imperfection or incompleteness and treat it as the opposite of form are driven to suppose that matter desires its own extinction. Surely it is impossible either for form to desire itself (since it is not defective or incomplete) or for its contrary to desire it (contraries being mutually destructive). What desires form, then, is matter; and it desires it as the female desires the male, or as the foul desires the beautiful [12]—not that such desires are present in femininity or foulness as such, but in persons who happen to have these characteristics.

Matter may be regarded from one point of view as becoming and perishing, from another as not. Considered as that in which there is incompleteness, it perishes in its very nature, because the incompleteness which perishes is a part of it. Considered as a potentiality of change, however, it does not perish essentially, but must be regarded as uncreated and imperishable. For if it had ever come into existence, we should have to suppose an original constitutive element 'already there' (*hypokeisthai*) for it to come out of. But this character of being 'a subject already there as a basis of change' is precisely the thing we have been inquiring about; hence, if the matter of what changes were itself to change, it would have to exist before its own coming into existence. For what I mean by matter is just this: the ultimate subject (*proton hypokeimenon*) of things, on which their origination and their existence essentially depend. By the same argument, therefore, matter in the sense of basic potentiality cannot perish; for if it did it could only pass into itself, and so after perishing it would continue to exist.

[So much for the problem of matter.] As for form (*eidos*), the general questions about it—whether it is one or many, and of what kind—fall within the province of basic philosophy, and may accordingly be postponed until we reach that study.[18] In the re-

---

[12] Cf. Plato's *Symposium*, to which Aristotle may be referring.
[18] I.e., the *Metaphysics*.

mainder of this treatise we shall deal only with forms of a natural and perishable sort.

The existence, nature, and number of principles in the universe have now been demonstrated. [In the next book] we shall approach our subject-matter from another standpoint.

BOOK II

THE CONDITIONS OF NATURAL OCCURRENCES

i. The meanings of nature

SOME THINGS EXIST by nature, some from other causes. Animals and their bodily organs, plants, and the physical elements—earth, fire, air, and water—such things as these we say exist 'by nature.' There is one particular in which all the objects just named are observed to differ from things that are not constituted by nature: each of them has within itself a principle of movement (*kinêsis*) and rest (*stasis*)—whether this movement be locomotion, or growth and decrease, or qualitative change. In such objects as beds and coats, on the other hand—provided we are speaking [not of their materials but] of the beds and coats themselves as products of craftwork (*technê*)—there is no inherent tendency to change (*metabolê*). Of course, in respect of the stone or earth or composite matter of which such things are made, they do to that extent have such a tendency.[1] This, however, is a purely incidental aspect; [although it offers, to be sure, additional evidence that] what causes a thing to change (*kineisthai*) or be at rest is its 'nature' (*physis*)—i.e., the nature that belongs to it primarily, not as an incidental attribute. As an illustration of what is meant by this last qualification, consider the case of a physician who cures himself. It would not be quâ patient that he possessed the art of healing; it would merely happen that in this exceptional case the same man was doctor and patient. So it is with all

---

[1] It is quâ wood or other heavy material that a bed tends to fall, not quâ bed.

artificial products: none of them has within itself the principle of its own production. But while in some cases (e.g., a house or any other such product of manual labor) the moving principle resides in some external agent, there are also cases where the principle is found as an incidental attribute within the thing produced.

Since this is what is meant by 'nature,' anything may be said to 'have a nature' so far as it possesses within itself a principle of the sort just described. Whatever possesses such a principle is 'something substantial, a concrete thing' (*ousia*); for it is *subject* [to change], and subjects are what have inherent natures. We may note also the phrase 'according to nature,' which is applied not only to the things themselves but also to their essential attributes. When, for example, fire is borne upwards, that phenomenon *is* not nature, nor does it *have* a nature, but it takes place *in accordance with nature*. This, then, is the distinction between nature (*physis*), [existing] by nature (*physei*), and [being or occurring] in accordance with nature (*kata physin*).

To try to prove that nature exists would be absurd. Obviously there are many undemonstrable truths of this kind; and to seek to prove what is obvious by what is not shows a lack of ability to distinguish the self-evident from the not self-evident. There are people, of course, in whom such an ability is lacking. But like a man born blind who argues about colors, they are only arguing about names, without any corresponding thought.

Some thinkers identify the nature, or 'substantive existence' (*ousia*) of a physical object with its proximate constituent, which considered in itself lacks the arrangement that characterizes the object: a bed, they say, is nothing but wood, a statue nothing but bronze. In support of this theory Antiphon points out that if you were to bury a bed, which in rotting were to generate enough force to send forth a shoot, the offshoot would be wood but not a bed—showing that the artificial arrangement produced by the craftsman is merely an incidental attribute, while that which persists uninterruptedly through the process of change determines 'what a thing really is' (*ousia*). By an extension of this argument it is declared that if the same relation that exists between a thing and its materials is found also between the materials themselves and certain ulterior elements—as water might be an ulterior constituent of bronze and gold, or earth of wood and bones, and so on—these elements will constitute the 'real nature' (*physis kai ousia*) of the thing. That is why some declare earth, others fire or air or water, still others a partial or total combination of these, to be the true nature of things. And when any such element, or combination of such elements, is taken as primary, a thinker will often declare this to be 'all that a thing really is' ('all the *ousia*'), dismissing its other aspects as 'temporary modifications' (*pathos*) or 'habitual states' (*hexis*) or 'habitual dispositions' (*diathesis*) of it. He will regard it moreover as eternal, on the ground that it cannot be transformed into anything other than itself—other phases of existence, however, becoming created and destroyed ceaselessly.

Here, then, is one meaning of the word nature: the proximate material [2] of whatever contains a principle of movement or change. But from another point of view we may regard the nature of a thing as consisting in its form (*eidos*), in the 'way it shapes up' (*morphê*) by definition. Just as we apply the word art (*technê*) to a thing both as having been produced by art and as having an artistic character, so we apply the word nature (*physis*) to what is 'in accordance with nature, or has a natural foundation' (*kata physin*) as well as to the 'natural basis itself' (*physikon*). And as in the one case we should not call a bed artistic if it were only potentially a bed and had not yet received a bed's actual form; so in the case of natural products, what is potentially flesh or bone does not possess its proper nature and does not exist 'naturally'

---

[2] *Protê hylê*: i.e., the material that we discover on first analysis—the bronze or wood or bone—as distinguished from the ultimate constituents. Aristotle sometimes, however, uses *protê hylê* to mean 'ultimate matter'—i.e., first in order of being rather than first in order of investigation.

(*physei*) until it actually assumes the form implied by its 'logical meaning' (*logos*). This logical meaning is made explicit by defining what flesh or bone properly is. Thus in this second sense of the word, nature means the 'shape' (*morphê*) or form (*eidos*) of such things as have an inherent tendency to change—this natural form being distinguishable in meaning although inseparable in fact from the matter that receives it. But while the word nature may sometimes connote the matter and sometimes the form it is never directly synonymous with the composite thing of which these are the complementary aspects: we say of a man not that he is nature, but that he exists by virtue of a certain nature.[3]

Of these two meanings of nature the second is the more fundamental. For a thing is more truly said to have a certain nature when it has actually realized that nature than when it merely is capable of it. Besides, man is born from man, but not bed from bed. Hence it is generally held that the real nature of a bed is not its 'visible form' (*schêma*), but the wood; on the ground that if the bed were to sprout, its offshoot would be merely wood, not another bed. If we agree that any such 'visible form *not* capable of reproducing itself' (*schêma*) is [a product of] art, it would seem that nature must be 'essential form capable of reproducing itself' (*morphê*); for man reproduces [the essential form of] man.

This is further shown by our practice of using the word nature for the process of growth by which the nature of a thing is attained. Herein nature differs from the art of healing, which aims not simply at healing but at health. The healing art stands at the beginning of the process, not at the end as a goal. Nature's relation to nature is different from this. A growing thing, quâ growing, must grow out of something and into something else. What is it that it grows into? Not what it arose from, but what it tends toward. Its 'final shape' (*morphê*), then, is its nature.

The words shape (*morphê*) and nature, we may observe in

[3] Lit., "that he exists 'by nature' (*physei*)"; which has previously been identified with 'having a certain nature.'

passing, are used in a twofold sense: i.e., there is a sense in which even deficiency is a sort of form (*eidos*), [since it is the lack of something with a definite character]. But whether a specific deficiency is involved in cases of absolute creation is a question to be considered later.[4]

ii. *The province of natural science*

Now that we have distinguished the various meanings of 'nature,' we may consider next in what way the mathematician differs from the 'natural scientist' (*physikos*). Their connection is suggested by the fact that the surfaces and volumes, lines and points, which the mathematician studies, are all present as aspects of natural objects. We may also ask whether astronomy (*astrologia*) is distinct from 'natural science' (*physikē*) or a subdivision of it. Here too there appears to be a connection: it would be unreasonable to expect the natural scientist to know the essential nature of sun and moon while entirely ignoring their more particular astronomical characteristics; especially since writers on natural science do discuss such questions as the shape of the moon and sun, and whether or not the earth and even the universe as a whole are spherical.

As for the relation between the mathematician and the natural scientist, it should be observed that while the former also busies himself with volumes, surfaces, lines, and points, he does not treat of these objects quâ belonging to physical bodies, nor is he interested in the special properties that they derive from this relation. Hence he abstracts them—that is, he separates them in thought from the physical mutations with which they are normally found; and their essential nature is not changed or falsified by this abstraction. . . .

With which of nature's two aspects, form or matter, is the natural scientist properly concerned? With both of them, no doubt. But even so, he still must examine each of them individually, and the

---

[4] The reference may possibly be to *De Gen. et Cor.*. Bk. I, Chap. iii.

question then arises whether the same type of inquiry is appropriate to each.

A study of the ancients would suggest that natural science is exclusively concerned with matter. Even Empedocles and Democritus tell us little about the form (*eidos*) and 'enduring essence' (*ti ên einai*) [5] of things. But if we admit that art (*technê*) imitates nature, and that to a certain extent it is the business of every 'scientific technique' (*epistêmê*) to understand not only its own 'distinctive character' (*eidos*, 'form') but also the 'material appropriate to it' (*hylê*, 'matter')—e.g., the doctor must understand not only health but also the bile and phlegm in which health is or is not to be found, the builder must have knowledge not only of the way in which a house is to shape up but also of the bricks and beams that are its materials, and so in other cases—we must conclude that it is the business of the natural scientist to study both the formal and material aspects of nature. . . .

To what extent, then, must the natural scientist study the form and 'essence' (*ti esti*) of things? To a certain extent of course he must, inasmuch as his investigation must include the 'goals toward which things strive' (*tinos heneka*); [not, however, to the extent of neglecting their material basis]—any more than the doctor [in studying health] should neglect the sinew, or the smith overlook the material properties of bronze. For the objects of natural science, while distinguishable ideally from the matter in which they reside, are not actually separable. Man and the sun must both be taken account of in explaining the generation of man. As for entities that can be separated from their matter, what they are and what their mode of existence, this is a question that belongs more properly to basic philosophy.

iii. The four types of explanation

We have next to consider the question of 'the factors that make a thing what it is' (*aitia*): what they are and how they are to be

[5] Lit., '[that aspect of a thing which continues] to be what it has been.'

classified. For knowledge is the object of our studies, and we can hardly be said really to know a thing until we have grasped the 'why' of it—i.e., until we have grasped 'the factors that are most directly responsible for it' (*protê aitia*). Clearly, then, this must be our aim also with regard to the phenomena of becoming and perishing and all forms of physical change, so that having grasped the underlying principles we may employ them in the explanation of particular phenomena.

[1. *Material factor.*] In one sense, then, 'the reason for anything' (*aitia*) means the material out of which an object is generated and which is immanent in the generated object: e.g., the bronze of a statue, the silver of a bowl, and also the genera to which such materials belong.

[2. *Formal factor.*] Next, it may mean the form (*eidos*) or pattern (*paradeigma*), i.e., what the thing is defined as being essentially; and also the genus to which this essence belongs. Thus the ratio 2:1 is a formal condition of the musical octave. Generally speaking, number and the factors that make up the definition of a thing are what constitute its formal condition.

[3. *Propelling factor.*] A third meaning is the immediate source of change or of cessation from change. In this sense a man who gives advice acts as 'determining agency' (*aitia*) [on him who receives it], a father on his offspring, and generally speaking whatever produces or changes anything on the product or on the thing changed.

[4. *Telic factor.*] Finally the reason for anything may mean the end (*telos*) or purpose for the sake of which a thing is done: e.g., health may be a determining factor in going for a walk. "Why is he taking a walk?" we ask. "In order to be healthy": having said this we think we have given a sufficient explanation. Under this category must also be put all the intermediate steps which the agent must take as means to the end—e.g., taking off weight, loosening the bowels, also drugs and surgical instruments, as means to health. All these are for the sake of an end, although they differ in that some are actions to be performed while others are instruments to be used.

Thus we have enumerated the various ways in which one thing can determine another. Frequently it happens that more than one type of determining factor bears an essential (not merely an incidental) relation to a single thing. It is quâ statue and not by virtue of an incidental aspect that a statue owes its existence both to the sculptor who makes it and to the bronze from which it is made; although these are of course related to it in different ways —the one as the force that produces it, the other as its material. Again, some things may be regarded as determining each other reciprocally—e.g., exercise and physical fitness—but not in the same sense, for while exercise is the actual source from which physical fitness proceeds, physical fitness is rather the end toward which exercise is directed. Again, a given factor will often account for quite opposite results: if a certain result can be attributed to its presence we may blame the opposite result on its absence. Thus we attribute a shipwreck to the absence of the pilot whose presence would have brought the ship to safety.

But all of the determining factors just mentioned come under our fourfold classification. In the sense of 'that out of which,' letters are the determinants of syllables, raw materials of manufactured goods, fire and the like of physical bodies, the parts of the whole, and the premises of the conclusion. In each of these cases the first of the related terms is a substratum [or material factor], as parts are to a whole; while the second is the essential character which the substratum receives—its whole or synthesis or form [formal factor]. Again, the seed or sperm, the doctor, the man who gives advice—in short, any agent—is the source in which the starting or stopping of a motion or change originates [propelling factor]. And finally, there are those things which determine in the sense of being a goal (telos), i.e., a good toward which other things tend [telic factor]; for the phrase 'for the sake of' connotes both a goal and a highest good—whether the good be real or apparent.

Such, then, are the number and kinds of determining factor; and while there are several other ways in which these may differ from one another, their differences are reducible to a few main heads:

(1) There are cases where one determining factor is logically prior to another of the same general type. Health, for example, may be attributed both to the doctor and to [the more general term under which he falls, namely] the expert; an octave is determined both by the ratio 2:1 and in a more abstract sense by number. This situation is found wherever one of the factors is more inclusive in meaning than the other which is subsumed under it.

(2) Again, what we call responsible for some result may be only an incidental characteristic of what has really been responsible for that result, or again it may be the genus under which such a characteristic falls. A statue, for example, may be attributed in one sense to Polycleitus, in another to 'sculptor'; but [from the standpoint of making the statue] it is an irrelevant accident that the sculptor happens also to be the individual Polycleitus. And as Polycleitus is also a man and a living organism, there is an incidental sense in which man and living organism are causes of the statue. Such indirectly related aspects of a cause may differ also in degree of nearness and remoteness: e.g., having a light complexion has less to do with producing a statue than being cultured has.

(3) Independently of whether they are proper and direct or merely incidental, determining factors may be further distinguished as potential and actual. The building of a house, for example, must be attributed in one sense to the builder [as a man who knows how to build], in another to the builder as one who is actually building.

The foregoing distinctions apply also to the effects which the determining factors produce. For example, *this* statue is also statue and more generally image; *this* bronze is also bronze and more generally material. Also effects, like causes, may be either direct or incidental. Incidental and direct aspects are sometimes conjoined in a single expression, as when we speak not of 'Polycleitus' nor of 'the sculptor' but of 'Polycleitus the sculptor.'

All of these various uses may be brought under six heads, each of which again may be meant in two ways. By 'the reason for anything' (*aitia*) we may mean either (1) the specific thing that is directly responsible for the effect, or (2) its genus, or (3) an incidental attribute or aspect of the principal factor, or (4) *its* genus; and either (5) some combination of these or (6) some one of them alone. Finally, in any of these cases we may be referring either to what is actually as we describe it or to what is merely potentially so. It should be observed that regarded as something both actively at work and particular, a reason for anything exists and ceases to exist simultaneously with its effect: e.g., 'this man actually doctoring' with 'this patient actually getting well,' or 'this man actually building a house' with 'this house actually being built.' Of merely potential determining factors, on the other hand, this is not necessarily true, for the house and the house-builder need not perish together.

In seeking the reason of anything (as indeed in any other investigation) we ought to strive to get our results in the most exact form possible. Thus when a man builds he does so quâ builder, and when a builder builds he does so by virtue of his possession of the building art. This last, therefore, is more directly the reason; and so in other cases.

Again, generic effects go with generic reasons, particular effects with particular reasons: e.g., statue with sculptor, and this statue with this sculptor. In like manner potential reasons are related to potential effects, actually operating reasons to actual effects.

This concludes our exposition of the types of 'explanatory factor' (*aitia*) and of the ways in which they work.

iv. Chance and luck

'Luck' (*tychê*) and 'pure spontaneous chance' (*automaton*) are sometimes included in the list of explanatory factors, and many things are said to come about 'as luck would have it' or 'by chance.' In what sense may luck and chance be included among the types of determining factor just enumerated? Further, is luck the same thing as pure chance or something different? And exactly what is each of them?

Some people question even their existence. Nothing, they declare, happens fortuitously; whatever we ascribe to luck or pure chance has been somehow determined. Take, for instance, the case of a man who goes to market and 'as luck would have it' meets someone whom he wanted but did not expect to meet: his going to market, they say, was responsible for this. So they argue that of any other occurrence ascribed to luck there is always some more positive explanation to be found. Luck [they say] cannot have been the reason (*aition*), for it would be paradoxical to regard luck as something real. Further, they consider it noteworthy that none of the ancient philosophers mentioned luck when discussing the reasons of becoming and perishing—an indication, apparently, that they disbelieved in the possibility of fortuitous occurrences.

Yet it is odd that while people theoretically accept the venerable argument which assumes that every chance happening and stroke of luck can be attributed to some reason or other, they nevertheless continue to speak of some things as matters of luck, others not. The earlier philosophers ought to have taken some account of this popular distinction, but among their various principles—love and strife, mind, fire, etc.—luck finds no place. The omission is equally surprising whether we suppose them to have disbelieved in luck or to have believed in but disregarded it; for at any rate they were not above employing the idea in their explanations. Empedocles, for example, remarks that air is sifted up into the sky not uniformly but 'as it may chance' (*tychein*); or, in the words of his *Cosmogony*, "Now it 'happened' (*syn-kyrein*) to run this way, now that." And the parts of animals, he declares, came to be what they are purely by chance (*tychê*).

Some go so far as to attribute the heavens and all the worlds to 'chance happenings' (*automaton*),[6] declaring that the vortex—i.e., the motion which separated and arranged the entire universe in its present order—arose 'of itself' ('from *automaton*'). We may well be surprised at this assertion that while the existence and generation of animals and plants must be attributed not to chance (*tyché*) but to nature or mind or something of the sort (what issues from a particular sperm or seed is obviously not a matter of chance, since from one kind of seed there comes forth an olive, from another a man), yet the heavens and the divinest of visible things have come into existence spontaneously ('from *automaton*') and have no determining factors such as animals and plants have. Even if this were true, it would be something to give us pause, and ought to have elicited some comment. For apart from the generally paradoxical nature of such a theory it is rather odd that people should accept it when they can find no evidence of spontaneous occurrences among celestial phenomena but plenty of such evidence among the things in which they deny the presence of chance. The evidence is just the opposite of what should have been expected if their theory were true.

There are other people who, while accepting luck as a determining factor of things, regard it as something divinely mysterious, inscrutable to human intelligence.

Accordingly we must investigate the nature of luck and chance, and see whether they are the same as each other or different, and how they fit into our classification of determining factors.

v. Luck vs. purposive activity

To begin with, when we see certain things occurring in a certain way either uniformly or 'as a general rule,' we obviously would not ascribe them to mere luck. A stroke of luck is not something that comes to pass either by uniform necessity or as a general rule. But as there is also a third sort of event which is found to occur, which

[6] Democritus is probably meant. He taught that there exist worlds without limit in empty space.

everyone speaks of as being a matter of luck, and which we all know is meant when the word 'lucky' is used, it is plain that such a thing as luck (*tychê*) and 'pure spontaneous chance' (*automaton*) must exist.

Some events 'serve a purpose' (*heneka tou*), others do not. Of the former class, some are in accordance with the intention of the purposer, others not; but both are in the class of things that serve a purpose. Evidently, then, even among occurrences that are not the predictable (i.e., neither the constant nor normal) results of anyone's actual intention, there are some which may be spoken of as serving a purpose. What serves a purpose may have originated either in thought or in nature: in either case when its occurrence is accidental [7] we call it a matter of luck. Just as everything has both an essential nature and a number of incidental attributes, so when anything is considered as a determining factor it may have similarly a twofold aspect. When a man builds a house, for instance, his faculty of house-building is the essential determinant of the house, while the fact that he is blond or cultured is only incidental to that result. The essential determinant can be calculated, but the incidentally related factors are incalculable, for any number of them may inhere in one subject.

As already explained, then, we attribute to chance or luck whatever happens [accidentally] in such a way as to serve a purpose. (The specific difference between chance and luck will be explained later; [8] for the present it is enough to emphasize that both of them refer to actions that happen to serve a purpose.) As an illustration, suppose that we wish to solicit a man for a contribution of money. Had we known where he was we should have gone there and accosted him. But if with some other end in view we go to a place which it is not our invariable nor even our usual practice to visit, then, since the end effected (getting the money) is not a spontane-

---

[7] *Kata symbebêkos.* I.e., when in the case of deliberate actions the result is unforeseen, and when in the case of natural occurrences the result is neither certain nor usual.

[8] In the next chapter.

ous process of nature, but is the type of thing that results from conscious choice and reflection, we describe the meeting as a stroke of luck. It would not be a matter of luck, however, if we were to visit the place for the express purpose of seeking our man, or if we regularly went there when taking up subscriptions. Luck, then, is e 'idently an incidental (*kata symbebêkos*) aspect of the real reason of something in the sphere of actions that involve purposive choice and reflection. Hence, since choice (*proairesis*) implies 'intelligent reflection' (*dianoia*), we may conclude that luck and intelligent reflection both refer to the same sphere of things and activities. . . .

According as the result of a fortuitous action is good or bad we speak of good and bad luck. In more serious matters we use the terms 'good fortune' (*eu-tychia*) and 'misfortune' (*dys-tychia*); and when we escape by a hair's breadth some great evil or just miss some great good we consider ourselves fortunate or unfortunate accordingly—the margin having been so slight that we can reflect upon the good or ill in question as if it were actually present. Moreover, as all luck is unstable (for nothing invariable or normal could be attributed to luck), we are right in regarding good fortune as also unstable.

Both luck and spontaneous chance, then, as has been said, are determining factors in a purely incidental sense and are attributed to the type of occurrence which is neither constant nor normal and which might have been aimed at for its own sake.

vi. Luck and chance distinguished

The difference between luck (*tychê*) and chance (*automaton*) is that 'chance' is the more inclusive term. Every case of luck is a case of chance, but not all cases of chance are cases of luck.

Luck, together with lucky or unlucky occurrences, is spoken of only in connection with agents that are capable of enjoying good [or ill] fortune and of performing moral actions. It follows, then, that luck always has some reference to conduct—a conclusion which is further enforced by the popular belief that 'good fortune' (*eu-tychia*) is the same, or practically the same, as 'happiness' (*eudaimonia*); and that happiness, as it involves 'well-doing' (*eupraxia*), is a kind of 'moral action' (*praxis*). Hence only what is capable of moral conduct can perform actions that are lucky or the reverse. Luck does not pertain to the activities of a lifeless thing, a beast, or a child, for these exercise no 'deliberate choice' (*proairesis*). If we call them lucky or unlucky we are speaking figuratively —as when Protarchus speaks of altar stones as fortunate because they are treated with reverence while their fellows are trampled underfoot. All such objects are affected by luck only in so far as a moral agent may deal with them in a manner that is lucky or unlucky [to himself].

'Pure spontaneous chance' (*automaton*), on the other hand, is found both among the lower animals and in many lifeless things. We say of a horse, for example, that it went 'by chance' to a place of safety, meaning that it was not for the sake of safety that it went there. Again, we say of a tripod that it fell onto its feet 'by chance,' because although it could then be used to sit on, it did not fall for the sake of that.

[The distinction, then, may be summarized as follows.] We attribute to 'pure chance' (*automaton*) all those events which are such as ordinarily admit of a telic explanation, but which happen on this occasion to have been produced without any reference to the actual result. The word 'luck' (*tychê*), on the other hand, is restricted to that special type of chance events which (1) are possible objects of choice, and (2) affect persons capable of exercising choice. . . . The difference between chance and luck becomes clearest when applied to the productions of nature: when she produces a monster we attribute it to chance but we do not call nature unlucky. Even this, however, is not quite the same type of situation as that of the horse who chances to escape; for the horse's escape was due to factors independent of the horse, while the reasons for nature's miscarriages are private to herself.

Thus we have explained the meaning of, and distinction between, chance and luck. Both, it may be added, belong to the order of 'propelling factors' or 'sources of movement'; [9] for the determining factors to which they are incidental are either natural forces or intelligent agents—the particular kinds of which are too numerous to mention.

Inasmuch as the results of chance and luck, while of a sort that nature or a conscious intelligence might well have intended, have in fact emerged as a purely incidental result of some determinative process, and as there can be nothing incidental without something prior for it to be incidental to, it is clear that an incidental connection presupposes a determinative relation that is authentic and direct. Chance and luck, then, presuppose intelligence and nature as determinative agents. Hence, however true it may be that the heavens are due to spontaneous chance, intelligence and nature must be the prior reasons, not only of many other things, but of this universe itself.

vii. Relations of the four determining factors

It is clear, then, that there are such things as 'determining factors' and that they are of four kinds, as we have stated. These correspond to the four meanings of the question 'why.' The 'why' of anything may be referred: (1) to the 'essential nature of the thing in question' (*ti esti*), when it is a question of things that do not involve change [10] (e.g., in mathematics, where our reasoning ultimately falls back upon the definition of a straight line or commensurability or the like); or (2) to the thing that started a movement going (e.g., "Why did they make war? Because they had been raided"); or (3) to the end in view (e.g., [they make war] in order to gain sovereign power); or (4) in the case of things that come into existence, to the material out of which they come. These, then,

[9] For although a chance event is such as would ordinarily admit of a telic explanation, the very fact that it happens by chance means that it lacks a telic determinant on this occasion.

[10] Also when it is a question of changeless aspects of changeable things.

being the four kinds of determining factor that there are, it is the business of the natural philosopher to understand them all; and his explanations, to be scientifically adequate, must take account of each of them—the matter, the form, the moving force, and the goal.

It sometimes happens that the last three of these determinants coincide. The essential nature of a thing may often be regarded as identical with the fundamental purpose which it serves; and both of these aspects must be identical in kind (*eidos*) with the source of the thing's movement—man, for example, being begotten only by man. This latter identity holds true in all cases where the propelling determinant is itself something that changes. As for the opposite sort of case (i.e., where the propelling determinant possesses within itself neither movement nor the power of movement, but is motionless),[11] this falls outside the province of natural science; whence we may distinguish three branches of inquiry—one of things to which movement is foreign, a second of moving but imperishable things, and a third of things that perish.

In short, then, when we explain anything we must take into account at once its material, its essential character, and the source of its movement; this being principally how explanations of occurrences are sought. "What comes into existence, and what has preceded it?" "What was the force or agent that started the process, and on what did it act?"—questions such as these, properly ordered, are essential to every [scientific investigation].

The 'principles that give rise to and govern' (*archê*) physical movement or change are of two kinds. One of them does not itself partake of change, and is therefore not physical: I refer to whatever produces movement or change in other things without itself being affected—the absolutely unalterable and primary [aspect of things], their essential character, or form; hence also their end and goal. And as nature is inherently 'goalful,' the natural scientist

---

[11] I.e., it *has* no principle (*archê*) of change or movement within itself, but it *is* such a principle for other things.

must not neglect this aspect. He must, in short, explain the 'why' of things in all four of its aspects, showing how one thing necessarily, or at any rate normally, arises from another [*propelling determinant*]; how one thing is a precondition of another's existence, as premises provide the material for a conclusion [*material determinant*]; how this or that [entity or aspect] manifests a thing's essential nature [*formal determinant*]; and why it is better that this or that should be as it is—not, of course, without qualification but relatively to the 'whole character' (*ousia*) of the thing in question [*telic determinant*].

viii. Evidence that nature is telic

We must now explain in what sense nature belongs to the class of telic determinants. Then [in the next chapter] we shall consider what is meant by necessity when spoken of with reference to natural phenomena; for people are constantly appealing to necessity as the cause of things, arguing that since the hot and the cold and all the other qualities are each of a certain definitive nature, the objects which they characterize [12] must exist and be created by necessity. Even those who admit some further determining principle of things, such as Love and Strife, or Mind, do not consistently adhere to their explanations [but fall back upon the idea of necessity].

[With reference to our first question] it may be objected that nature does not act with reference to a goal nor by reason of the fact that one thing is better than another, but for the same reason that it rains [13]—not to make the corn grow, but of necessity. When rain falls, so the argument runs, it is simply because the rising vapor has become cooled, and being cooled turns to water, which descends, causing the corn to grow; on the same basis as, when rain spoils the crops on the threshing-floor, we do not suppose that

[12] Or possibly: "they themselves"—i.e., all existing qualities.
[13] Lit., 'Zeus rains.' The personification, while awkward in English, was natural to the Greek idiom.

it fell for the sake of spoiling them but that it merely happened to do so. Why, then, should it not be the same with the organic parts of nature? Take the case of our teeth, for example—the front teeth sharp and suitable for tearing the food, the back ones broad and flat, suitable for grinding it—may they not have grown up thus by simple necessity,[14] and their adaptation to their respective functions be purely a coincidence? The same argument can be offered about any organic structure to which purpose is commonly ascribed; and it is further explained that where the organic structures happen to have been formed *as if* they had been arranged on purpose, the creatures which thus happen to be suitably organized have survived, while the others have perished—as Empedocles relates of his 'man-faced ox-creatures.'

While these and similar arguments may cause difficulties, they certainly do not represent the truth. For in the first place, (1) teeth and all other natural phenomena come about in a certain way if not invariably at least normally, and this is inconsistent with the meaning of luck or chance. We do not appeal to luck or coincidence in explaining the frequency of rain in winter nor of heat in mid-summer; we would, however, if the situation were to be reversed. As every occurrence must be ascribed either to coincidence or to purpose, if such cases as the foregoing cannot be ascribed to coincidence or chance, they must be ascribed to purpose. But since even our opponents will admit that all such occurrences are natural events, it follows that there is such a thing as purpose in nature and its processes.

(2) Furthermore, [in any human art or technique] where there is an end to be achieved, the first and each succeeding step of the operation are performed for the sake of that end. As in human operations, so in the processes of nature; and as in nature, so in each human undertaking—unless there is something to interfere.

---

[14] I.e., by virtue of material and efficient determinants only, and without reference to any telic determinant.

Human operations, however, are for the sake of an end; hence natural processes must be so too. If a house, for example, had been a natural product it would have been made by the same successive stages as it passed through when made by human technique; and if natural objects could be duplicated artificially it would be by the same series of steps as now produce them in nature. In art and in nature alike each stage is for the sake of the one that follows; for generally speaking, human technique either gives the finishing touches to what nature has had to leave incomplete, or else imitates her. Hence, if the operations that constitute a human technique are for the sake of an end, it is clear that this must be no less true of natural processes. The relation of earlier to later terms of the series is the same for both.

(3) This is most clearly true in the case of the lower animals, whose behavior is admittedly independent of any conscious technique or experimentation or deliberation—so much so, in fact, that it is debated whether the work of spiders, ants, and the like is due to intelligence or to some other faculty. Passing gradually down the scale we find that plants too produce organs subservient to their 'natural end' (*telos*): leaves, for instance, are put forth to provide shade for the fruit. Hence, if it is both 'by nature' (*physei*) and also 'for a purpose' (*heneka tou*) that the swallow builds its nest and the spider its web, and that plants put forth leaves for the sake of the fruit and push down rather than up with their roots for the sake of nourishment, it is evident that the type of determining factor which we have called telic is operative in the objects and processes of nature.

[What, then, is a telic determinant?] Consider first that nature exists under a twofold aspect—as 'composed of materials' (*hylê*) and 'as consisting in the ways in which things are shaping up' (*morphê*); that by the second of these aspects is meant 'the perfected results at which processes tend to arrive' (*telos*), and that all the earlier stages in any process are for the sake of such perfected results [i.e., are telically determined by them]: it follows that the telic determinant of a thing is nothing other than the 'way in which it tends to shape up' [i.e., its 'form'].

No human technique is free from error: the man of letters makes mistakes in grammar, and the physician may administer a wrong dose. Hence it is not surprising that there should be errors in the processes of nature too. Just as in the arts and other human techniques there are certain procedures which correctly serve their specific ends, while to aim at such ends and miss them is to fail; so it presumably is with nature, and what we call freaks are simply failures or errors in respect of nature's proper ends. . . .

[A consequence of Empedocles' theory [15]] is that it would be entirely a matter of chance what might spring up from a given seed. But such an assertion would be a denial of nature and of the whole natural order. For we call anything 'natural' when by virtue of an 'initiating principle' (*archê*) inherent in itself it progresses continuously toward some goal. Such principles do not all make for the same goal, nor, on the other hand, is the goal picked at random; but each inner principle makes always for the same goal of its own, if nothing interferes. There are other cases, to be sure, where a certain end, as well as the means of attaining it, may come about entirely by luck. Thus we call it a stroke of luck that a stranger should come and before departing pay the ransom; for the ransom is paid just as if payment of it had been the stranger's purpose in coming, although actually it was not. In this case the result achieved is incidental [to the stranger's real purpose in coming]; since luck, as we have already explained, is incidental causation. But when a certain result is achieved either invariably or normally, it is no incidental or merely lucky occurrence; and in

[15] That 'man-headed ox-creatures' and countless other such combinations originally arose at random, but being ill-adapted did not survive. Aristotle has just been discussing this theory of Empedocles, but the Greek text is here so obscure and corrupt that the passage has been omitted from the present edition.

the processes of nature each result is achieved if not invariably at least normally, provided nothing hinders.

There are some who deny the existence of purpose in nature on the ground that they can never detect the physical force in the act of deliberating. Such an argument is illogical, for human techniques also may be carried on without deliberation. Yet if the ship-building art were inherent in the timber the construction of the ship would then proceed naturally in the same way as it now proceeds by human skill—showing that if purpose is inherent in human techniques it must inhere in nature too.

The processes of nature are best illustrated by the case of a doctor who doctors himself. Nature similarly is agent and patient at once.

In conclusion, it is clear that nature is a 'determining principle' (*aitia*), whose manner of determination is telic.

ix. The meaning of necessity in nature

As for necessity (*anangkê*), does it exist conditionally or unconditionally? People tend to think of necessity as something inherent in the process of production; which is pretty much as if they should suppose that a wall might be built by [an accidental conjunction of] necessary forces—i.e., that as heavy things are naturally borne downward and light things toward the top, so the stones and foundations would necessarily fall to the lowest place, the earth more lightly rising above, and the wood, because it was lightest of all, forming the roof. But while it is true that the wall cannot be built unless these materials [with their respective properties] are present; still, being only its material conditions, they will not suffice to account for the completed wall, which is brought into existence for the sake of sheltering us and protecting our goods. And so with all other cases of working toward an end: although the end cannot be attained without certain materials possessing definitive properties, these are only the material precondition of its attainment; properly speaking, what brings it into existence is a certain purpose. Suppose, for example, we were to ask why a saw is what it is. In order that it may perform a certain work and thereby serve a certain end, we should reply. But [let us suppose] this work cannot be performed unless the saw is made of iron. We may then declare that if it is to be truly a saw and perform its function it 'must necessarily' be made of iron. Necessity, then, is conditional. It is not of the same order as the end (*telos*); for while necessity resides only in the 'material preconditions' (*hylê*), the 'end or purpose' (*heneka tou*) is found in the definition. . . .

From the foregoing analogy it is plain that when we speak of necessity we are referring to the 'material aspect' (*hylê*) of nature and the changes proper to that aspect. While the natural scientist must deal with the material aspect too, his primary concern is with the 'purposive aspect' (*heneka tou*); for the goal may determine the material changes, but these do not determine the goal. The principle that determines the goal, or inherent purpose, of a thing is to be found in its meaning (*logos*) and definition (*horismos*). In the case of human techniques, when we have determined what kind of a house we want, certain materials must then 'of necessity' be either had or got in order to build it; and when we have determined what we mean by health, certain things become necessary in order to secure it. [So it is with nature:] if man has a certain meaning, certain antecedent conditions are requisite to his existence, and these conditions will in turn presuppose others.

From another point of view we may refer necessity to the definition of a thing. For if we define sawing as a particular kind of scission, it will follow that this cannot be accomplished unless the saw possesses teeth of a particular character, and to have such a character the teeth must be made of iron. The definition, no less than the physical object, contains parts which are, so to speak, its matter.

BOOK III

MOTION, CHANGE, AND THE INFINITE

i. Definition of motion

SINCE NATURE, which is the subject of our general inquiry, has been defined as the 'originating principle' (*archê*) of motion (*kinêsis*) and change (*metabolê*), we must now consider what 'motion' means—a study which is essential to an understanding of nature. After we have determined the meaning of motion we shall then have to take up in the same manner each of the terms implicit in its definition.

Evidently motion belongs to the class of things that are *continuous*. In defining continuity it is usual to appeal to the concept of the infinite, for this concept is first apprehended in terms of continuity: accordingly we say that the continuous is what is infinitely divisible. In addition to these concepts it is generally held that motion also presupposes place (*topos*), 'empty space' (*kenon*), and time (*chronos*) as necessary conditions of its existence. This being the case, and because all of these properties are universally characteristic of natural phenomena, we must take up and examine each of them in turn. For we can hardly expect to understand the properties that differentiate one thing from another until we have first considered the properties which all things share.

Let us begin, then, as we have proposed, with 'motion, in the broadest sense of the word' (*kinêsis*). First we must distinguish between what exists only in a 'state of perfect fulfillment' (*entelecheia*) and what exists as incompletely actualized, possessing a 'capability of becoming something further' (*dynamis*). Its capability may be to develop into 'a certain kind of individual thing' (*tode ti*) or to change in quantity or quality or in respect of any of the other categories. Change with respect to the category of relation may be a change of relation between excess and deficiency; or again, between agent and patient, i.e., between the source and the recipient of any motion, inasmuch as to impart motion and to receive motion are processes that entail each other mutually.

There is no motion [or change] apart from things that are changing. For motion can take place only with respect either to substance, to quantity, to quality, or to place. Now our doctrine denies that there can be any larger category distinct from quantity, quality, and the other determinate categories, and embracing them. Hence motion and change can have no existence apart from the categories; since apart from them there is nothing.

With respect to each category there are certain pairs of terms between which motion [and change] take place. With respect to substance there is the 'proper character' (*morphê*) of a thing and the 'not-yetness' (*sterêsis*) of that character; with respect to quality, white and black; with respect to quantity, complete and incomplete amounts; and with respect to 'locomotion' (*phora*) [1] there is the antithesis of up and down, the states of being light and heavy. Thus there are as many types of motion (*kinêsis*) and change (*metabolê*) [2] as there are meanings of the verb 'to be.' Applying to each of these four meanings our earlier distinction between capability ('potentiality,' *dynamis*) and fulfillment ('actuality,' *entelecheia*) we may define motion (*kinêsis*) as the *fulfillment of a potentiality* quâ *potentiality*. Thus 'qualitative alteration' (*alloiôsis*) is the fulfillment of a qualitatively alterable thing quâ qualitatively alterable; increase and decrease (there is no single

---

[1] The word connotes 'being borne along.'

[2] Aristotle probably intends by the wider term, *metabolê*, types of change with respect to the categories other than those here specified. *Kinêsis* includes changes with respect to quantity, quality, and place; also, according to the present chapter, changes with respect to substance, although this is contradicted in Bk. VIII, Chap. vii.

word covering both) are similarly the fulfillment of what is capable of being increased or diminished; generation (*genesis*) and annihilation (*phthora*), the fulfillment of what can be created and destroyed; locomotion, the fulfillment of what can be borne through space. Examples will confirm this interpretation of motion. To just the extent that the buildable in its buildable aspect is being built, to that extent it has attained fulfillment; and this fulfillment is what is called building. Other processes, such as learning, doctoring, rolling, leaping, maturing, and growing old, may be analyzed in the same way.

As a given thing may be both potential and actual—though not, to be sure, at the same time, or else not in the same respect, but, e.g., potentially hot and actually cold—things will both act on and be affected by each other in a variety of ways; each of them being capable both of acting and of being acted upon. Every physical cause of motion [change],[3] then, is itself mutable; and whenever anything in the physical world produces such a motion it does so by virtue of being in motion itself. Hence some have been led to suppose that anything *whatever* that produces motion in some other thing must itself be in motion. The true state of the case will be explained at a later point, and by another set of arguments;[4] for the present we shall simply affirm that there does exist a motionless cause of motion—an unchanging cause of change.

Motion, then, is the functioning of something mutable in making active the potentiality which it possesses not quâ that thing but quâ mutable. What I mean by 'quâ' will be clear from an illustration. A piece of bronze is potentially a statue. When it is being fashioned into a statue the process does not consist in the actualization of bronze quâ bronze, for 'to be bronze' and 'to be mutable' are essentially distinct. If they were identical without qualification —i.e., identical in meaning (*logos*)—then indeed the process which the bronze undergoes would be its actualization quâ bronze;

[3] From the verb *kinein*.
[4] Bk. VIII, Chap. i–vi; esp. Chap. v.

but as we have said, they are not identical in this way. This is illustrated more clearly by the case of opposites. Being capable of health and being capable of illness are not identical, for if they were there would be no difference between being well and being ill. Yet whether the ailment be excess of blood or excess of moisture, it is in any case one and the same subject who is both well and ill. Hence as these states are not identical with each other—any more than color and visibility [which similarly have reference to an identical subject] are identical with each other—it is clear that when we define motion as the fulfillment of a thing's potentialities, we must be careful to add 'quâ potentialities.'

This being the nature of motion, it is clear that motion may be predicated of a thing only while the thing is actually functioning in the manner explained, and not before or after. Every physical thing is capable of being at one time actual, at another not. In the case of 'building materials' for example, the fulfillment of their proper nature as 'capable of being built with' is found in the process of building. For the fulfillment must be either this process or else the completed edifice. But when the edifice is completed the building materials are no longer capable of being built with. Their fulfillment quâ building materials must therefore be the process of building; and building is a species of motion. This same argument will apply to other kinds of motion as well.

BOOK VIII

MOTION AND THE UNMOVED MOVER

i. The eternity of motion

WAS THERE EVER a time when motion (*kinêsis*) first began to exist? And will there ever be a time when it at length ceases to exist? Or must we suppose that motion is without beginning and end, that it always has existed and always will exist, and that it is a deathless and unfailing property of things—the 'vital essence' (*zôê*), so to speak, of everything in nature?

That motion does exist is tacitly admitted by all who discuss natural science; for if there were no such thing as motion, they would be unable to theorize as they do about the making of the cosmos and the genesis and disappearance of things. . . .

Let us start from certain definitions already arrived at. We have said that motion is the fulfillment (*entelecheia*) of the movable character of whatever can be moved; and from this it follows that the existence of a given kind of motion presupposes the existence of objects capable of being moved or changed in that particular way. Moreover there is no need of appealing to definitions: everyone will agree that for anything to move or change in a given way it must be intrinsically capable of that sort of motion. What undergoes qualitative change is intrinsically changeable with respect to qualities, and what moves from place to place is intrinsically capable of locomotion: e.g., there can be no combustion or burning unless there already exists something combustible and capable of being burned. Accordingly, instead of asking about motion in the abstract we may turn our inquiry to mutable entities: have these had a definite beginning or have they existed from eternity? If, on the one hand, we suppose each mutable entity to have had an absolute beginning, it will follow that there must have been some preëxisting change (*metabolê*) or motion to account for the creation of those very entities that we have postulated as a precondition of all motion or production of motion. On the other hand, if we suppose that although there was at first no actual motion yet potential movers and potentially mutable objects have existed from eternity, our supposition will appear illogical to any thoughtful man, especially if he undertakes thoroughly to examine it. For supposing that there had once been mutable entities and potential movers both existing in a state of absolute rest and that all at once a mover moved something for the first time, it is evident that there must have been some antecedent change to account for this. [As potential movers and potentially mutable objects were both present] there must originally have been some specific cause [1] to account for the lack of actual motion—i.e., the state of rest. Hence, as no motion could arise until this hindering cause was removed, there must have been a change of some sort prior to the supposed first change.

[To make clear what I mean about a hindering cause, we may consider the matter as follows.] Certain movers can produce motion of one sort only, while others can produce either of two contrary motions: fire, for example, can apparently heat but not chill, whereas one and the same intelligence seems able to produce contrary effects. Nevertheless there is a sense in which the former class of movers may be considered as a variant of the latter class; for coldness by turning around and withdrawing may produce heat, in much the same way as an expert (*epistêmôn*) by employing his skill in a contrary direction may do conscious mischief.

At any rate, a thing that is capable of acting or of being acted upon—that is, of producing or of undergoing motion—possesses

---

[1] The mover might, for instance, (as Aristotle suggests later) have been too far away from the movable object to have any effect upon it.

this capability not with respect to all circumstances, but only so far as mover and mutable object are suitably disposed and sufficiently close to each other. Hence we may say that motion occurs when both a mover and a mutable object exist and are in sufficient proximity to each other. If we suppose that although both of them have existed from eternity there was nevertheless a time when no actual motion had ever up till then occurred, this must evidently have been because they were not so situated that they could respectively produce and receive motion. Accordingly, one or the other of them must have been changed in order that any motion should have occurred. It is the same way with all cases of relatedness: e.g., if a thing is at one time double another and at another time not, it follows that either or both of the things in question must have changed. Thus [on the supposition that movers and mutable entities had existed from eternity without actual motion] there would have had to be a change prior to the supposed first change.

Furthermore, how could we speak of a 'before' and an 'after' if time did not exist, and how could time exist if there were no motion? For whether we conceive of time as the measure (*arithmos*) of motion or as itself a kind of motion, it follows in either case that if time is eternal motion must be eternal too. And as to the eternity of time all thinkers, with but a single exception, appear to agree; for they declare it to have had no origin. Democritus, for example, takes this as the ground on which to refute the claim that everything has had an origin: for time, he says, has had none. Plato is the only thinker who ascribes an origin to time: it originated, he declares, simultaneously with the universe, to which he also ascribes an origin.

Finally, time can neither exist nor be conceived apart from an actual 'now.' But what we call 'now' is a kind of intermediate state, having the twofold character of a beginning and an end —a beginning, that is to say, of future and an end of past time. Hence time must always have existed; for whatever you take as time's ultimate limit must consist in a certain 'now' (you can take absolutely no point in time that will not have the character of a 'now'), and since every 'now' is an end as well as a beginning, it follows that time must necessarily extend backwards from that 'now' as well as forwards from it. And if this is true of time, it clearly must be no less true of motion—since time is a derivative (*pathos*) of motion.

By the same reasoning we may discover motion to be imperishable. Just as the supposition that motion has had a beginning implies that there was a change prior to the first change, so the supposition that motion will have an end implies that there will be a change subsequent to the last change. The potential mover and the potentially mutable object do not lose their characters merely because actual motion happens to have ceased: for instance, a combustible object remains combustible even though it is not actually being burnt; and in the same way a movent force does not cease to be a force when it ceases to cause actual motion. On any other supposition we should have to think of a destructible object, after it had destroyed something, as being itself destroyed, and its destroyer as destroyed in turn. This would mean, since destruction too is a kind of change (*metabolê*), [that if motion were perishable there would have to be motion after the last motion had been finally destroyed]. As such a consequence is inadmissible, we must conclude that motion is something eternal, that it cannot exist at one moment and be non-existent at another: in fact, any denial of this can be little more than a figure of speech. . . .

iii. *Alternations of motion and rest demonstrated*

We must now examine a question previously mentioned [2]—why it is that certain things are now in motion, now at rest. There are three general possibilities: (1) either everything is always at rest, or (2) everything is always in motion, or (3) some things

[2] In Chap. ii, omitted from the present edition.

are in motion and others at rest. From the last of these alternatives three further possibilities arise: (a) either the objects in motion are always in motion and the others always at rest, or (b) everything has a natural capacity of motion and rest alike, or third and finally, (c) it may be the case that some things are always motionless, others always in motion, while still others pass from one state to the other. This last possibility is the one that we shall have to adopt, for it alone can solve all our difficulties and ensure a successful outcome to the present inquiry.

(1) To suppose that everything is constantly at rest, and to seek to establish this rationally with no reference to sense-perception, is a kind of paralysis of the intelligence, with respect not only to natural science but to other fields as well; for motion is a presupposition not only of the science of nature but likewise of all the other sciences and doubtless of all 'popular thinking' (*doxa*) too. Besides, just as no mathematician can discuss mathematics with a man who challenges its basic principles (a rule which holds similarly true of other subjects), so no natural scientist can discuss his science in the face of a similar denial: it is a presupposition with him that nature finds its basic principle in motion.

(2) The proposition that everything is always in motion, while no less false, is less flatly opposed to the methods of natural science than the alternative just considered. Although our lectures on nature [3] have laid down the postulate that nature is the principle of both motion and rest, yet motion is its more essential phase. Some thinkers go so far as to assert that instead of there being some things in motion and others that stay at rest, everything is always in motion, even though the motions may be such as to escape the notice of our senses. Such thinkers, despite their failure to explain whether they mean a specific kind of motion or motion in general, are not hard to deal with. For, (a) neither growth

---

[3] I.e., Books I–IV of *Natural Science*, between the two halves of which Aristotle frequently makes a distinction. The reference is evidently to the first paragraph of Bk. II, Chap. i.

nor dissolution can go on incessantly: there must be an intermediate point [which is neither the one nor the other]. A similar
argument may be drawn from the case of a rock that is worn away
by dripping water or split by a growing plant: if in a certain
period of time it has been worn away or dislodged to a certain
degree there is no assurance that it would have been affected
just half that much in half the time. Rather it is like hauling a
ship onto land; [4] and if a certain amount of dripping produces
a certain effect, it may be the case that a mere portion of that
dripping would never have produced any effect at all. Granted
that the amount of rock worn away is divisible, still the parts
may not have been removed separately. Plainly, then, although
a given amount of decomposition may be subdivided without
limit, it does not follow that the process has lasted over the whole
period [in which the drops have been falling], for it may have
occurred all at once. So it is with 'changes of quality' (*alloiôsis*)
in general. The fact that the object undergoing the change is infinitely divisible does not prove the process of change itself to
be so. As in the case of freezing, it may take place as a unit. Again,
(b) a man who is recovering from an illness takes a certain time
in which to get well. But at the point where his recovery is complete he is not changing—since the only change with which we
are here concerned is the change from sickness to health. Inasmuch as all changes of quality, therefore, are changes from
opposite to opposite, we fly in the face of evidence if we suppose
change to go on unceasingly. Nor again, (c) do stones grow either
harder or softer,[5] and (d) it would be astonishing if we were
deceived in thinking that a stone moves when it is falling and
is really at rest when lying on the earth. Finally, (e) it is axiomatic

---

[4] I.e., supposing that a dozen men can pull the ship a certain distance,
it may nevertheless be the case that no one of them alone would have been
able to move it at all.

[5] I.e., these particular qualities of stones remain unchanged—a further
refutation of the thesis that change is in every respect universal and in-
cessant.

that the earth and every other physical body must stay in the place proper to it unless dislodged by some force. If some things, therefore, are already in the places proper to them it follows that not everything has motion with respect to place. These and other such considerations should convince us that neither can everything be always in motion nor can everything be always at rest.

(3, *a*) It is likewise impossible that some things should be always in motion and everything else always at rest, with nothing in motion at one time and at rest at another. The impossibility of this may be demonstrated by much the same arguments as those just employed. We actually see things changing from rest to motion and the reverse; to deny this is to fly in the face of evidence. The growth of living things further demonstrates the point; [6] so too does the act of forcible motion, because by force there is produced an unnatural motion in things that were formerly at rest.[7] Thus the supposition just mentioned is incompatible with the phenomena of becoming and perishing; for all motion,[8] considered from one point of view, is a kind of becoming and perishing—i.e., when anything changes it ceases to exist in its former character or in its former place, and begins to exist in a new character or in a new place: proving that there are cases of alternate rest and motion.

We may now take in connection with the preceding arguments the hypothesis (3, *b*) that everything is sometimes at rest, sometimes in motion [and that nothing is either wholly the one or wholly the other]. First, let us recapitulate the possibilities as outlined at the beginning of the discussion. Either (1) everything is at rest, or (2) everything is in motion, or (3) some things are at rest and others are in motion. And if both rest and motion actually exist, there are three possible sub-alternatives: either (*b*) everything is sometimes at rest and sometimes in motion,

---

[6] Because they stop growing after reaching maturity.

[7] E.g., as when a stone is dislodged from its natural resting-place on the ground and thrown into the air.

[8] I.e., each of the four kinds distinguished in Bk. III, Chap. i.

or (*a*) things at rest are always at rest, while things in motion are always in motion, or (*c*) some things are always at rest, others always in motion, while still others are now the one and now the other.

(1) It has already been declared that everything cannot be in a state of rest; and in support of this a further consideration may now be added. Suppose we grant what certain thinkers [9] contend—that reality (*to on*) is something infinite and motionless. At the same time we should have to grant that this is not how things appear to our senses, for we perceive many things as moving. But if we thus admit that false opinion (or indeed any *opinion*) exists, it follows that motion must also exist. This is likewise the case if we admit that imagination exists, or that it is possible to change one's mind; for imagination and opinion are generally admitted to be species of motion. But after all, to trouble ourselves much over such arguments and to seek proof of matters for which we already possess clearer evidence than any proof can afford, is to confuse the better with the worse, the plausible with the implausible, and the basic with the derivative.

We have further refuted (2) the hypothesis that everything is always in motion, and (3, *a*) the hypothesis that things in motion are always in motion, things at rest always at rest. To all such contentions one reply is convincing and sufficient: simply that we *see* some things now moving, now at rest. Evidently, then, it is impossible either (1) that everything should be continuously at rest, or (2) that everything should be continuously in motion, or (3, *a*) that each thing must either be such as always to be at rest, or such as always to be in motion. It remains to consider whether (3, *b*) all things are such as sometimes to move and sometimes to be at rest, or (3, *c*) whether some things are of this sort while others are always at rest and still others always in motion. It is this last alternative that we shall demonstrate to be true.

[9] The Eleatic philosophers, principally Melissus.

iv. External and internal causes of motion

To some of the things that produce or undergo motion the motion is merely incidental; in others it is an essential part of their natures. The former class comprises (1) properties belonging to things that produce or undergo motion, and (2) wholes to which such things belong as parts; the latter class comprises whatever produces or undergoes motion directly and not in either of the aforesaid ways.

Of the things to which motion belongs essentially, some produce the motion themselves, others derive it from an external source; moreover in some the motion is natural, in others violent and contrary to nature. (a) In things whose motion has its source in the moving things themselves (e.g., animals, since every animal is self-moved) the motion is natural; and where the 'originating principle' (arché) of the motion is in the moving things themselves the motion is again declared to be natural. Thus an animal taken as a whole is the source of its own motion, and its motion is in this respect natural; but the 'physical body' (sôma) of the animal may partake both of natural and unnatural motions—depending on the kind of motion that it happens to be undergoing and the kind of 'material element' (stoicheion) of which it is composed. (b) In things which derive their motion from an external source, the motion may be either natural or (as in the case of earthly objects moving upwards and fire moving downwards) unnatural. . . .

We must now seek the reason for the motion of light and heavy objects into their respective positions. The reason is that they each have a natural tendency in some direction or other, and that this tendency constitutes the essence of lightness and heaviness, the former consisting in an upward, the latter in a downward tendency. As has already been observed, there is more than one sense in which a thing may be potentially light or heavy. When it passes into the form of water its lightness is potential in one sense; [10] when it becomes air its lightness may again be only potential, but in this sense—that its rising may be prevented by some obstacle, upon the removal of which its upward tendency will unfailingly find active expression. This is similar to the process by which a quality begins to function actively: the state of being intelligent finds prompt expression, if nothing hinders, in the activity of intellectual inquiry. So too, what is of a certain quantity will spread itself over a certain area unless something intervenes to compress it.

Whatever removes the obstacle that is preventing a thing's natural motion, is in one sense the mover, in another not. The person who dislodges a pillar or removes the stopper from a leathern flask held under water is but an incidental factor in determining the ensuing motion, [the primary determinant of which is the upward and downward tendencies of things]. In a similar fashion we attribute the motion of a ball not to the wall from which it bounces, but to the thrower.

Plainly, none of the things here mentioned is self-moved. The principle of motion that each of them contains is not that of causing or producing motion, but of receiving it. If, then, all moving things move either naturally or violently and unnaturally; and if things whose motion is violent and unnatural are moved by some agency distinct from themselves, while things whose motion is natural are also moved by some agency (whether by themselves or by an entity distinct from themselves—e.g., light and heavy objects, whose motion may be regarded as caused either by what originally brought them into existence and made them light and heavy, or by what released them from the thing that was obstructing and preventing their proper motion); it follows that whatever is in motion must be moved *by* something.

[10] I.e., lightness, while not a property of water quâ water (since water tends to move down rather than up), is in the water 'potentially' in the sense that water has the potentiality of changing into air (i.e., into a gaseous state), the lightness of which, if not actual, is potential in the second sense mentioned.

v. The original Mover not further moved

There are two senses in which we may regard one thing as producing motion in another. Either the mover is ultimately responsible for the motion, or else it is not ultimately responsible but transmits the motion from an ulterior source; and in the former case, either the action of the mover immediately precedes the result or else there are intermediate steps. Thus a cane that pushes a stone is itself moved by a hand which is in turn moved by a man; the man himself, however, is not moved by anything further. The resultant motion in such a case may be ascribed either to the last or the first of the movers in the series, but more correctly to the first; for the first mover moves the last without being moved by it, and moreover may produce motion without the presence of the last whereas the last can produce no motion without the first—e.g., the cane does not push anything unless it is set in motion by the man. If, then, every moving object is set in motion by some cause, and if the immediate cause of its motion is either some other moving object or not; and if where the source of the motion is another moving object there must be some original mover that is not itself moved by anything else (while in cases where the *immediate* source of the motion is not moved by anything else, there is of course no need of looking further); . . . we may conclude that the original mover, since it is not moved by anything else, is necessarily the cause of its own motion. . . .

This, when we stop to examine it, is a most reasonable conclusion. For there are three things which any motion entails: an object moved, a mover, and an instrument. [*A priori* we might suppose] that the object in motion, while certainly moved, does not necessarily produce motion; that the instrument must both produce motion and also be moved itself, since it changes along with the object which it sets in motion (this is illustrated by the case of locomotion, where there has to be a certain period of contact between the instrument and its object); and that the real mover, as distinguished from the instrument of motion, must itself be unmoved. [The first two parts of this hypothesis are verified by everyday experience:] we see cases of objects in motion that have no inherent power (*archê*) of motion; we also see cases of objects in motion that supply their own power of motion. It is reasonable, therefore, not to say necessary, to infer that the third condition which we have supposed requisite to motion also exists —namely, an unmoved source and producer of motion. Hence Anaxagoras was right in declaring that Mind (*nous*), which he takes to be the source (*archê*) of all motion, is impassive and unmixed; for it could be a genuine mover only by remaining unmoved, and a supreme power only by being unmixed. . . .

Let us start afresh and ask in what respect and in what manner a thing may be the cause of its own motion. Whatever moves must be divisible into infinitely divisible parts; for as our general [lectures] on natural science have shown, whatever possesses motion as an essential attribute of itself is continuous. Now when anything is the cause of its own motion we cannot suppose that the object in motion taken as a whole is at once cause and effect; for this would mean that a single unanalyzable whole might be receiving the same push or the same alteration that it was producing. On such a hypothesis there would be, in any given case, no distinction between teaching and being taught or between curing and being cured.

Moreover, what receives motion is, by our previous definition, something mutable—i.e., something potentially but not actually in motion. But to be potentially such and such is to be on the road to becoming actually that. Motion, then, may be regarded as *an incomplete actualization of what is mutable*. The nature of the mover, on the other hand, is already fully realized: e.g., what produces heat must be something already hot; and more generally, whatever produces any 'specific character' (*eidos*) must already be in possession of that character. [If, then, the same thing in its entirety could be both producer and receiver of the same motion] it would follow that the same thing could be both hot and not hot at the same time and in the same respect. In all cases where the same word is applied to what produces and to what receives motion, a similar analysis is applicable. That is to say, wherever anything is self-moving we should distinguish between the aspect wherein it produces the motion and the aspect wherein it receives it.

From the foregoing arguments it is plain that the primary producer of motion is itself unmoved. For whether the series of moved objects and external movers leads directly back to an original unmoved mover, or whether the immediate cause to which it leads is something self-moved and self-halted [i.e., an animal]; [still, since even a self-moved animal requires something further as an explanation of its coming-to-be and passing-away,] it follows on either hypothesis that in every case where objects are moved there is an original unmoved mover.[11]

vi. The Unmoved Mover is eternal and one

As motion exists always and unintermittingly, there must be something eternal—whether one thing or many—that is the basic producer of motion; and this prime mover must itself be motionless. It is irrelevant to our present inquiry to ask whether each individual unmoved mover [i.e., each living soul] is eternal. That there must, however, be something capable of producing motion in other things while not possessing, either directly or incidentally, any motion or change of its own, will be clear from the following argument.

Let us suppose, if we like, that there are certain entities [i.e., individual souls] that are capable of existing and ceasing to exist without going through a process of formation (*genesis*) and dis-

[11] On the second hypothesis, as demonstrated in the preceding paragraph, it is only because of insufficient analysis that the moving cause may be regarded as producing motion in 'itself.' Strictly speaking, one part or aspect of it is the producer of motion, another the recipient. On the second hypothesis too, therefore, there will be an original unmoved cause.

integration (*phthora*).[12] As a matter of fact, if an entity without parts exists at one time and not at another, it would seem to be a necessary assumption that the entity begins to be and ceases to be without undergoing any *process* of change.[13] Let us even suppose that among the unmoved 'principles' (*arché*) of motion there are some that begin and cease to be.[14] Still, this could not hold true of all such principles; for even though the principles were self-moved, there would have to be some ulterior principle which caused them to begin and cease to be. . . . Hence the process of generation and annihilation, and the continuity of this process, cannot be accounted for by any unmoved entity whose existence is intermittent, nor by any group of entities some of which move some things and others others. The eternity and continuity of the process cannot be caused either by any one such entity nor by all of them combined; for the process must be caused by something eternal and necessary, whereas the individual movers are indefinitely numerous and do not all exist at the same time. Clearly then, although innumerable unmoved principles of motion may perish, and although many self-moving entities may perish and others begin to exist, and although one motionless entity may cause one thing's motion and another another's; there must nevertheless be something distinct from all these which comprehends them all, which is the cause (*aition*) of their existence or non-existence and of their continuous 'process of change' (*metabolé*), and which is the ultimate source of the motion that particu-

[12] Aristotle more frequently uses *genesis* and *phthora* to connote simply the bare fact of creation and annihilation, of coming-into-existence and passing-out-of-existence. In the present context, however, since the terms are contrasted with the bare facts of beginning-to-be and ceasing-to-be, they evidently connote the *processes* ordinarily attendant upon these phenomena.

[13] So that even if individual souls are created and annihilated, they may still be 'unmoved movers.'

[14] I.e., let us make the false but theoretically conceivable supposition that certain 'laws of nature'—such as the upward tendency of air and the downward tendency of earth—might at one time hold good and at another time not.

lar movers produce in other things. And since motion is eternal, this prime mover, if there is but one, must be eternal too; or if there are more of them than one, these will all be eternal.

We ought, however, to postulate one prime mover rather than many, and a finite number of them in preference to an infinite number. The assumption that things are finite is always to be preferred, provided it can equally well explain the facts in question; for in the realm of nature we ought wherever possible to suppose the existence of what is finite and better rather than [of what is infinite and worse]. It is enough, then, that there should be one ultimate mover, which, being the first of unmoved entities as well as eternal, will be the 'originating principle' (*archê*) of motion in everything else.

vii. Locomotion, the primal kind of motion

. . . Of the three kinds of motion (*kinêsis*)—change of magnitude, change of quality (*pathos*), and change of place [15]—it is the last, which we call locomotion (*phora*), that must be regarded as primary. [We may demonstrate this as follows.] Any increase (*auxêsis*) presupposes the occurrence of 'qualitative alteration' (*alloiôsis*). For a thing is increased partly by what is like itself, partly by what is unlike: opposite is said to nourish opposite, while on the other hand development involves an assimilation of like to like. Increase involves, then, a change from opposite to opposite, and this change may be described as 'qualitative alteration.'

Now when anything is altered there must be something that alters it—e.g., something that turns the potentially hot into the actually hot. But [inasmuch as alterations occur intermittently] it is evident that what produces and what receives the alteration do not stand in a uniform relation to each other, but are at one time nearer, at another farther apart; and this implies locomotion.

[15] Cf. Bk. III, Chap. i (p. 44); where change of substance or thinghood is also included as a species of *kinêsis*. In the present passage, as frequently elsewhere, Aristotle evidently regards change of substance as falling under the broader term *metabolê*, but not under *kinêsis*.

Hence if motion is eternal, locomotion as the basic form of motion must also be eternal; and if one type of locomotion is prior to another, it is the prior type that we are speaking of.

[The same conclusion may be reached also in another way.] The 'originating principle' (*archê*) of all 'passive qualities' (*pathêma*) is condensation and rarefaction: heavy and light, soft and hard, hot and cold are recognized to be forms of density and rarity. Now condensation and rarefaction are simply the conflux and dispersion [of elements]; indeed, the generation and annihilation of substances is also interpreted in this way. And if elements are thus conjoined and separated, they must evidently undergo change of place.

Moreover, whenever a thing increases or decreases, its magnitude changes with respect to place. . . .

ix. Rotation, the primal form of locomotion

It is evident that the primary form of locomotion is rotation. Every locomotion, as we have already remarked, is either rotatory or straight or a combination of both; and the first two of these types must be prior to the last since they are the elements of which it is composed. Rotation, moreover, is prior to motion in a straight line, for it alone is simple and complete, [as the following considerations will show]. A straight line cannot be infinite: first because an actual infinite does not exist; secondly because even if an actual infinite did exist it could not be traversed by a moving object—for the impossible does not occur, and to traverse an infinite distance is impossible. Granted, then, that a straight line is finite, motion along such a line must, if reversed, be composite and consist of two motions; while if not reversed, it will be incomplete and perishable. But the complete and imperishable is prior to the incomplete and perishable, whether in respect of nature, of definition, or of time. . . .

x. The Unmoved Mover is without magnitude

. . . From the foregoing considerations it is clear that the original Unmoved Mover cannot have any magnitude. For if it had magnitude, its magnitude would have to be either finite or infinite. The impossibility of an infinite magnitude has already been demonstrated in [this course of lectures on] natural science; and we have just finished demonstrating that a finite magnitude cannot have an infinite force, and that it cannot produce motion during an infinite time.[16] But the prime mover produces a motion that is eternal, and continues to produce it during an infinite time. It follows, therefore, that the prime mover is indivisible, without parts, and without magnitude.

[16] The impossibility of an infinite magnitude is demonstrated in Bk. III, Chap. v, omitted from the present edition. The thesis concerning a finite magnitude is demonstrated in the omitted portion of the present chapter.

The Metaphysics

The Metaphysics

BOOK I. ALPHA MAJOR

ON PHILOSOPHICAL WISDOM

i. The evolution of knowledge

ALL MEN by nature have a desire for knowledge. An indication of this is the joy we take in our perceptions; which we cherish for their own sakes, quite apart from any benefits they may yield us. This is especially true of sight, which we tend to prefer to all the other senses even when it points to no action, and even indeed when no action is in prospect; a preference explained by the greater degree to which sight promotes knowledge by revealing so many differences among things.

It is by nature, again, that animals are born with a faculty of perception, and from this there arises memory in some of them, though not in others. The former class are more intelligent and more capable of learning than those without memory.[1]

But while the other animals live by means of impressions (*phantasia*) and memories (*mnêmê*), with only a small amount of 'what can properly be called experience' (*empeiria*), the human race lives also by art (*technê*) and reasoning (*logismos*). Memory is what gives rise to experience in men, for it is by having repeated

[1] "Animals that cannot hear sounds, like the bee and similar species, cannot learn, although they have intelligence. Where, on the other hand, an animal has the sense of hearing in addition to memory, it is able to learn."—Aristotle's gloss.

memories of the same thing that our ability to have a single whole experience arises. At first sight experience seems much like knowledge (*epistêmê*) and art, but it is truer to say that experience is the means through which science and art can be acquired; thus Polus rightly declares that "experience has produced art, inexperience chance."

Art arises when out of many reflections upon experience there is produced a single universal judgment (*hypolêpsis*) about some class of similar objects. To make the judgment that when Callicles was ill of a certain disease a certain remedy was beneficial, and to make a similar judgment about Socrates, and so on, is a matter of experience. Art would consist rather in judging that the remedy is beneficial for all persons of a given type who are suffering from a given disease—e.g., for phlegmatic or bilious people suffering from fever.

From a practical standpoint experience may well be quite as good as art; indeed we often see men of experience succeeding better than those who have theory (*logos*) without experience. The reason for this is that experience is knowledge of particulars, art of universals, and that actions and their effects are always particular. That is to say, the physician does not cure man, except in an incidental sense; he cures Callicles or Socrates or some other namable individual, who has the incidental characteristic of being 'man' as well. Hence, if someone has the theory without the experience, and knows the universal but is ignorant of the particular instance which is before him, he will often fail to cure, for what has to be cured is always the particular. Nevertheless we think of knowledge and understanding as belonging rather to art than to experience, and we judge artists (*technitês*) to be wiser than mere empirics on the ground that wisdom must always involve some knowledge. Empirics know *that* something is, but not *why* it is; artists, on the other hand, know the why and the reason (*aitia*). Similarly, in any craft we regard master-craftsmen as more estimable and as having a wiser understanding of their craft than manual workers because they know the reasons why things are done, whereas we look on manual workers as analogous to those inanimate things which act without knowing what they do, as fire burns for instance, the only difference being that inanimate things behave as they do by nature, manual workers by habit. In short, we regard master-craftsmen as superior not merely because they can do things but because they have a grasp of theory and know the reasons for acting as they do. Broadly speaking, what distinguishes the man who knows from the ignorant man is an ability to teach, and this is why we hold that art and not experience has the character of 'genuine knowledge' (*epistêmê*) —namely, that artists can teach and others [i.e., those who have not acquired an art by study but have merely picked up some skill empirically] cannot.

Sense perceptions (*aesthêsis*), too, we should avoid confusing with wisdom; for although it is true that they are our chief source of knowledge (*gnôsis*) about particulars, still they do not tell us the 'why' (*dia ti*) of anything—e.g., they do not tell us why fire is hot, but only that it is hot.

No doubt the first discoverer of any art that went beyond man's ordinary sense-perceptions was admired by his fellows, not merely for whatever utility his discoveries may have had, but because his wisdom seemed to set him above the others. And as further arts were discovered, some supplying the necessities of life, others its leisure moments, the discoverers of the latter were always considered wiser than the discoverers of the former, because theirs was a sort of knowledge that did not aim at utility. The next step, when all such discoveries as these had been made, was the discovery of the sciences that do not aim either at pleasure or at the necessities of life; and this first occurred in those places where men enjoyed leisure: which explains why the mathematical disciplines (*technê*) first arose in Egypt, because in that country the priestly caste was permitted to live in leisure.

How art, science, and the other faculties of that kind are dis tinguished from one another has been explained in the *Ethics*.[2] The aim of our present discussion is to inquire about wisdom (*sophia*), which is generally understood to deal with the basic 'determining factors' (*aition*) and 'initiating principles' (*archê*). For consider what has already been said: that the man of experience is agreed to be wiser than one who is limited to mere sense-awareness, the artist than the man of experience, the master-craftsman than the manual worker, and the contemplative (*theôrêtikos*) sciences to partake of wisdom more than the productive (*poiêtikos*). From this progressive relation it becomes clear that wisdom (*sophia*) is that kind of knowledge (*epistêmê*) which concerns ultimate principles and reasons (*aitia*).

ii. The nature of wisdom

Since wisdom [as here defined] is the sort of knowledge under investigation, we must consider the nature of those reasons (*aitia*) and basic principles the knowledge of which constitutes wisdom. The matter will perhaps be somewhat clarified if we look first at our commonly held opinions concerning the wise man. It is supposed, in the first place, that the wise man has knowledge of all things, so far as possible, although not in every particular detail. Secondly, that a man is wise if he can know about difficult matters, such as cannot be learned easily. Here, incidentally, is further proof that sense-perception, which as it is common to all must be easy to acquire, cannot be the same as wisdom. Thirdly, we regard as the wiser man him whose knowledge, in whatever field, is more exact and who is better able to expound the 'determining principles' (*aitia*) of things. Fourthly, with reference to the subject-matter of wisdom, we consider a science which is valued in itself and for the sake of knowledge as partaking more of the nature of wisdom than one which is valued for its results. And finally, we regard the more ruling science as being more of the nature of wisdom than the subordinate: for the wise man

2 See pp. 225–231.

is not one to be ordered but to order, not one to obey another but to be obeyed by the less wise. These are the various notions commonly entertained about wisdom and wise men.

The first of the foregoing characteristics, that of knowing all things, must necessarily belong to him who has in highest degree knowledge of the universal, for he it is who, in a sense, can be said to know all the subsumed instances. As for the second of them, let it be noted that the most universal things are the hardest for men to grasp, because they lie at farthest remove from the impressions of sense. To the third point it may be added that the most exact of the sciences are those which deal mainly with what is logically primary, for sciences that rest on fewer [presuppositions] are more exact than those that involve supplementary ones as well: thus arithmetic is more exact than geometry. Moreover, the sciences that deal with [such fundamental] determining principles really teach us most, for scientists who refer each particular to its determining principles are the ones who most truly teach us. With reference to the fourth point, the pursuit of knowledge and understanding which are valued for their own sake are most fully attained in the 'conceptual knowledge' (*epistêmê*) of what is intrinsically most knowable; for he who really wants to know (*epistasthai*) for the sake of knowing will want knowledge (*epistêmê*) in the fullest sense of the word, which is to say knowledge of what is intrinsically most knowable; and the intrinsically most knowable things are the primary 'determining factors' (*aitia*)—it being through these that other things, namely the 'subsumed particulars' (*hypokeimenon*) are known, and not vice versa. And lastly, [with reference to the fifth and final point], the most authoritative science, as distinguished from what is subsidiary, takes cognizance of the end for which each thing is done: i.e., of the good in each instance, and more generally of the highest good in nature as a whole.

Reviewing all the considerations here enumerated we may conclude that the concept in question [namely, wisdom] falls within the scope of a single science—the science, that is to say, which examines basic principles [which have the character of] 'determining factors' (*aitia*); for the *good*, which is to say the *end*, is one of the types of determining factor.

That the science in question is not of a productive (*poiêtikos*) nature is clear even on the evidence of the earliest philosophers. It is through wonder that men begin to philosophize, whether in olden times or today. First their wonder is stirred by difficulties of an obvious sort, and then gradually they proceed to inquire about weightier matters, like the changes of the moon, the sun and stars, and the origin of the universe. Now the result of wonderment and perplexity is to feel oneself ignorant; [3] if, then, it was to escape ignorance that men began to philosophize, it is evident that they were pursuing this sort of study (*epistasthai*) in order to know (*eidenai*) and not from any motive of utility. An incidental confirmation of this view is that such thinking (*phronêsis*) began to be undertaken as a pastime and recreation at a time when all the main necessities of life had been supplied. Clearly, then, knowledge of the kind that is under discussion is not sought for the sake of any external advantage; but rather, as we call that man free who exists in and for himself and not for another, so we pursue this as the one free and independent science, because it is the only one that exists for the sake of itself.

Such considerations might lead us to suppose, reasonably enough, that to acquire the kind of knowledge we are discussing is beyond the range of human power. For in many respects human nature is in bondage, being unfitted for the quest of such knowledge as lies beyond human reach: as Simonides says, only a god may enjoy that privilege. Indeed, if there were any truth in the poet's view that divinity naturally tends to be jealous, the jealousy would doubtless manifest itself in this direction especially, which would mean that those who excel in the pursuit of wisdom are less

---

[3] "Hence even the myth-lover (*philomythos*) is a sort of philosopher (*philosophos*), for a myth is composed of wonders."—Aristotle's gloss.

fortunate than other men. Divinity, however, cannot be jealous;
and, as the proverb says, "Bards tell many a lie." And let us not
esteem any other knowledge higher than this, for the most divine
knowledge is always the most estimable. Such knowledge, and
such only, is divine in two respects. Knowledge is divine if (*a*)
it is such as we may properly suppose God to possess, or again
(*b*) if it is concerned with divine matters. And the knowledge
under discussion is the only knowledge that fulfills both of these
conditions; for (*b*) God is commonly agreed to be one of the
reasons of things and an ultimate principle, and (*a*) God possesses
this kind of knowledge, if not exclusively at least in the highest
degree. Hence, even though other kinds of knowledge might be
more necessary [for everyday life] than this one, no other is of
higher excellence.

Let it be noted, however, that the acquisition of such knowledge
leads to a point of view which is in a way the reverse of that from
which we began. Everyone begins, as we remarked earlier, by
wondering that things should be as they are—whether the movements of marionettes or the solstices or the incommensurability of
the diameter of a square with its side: because it seems remarkable
to those who have not yet fathomed the reason-why, that there
should exist no smallest common unit by which any two lengths
could be measured. But in the end we come to the opposite point
of view—which moreover is the better one, for surely the adage
that "second thoughts are better thoughts" is most applicable in
these cases where learning takes place. From the new standpoint
there is nothing a geometer would so greatly wonder at as if the
diameter *were* to be found commensurable.

ON PHILOSOPHICAL WISDOM (*Continued*)

i. Character of philosophical truth

THE STUDY (*theoria*) of truth is difficult in one respect, easy in another. This is shown by the double fact that while no individual can grasp truth adequately, yet collectively we do not entirely fail. Each individual makes some report on the nature of things, and while this by itself contributes very little to the inquiry a combination of all such reports amounts to a good deal. That is to say, in so far as truth can be likened to the proverbial door that no one can miss,[1] it is easy; but the fact that we can know a large general truth and still not grasp some particular part of it shows how difficult truth-seeking really is. However, there are roughly two ways of accounting for a difficulty, and it may be that in the present case the reason for it lies not in the subject-matter but in ourselves, and that as bats' eyes are dimmed by daylight so the 'power of reason' (*nous*) in our souls is dimmed by what is intrinsically most self-evident. . . .

Philosophy is rightly called a 'knowledge and understanding' (*epistêmê*) of truth. It is contemplative (*theorêtikos*) knowledge that has truth as its end, as distinguished from 'practical and moral' (*praktikos*) knowledge, whose end is action.[2] Now we cannot

---

[1] The simile is drawn from archery. Anyone, even the poorest marksman, can hit a big target like a door in some spot or other, but to hit an exactly defined target is another matter.

[2] "For practical men, even when they are investigating the *how* of things, study this not in its eternal but in its relative and temporal aspect." —Aristotle's gloss.

know the truth of anything without also knowing its explanation (*aitia*). And just as a thing possesses a quality in higher degree than other things when it is able to infect those other things with that quality (e.g., fire is the hottest of all things because it is the cause (*aitia*) of heat in everything else), so in the same way that is the most true which is the explanation (*aitia*) of other truths. Consequently the 'ultimate principles' (*archê*) of the permanent [aspects of things] must necessarily be true in the fullest sense; for such principles are not merely sometimes true, nor is there any ulterior explanation of their being, but on the contrary *they* are the explanations of other things. And so, as each thing stands in respect of being, it stands likewise in respect of truth.

ii. Finitude of the explanatory process

It is evident that there must be an 'ultimate principle' (*archê*) and that the 'determining factors' (*aitia*) of things are not infinite, either serially or in kind.

(1) When one thing emerges out of another which is its 'material stuff' (*hylê*) the process cannot have an infinity of stages —e.g., flesh from earth, earth from air, air from fire, and so on without limit.

(2) Nor can motion (*kinêsis*) arise out of its source (*archê*) by an infinite number of steps—e.g., man being moved by air, air by the sun, the sun by Strife, and so on without limit.

(3) Similarly, it is impossible that 'that for the sake of which' should form an infinite series—e.g., walking for the sake of health, health for the sake of happiness, happiness for the sake of something else, and so on, everything being always for the sake of something else. . . . 'That for the sake of which' is an end (*telos*) for the sake of which other things occur but which does not in turn occur for the sake of anything. Accordingly, if there is to be a last term of this sort, the series [of telic determinants] is not infinite; if there is no such term, there will not be anything for the sake of which other things really occur. Those who make the process

infinite inadvertently destroy the nature of the good, failing to see
that no one would undertake to do anything if there were not some
limit to which he might attain. Moreover, [if their hypothesis were
true] there could be no 'rational intelligence' (*nous*) in the world:
because the man who has rational intelligence always acts for the
sake of something, and this is in the nature of a limit, any end being
a limit.

(4) Nor can the essence (*to ti ên einai*) be carried back [with-
out limit] to another definition which is [always] logically more
complete. For the first definition [of such a series] more truly defines the essence than do the later ones, and if the first definition is
not adequate the subsequent ones will not be any more so. Moreover, those who argue in that way destroy the possibility of valid
knowledge, for it is impossible to know anything unless one can
presuppose certain unanalyzable terms. Even ordinary recognition
becomes impossible; for how could one mentally grasp an [actual]
infinite of this sort? . . . For [even if there be a sense in which
infinity exists, still] the concept of infinity cannot be infinite.

On the other hand, if the *kinds* of 'determining factor' (*aitia*)
were numerically infinite it would again be impossible to have any
knowledge. For we only suppose that we know a thing when we
have become acquainted with the factors that determine it, and
it would be impossible in a finite time to go through what is dis-
cursively infinite.

BEING AND 'OUSIA'

i. The science of abstract Being

THERE IS A science (*epistêmê*) that studies Being quâ Being, together with those properties which belong to it by reason of its essential nature. This science is quite distinct from what we may call the special sciences, none of which investigates Being in its purely general aspect as Being, but each of which rather cuts off some partial aspect of Being and studies the set of properties belonging to that partial aspect: as do the mathematical sciences. But it is first principles and the highest reasons that we are seeking, and clearly these must constitute a subject-matter with a nature of its own. . . .

ii. Primary Being and essential thinghood

The term 'being' has several meanings; these, however, are not unrelated meanings that happen to be expressed by a common epithet, but along with their diversity they share a common identity of content and reference. In much the same way anything that is called healthful relates somehow to health, whether in the sense of preserving it, or producing it, or being a symptom of it, or being receptive to it. Again, anything called medical relates somehow to the art of medicine, whether in the sense of possessing this art, or being naturally adapted to it, or being a function (*ergon*) of it. And other terms might be found which illustrate the same point. Similarly the term 'being' has several meanings, but all of them share a single basic reference. Something may be said to 'be' in the sense that it is a 'concrete thing' (*ousia*), or as the modification (*pathos*) of a concrete thing, or as tending toward the condition of concrete thinghood, or as the destruction or lack or attribute of concrete thinghood, or as what produces or generates concrete things or in some general way relates to them, or even as what negates concrete thinghood or any of its foregoing relata. Thus [in this last sense] we can even say of non-being that it *is* non-being.

And as there is a single science pertaining to whatever is healthful, so too in all analogous instances. For the unity of a science need not consist in investigating all such objects as fall [completely] under a single definable concept, but at the very least there must be some 'fundamental respect' (*physis*) in which they can all be said to fall under a single concept. Clearly, then, it belongs to a single science to take whatever *is* and study it solely under the aspect of its Being. Now knowledge is always principally concerned with what is primary—i.e., that on which other aspects depend and by which they are defined. If 'essential thinghood' (*ousia*, sing.) has this sort of primacy, it is of 'thinglike essences' (*ousia*, pl.) that the philosopher must grasp the principles and explanations.

Definition of 'Ousia' [1]

We give the name of *ousia* to (1) simple bodies such as earth, fire, water and the like; or, more broadly, to any bodies and to whatever wholes or parts, whether of an animal or divine nature, may be composed of them. Anything of the sort has *ousia* because it is a 'grammatical subject' (*hypokeimenon*) to which certain predicates may be ascribed, while there is no further subject of which it in turn can be predicated.

(2) Next, the word applies to that which is the immanent 'de-

---

[1] From Aristotle's lexicon of key-terms, published as Book V (Delta) of the *Metaphysics*. The word '*ousia*' is left untranslated here, in order not to prejudice Aristotle's explanation of it. '*Ousiai*' is the plural. Cf. p. 125.

termining principle' (*aitia*) of *ousiai* in the sense just defined: e.g., the soul.

(3) Next, it may mean any part immanent in a whole in such a way that while retaining its own specific meaning it also delimits the meaning of the whole to which it belongs, so that if it were destroyed the whole would be destroyed too. In this manner the line is related to the plane, and, as some say, the plane to a three-dimensional body. More abstractly, number is thought by some to be of this nature, on the ground that it furnishes limits to everything, so that if it were destroyed nothing would exist.

(4) Finally, the 'enduring essence' (*to ti ên einai*)—i.e., the 'formal meaning' (*logos*) which is expressed by a definition (*horismos*)—is also called an *ousia*.

Thus it can be seen that *ousia* has two main connotations: the ultimate subject of predication, which cannot be predicated of anything further in turn; and that which can be distinguished as an identifiable thing having its own shape (*morphê*) and form (*eidos*).

SCIENCE AND ITS OBJECTS

i. The three main divisions of science

IT SHOULD BE SUFFICIENTLY CLEAR by now that what we are seeking are the 'initiating principles' (*archê*) and 'determining factors' (*aition*) of *whatever is,* considered solely under the abstract aspect of its *being.* Health and physical condition have their determining factors, mathematics has its principles and elements and determining factors, and generally speaking every science that is intellectual or in any way involves intellect (*dianoia*) must take account of determining factors and initiating principles, whether in a precise or in a rough-and-ready way. But each of these sciences picks out some entity or class of entities and confines its attention to that. It does not deal with Being in its most general aspect, Being quâ Being, nor does it offer any 'logical account' (*logos*) of Essence (*ti esti*); rather, starting from some preconception of what essence is, whether as a datum of sense-perception or as a postulate (*hypo-thesis*) arbitrarily set up, it proceeds to demonstrate with more or less cogency the essential attributes (*hypo-archon*) of the class of things it is dealing with. Such a procedure obviously yields no real demonstration of the 'essential thinghood' (*ousia*) and whatness (*ti esti*) of anything, but contents itself with exhibiting them implicitly in the particular method it pursues. Indeed, these special sciences do not even inquire whether the class of entities they deal with really exists or not; because to show *what* something is and to show *that* it is fall under the same type of 'intellectual inquiry' (*dianoia*).

Since the 'science of nature' (*physikê epistêmê*), too, deals with a certain class of Being—namely, with the sort of thinghood that contains within itself the 'initiating principle' (*archê*) of motion and rest—it is clearly neither practical nor productive in nature. For in the case of anything produced the principle resides in the producing agent—whether this be mind (*nous*) or art (*technê*) or some 'simple ability' (*dynamis*). And in the case of anything done it resides in the doer as 'moral choice' (*proairesis*). Consequently if all 'intellectual procedure' (*dianoia*) is either practical, productive, or contemplative (*theôrêtikos*), the science of nature must be a contemplative science, but its contemplation is concerned with the kind of Being that admits of being moved, and with essences (*ousia*) so conceived as to be virtually inseparable from their material embodiments.

There is a modal distinction with regard to essences (*ti esti*) and their formulation, which we should not overlook lest our inquiry thereby become futile. Of things defined—i.e., of essences— some are like the term 'snub,' some like the term 'concave.' The difference here is that 'snub' is caught up in a world of matter—for 'snub' means a concave *nose*—whereas concavity itself [has a meaning that is] independent of the matter of perception. Accordingly, if all physical terms have meaning in a way analogous to 'snub'—e.g., 'nose,' 'eye,' 'face,' 'flesh,' and 'bone,' as well as the more general term 'animal' (for all of these involve matter and it is impossible to define them without reference to motion)—it is clear what our method of investigating and defining natural objects should be. This also explains why and how far even the soul falls within the natural scientist's scope of inquiry—so far, namely, as it is not independent of material conditions.

Thus it becomes evident that natural science is essentially 'contemplative' (*theôrêtikos*). Mathematics likewise is contemplative, but while it is not yet clear whether the objects it deals with are immutable and separable from matter, at least this much is clear— that some mathematical inquiries confine their attention to the immutable and separable aspect of their objects. As to whether there really is anything that is eternal and immutable and separable from the material world, this is evidently a question belonging to a contemplative type of science, yet not to the science of nature (which deals with mutable things) nor even to mathematics, but to a science prior to both. For natural science is concerned with entities which, though separable, are still mutable, while certain parts of mathematics concern themselves with entities which are immutable but not perhaps entirely separable. Primal Science, on the other hand, concerns itself with entities at once separable and immutable.

All 'determining principles' (*aition*) are necessarily eternal, but especially those belonging to Primal Science, for they are the determining principles of as much as we can see of the Divine. Accordingly we should distinguish between the three contemplative disciplines of mathematics, natural science, and [Primal Science, which we may also call] theology on the ground that if the Divine has pertinence anywhere it must be especially pertinent to the kind of entity that Primal Science studies. . . .

ii. On the accidental

The simple term 'being' has been found to have several meanings: on the one hand the *accidental,* on the other the *true* (in which sense 'not-being' connotes *false*), and besides these the various forms of predication, e.g., the 'what' or essence of anything, as well as the quality, amount, place, time, and other such predicable meanings; while cutting across these distinctions is the further distinction between what is potentially and what is actually.

Granted these various meanings, let us begin by considering the accidental. And first let it be noted that the accidental cannot be made the object of 'scientific contemplation' (*theôria*), as is indicated by the fact that no one of the sciences—moral (*praktikos*), productive, or contemplative—actually deals with it. The builder of a house cannot be considered the real producer of all the incidental properties and results that come into existence as the house is built. These, indeed, are innumerable. No doubt the house when it is built will be pleasing to some people, injurious to others, and useful to still others, and it will be somehow uniquely different from all other existing houses, but the science of construction does not concern itself with such accidental aspects as these. . . .

Our next step with regard to the accidental must be to explain, so far as we can, its nature and what brings it about. Therein it will be shown why there can be no science of it.

There are cases where we can say that something is so without exception and necessarily—i.e., not in the sense of being physically compelled but in the more general sense of the impossibility of being otherwise—and there are other cases where we cannot say that something is always and necessarily so but only that it is *usually* so. From this distinction we can derive both the initiating principle and the real reason (*aitia*) of the accidental, for the meaning of accidental is precisely this: what is neither always nor usually so. For example, we say that it happens by accident when there is cold stormy weather during the dog days of midsummer [1] but not when there is stifling heat at that season, and this is because the latter occurs either always or usually at that season, the former not. It may happen by accident that a man is pale (since the phenomenon occurs neither always nor usually), but it is no accident that he is an animal. A pale man, in turn,[2] is neither always nor usually cultured; but since this happens sometimes, it must be regarded as accidental. Again, a builder who cures someone does so by accident, because to do this is a function of the doctor's nature and not of the builder's: we say that in this case

[1] I.e., July and early August, when Sirius, the dog star, rises and sets approximately with the sun.
[2] This sentence is transposed from a later place in the paragraph, where logically it does not belong.

the builder happened accidentally to be a doctor. Again, a confectioner while aiming to please the palate may produce something wholesome: but as this does not derive from the confectioner's art we call it accidental; i.e., he produces something wholesome, to be sure, but not in an absolute and unqualified sense [of the word 'produce']. Other results can be referred to corresponding potencies, but there is no potency corresponding to an accidental result, and no art of producing it; for when anything exists or occurs accidentally, the only explanation (*aition*) that we can assign to it is 'accident.'

Now since not everything exists or occurs necessarily and with absolute uniformity, but most things happen merely as a general rule, it follows that the accidental must exist: for if this were not so, then all things would have to be by necessity. The explanation of the accidental, then, resides in the 'material condition' (*hylê*), which is such as to allow some variation from the usual. The primary question to be faced is this: does nothing whatever exist save what can be described by the words 'always' or 'usually'? Surely this cannot be true. There must be something else, then, namely what is fortuitous and accidental.

Shall we then say that all things are but usually so, and nothing always? Or is there anything eternal? These questions will be examined later on.[3]

That there can be no science of the accidental is clear from the consideration that any science must deal with what is either always or usually so. Otherwise how could one learn it or teach it to anyone else? The object of scientific inquiry must be defined in terms of the 'always' or the 'usually': that honey-water helps to cure fever, for example, is usually the case. But suppose that it should happen *not* to be helpful—e.g., on the day of the new moon: science will not be able to explain [the peculiar character of] the exception. The 'always' and the 'usually' may apply also, of course, to [much] that happens on the day of the new moon; but the

---

[3] See Bk. XII, Chap. vii, pp. 99–102.

accidental stands aside from either of these [patterns of explanation].

This concludes our discussion of what the accidental is, why there is such a thing, and why there can be no science of it.

ON THE ACTUAL AND THE POTENTIAL

i. Active and passive potencies

WE HAVE NOW DEALT with that primary mode of being to which all the other categories of being are referred: namely, 'essential whatness' (*ousia*). For it is only by reference to such 'whatness, or thinghood' (*ousia*) that the other modes of being—quantity, quality, and so on—can be significantly spoken: all of these necessarily involving the concept of a 'thing' (*ousia*), as we said in the first part of that earlier discussion. Inasmuch as the term 'being' has to be distinguished not only according as it means the individual subject, the quality, the quantity, and so forth, but also according as it connotes potency (*dynamis*) or actuality (*entelecheia*) or function (*ergon*), our next task will be to clarify the distinction between potency and actuality.

First let us consider potency in its most basic sense (though not the most useful one for our present purpose); for the distinction between potency and actuality is not limited to the realm of mutable things. After discussing potency in this basic sense we will explain its other meanings in the course of our exposition of actuality.

We have pointed out elsewhere [1] that the terms 'potency' and 'can' have several meanings. We may dismiss those meanings which rest on mere equivocation: as when, by analogical extension, we speak of 'potencies' [in the sense of functions] in geometry, or when [in everyday speech] we call something possible or impossible because it does or does not exist in some particular way. But

[1] In the lexicon which appears in the *Metaphysics* as Book V (Delta).

all potencies that belong to a single 'recognizable type' (*eidos*) are 'initiating principles' (*archê*) and are spoken of in the basic sense of being 'initiating sources' (*archê*) of change either in something other than themselves or in themselves under the aspect of otherness.

Potency may also connote 'capable of being affected.' The source (*archê*) of a change considered passively is in the patient [i.e., the thing affected] itself, although it comes about through the *agency* of something else (or of itself under the aspect of otherness). . . . From this it is evident that the potency of acting and the potency of being affected are in a sense one and in another sense not. They are one inasmuch as 'can' (*dynaton*) connotes at once the power of being acted upon and the power of acting upon something else. But they are also distinct, inasmuch as the thing affected contains a 'principle or initiating source' (*archê*) which allows of its being affected. For a thing's matter, too, is a kind of source (*archê*) of the thing's proneness to be acted upon, and more specifically of one thing's proneness to be acted on by one agency, another by another: it is the principle (*archê*) whereby what is oily can be burnt and what yields in a certain way can be broken, and so on. And in this sense the potency of the patient differs from a potency of the agent, such as the power of producing heat or of building a house. Hence, nothing can be acted upon by itself so far as it is a single nature, for in this respect its oneness allows of no otherness.

ii. Rational and non-rational potencies

Although some of the initiating principles under discussion reside in lifeless things, others are found in beings that possess souls, and some even in the rational part of the soul; whence it is evident that some of the potencies, correspondingly, will be non-rational and others rational. [The latter class includes in particular] the arts (*technê*), or 'productive forms of knowledge'(*poiêtikê epistêmê*), which are potencies inasmuch as they are the initiating principles of change in another thing (or in the artist or craftsman himself under the aspect of otherness). The difference between the two classes is that every rational potency admits of contrary outcomes, whereas a non-rational potency admits of only one outcome. Heat can produce only heat, but [the science and art of] medicine can produce either disease or health. The reason for this difference is that medical science is a 'set of rational propositions' (*logos*), and the same set of rational propositions must pertain both to the presence and absence (*sterêsis*) of the 'situation to which they refer' (*pragma*), although not in the same way, but rather more to the positive aspect. Hence, such sciences must pertain to contraries—to one contrary by virtue of its own nature, to the other not by virtue of its own nature; for a 'set of propositions' (*logos*) signifies a certain object by virtue of its own nature while signifying its contrary in an incidental sort of way, i.e., by negation and removal. For the contrary is the primary privation (*sterêsis*), in that it connotes the negation of that to which it is contrary. Consequently, since contraries cannot both exist in the same subject, and since science is a potency involving a set of rational propositions [and hence taking cognizance of both contraries of any relevant pair], and since the soul has an initiating principle of motion, it follows that whereas the healthful can produce only health, and hot and cold agencies can produce only hot and cold respectively, the man who has knowledge can produce either of two contrary results. For as his 'rational understanding' (*logos*) pertains in different ways to both of two contrary outcomes, and as the initiating principle of motion with regard to them resides in his soul, it follows that the soul can produce either of two contrary courses of action by linking them up with this one initiating source. This explains why rational potencies are sharply distinguished in nature from non-rational potencies: because the possible outcomes of the former are embraced by a single rational initiating principle.

In the case of rational potencies, which can produce contrary effects (as distinguished from non-rational potencies, each of which can produce but one effect), it is obviously impossible that a single potency should produce contrary effects at the same time. Hence there must be something else that makes the decision, namely desire (*orexis*) or 'deliberate choice' (*proairesis*). For whichever of two things a creature decisively desires to do, that thing it will do, when the existing circumstances permit and when there is an object at hand capable of being acted upon by the potency in question. In short, a creature which has a rational potency, when it desires that for which it has a potency, and when the circumstances are appropriate, must act accordingly.[2]

iii. Refutation of the Megaric fallacy

There are some who maintain, as the Megaric school [3] does, that a thing can do only when it is actually doing, and that when it is not functioning it cannot be said to 'be able' to function. A man who is not building, they declare, cannot build; the only one who can build is he who is building and at the very moment when he is building. Similarly of other instances. The absurd consequences of this view are not hard to see.

In the first place, because to be a builder is to be *able* to build, they assume that no one is a builder unless he is actually building; and similarly of the other arts. Now if we agree that it is impossible to possess such arts without taking time to learn and understand them, and impossible to lose possession of them without either forgetting them or being otherwise affected through the passage of time (for the *object* of the art cannot be destroyed, being indeed eternal), how can we claim that when the artist stops practic-

---

[2] I have transposed this paragraph from Chapter v (the remainder of which is not included in the present edition) in order to present the unresolved tension in Aristotle's treatment of what we nowadays call the problem of free will. I omit the rest of Chapter v, where Aristotle strikes me as confusing the distinction between rational and non-rational potencies with the independent distinction between self-sufficient potencies and potencies which require a patient to be acted upon. Each of these distinctions has been treated independently in the foregoing pages.—Tr.

[3] Founded by Eukleides of Megara, one of the companions of Socrates mentioned in the *Phaedo*.

ing his art he instantly stops possessing it? And if he does so, then how, if he suddenly starts building again, does he reacquire the art?

Likewise with inanimate things. On the one hand, it will follow that neither cold nor hot nor sweet nor any other perceptible quality will exist unless it is being perceived: which leads to an acceptance of Protagoras' theory. And on the other hand, nothing will have the power of perceiving unless it is actually perceiving —i.e., unless it is actually functioning as a perceiver. Hence, if by 'blind' we mean deprivation of sight in the case of a creature that would naturally have it, the conclusion follows that the same creatures must be blind many times a day. Or deaf, for that matter.

Moreover, since that which has no potency is incapable, it would follow [from the position here considered] that what is not actually occurring is incapable of occurring; and of course it must be erroneous—by the very meaning of 'incapable'—to say that what is incapable of occurring either *is* or *will be*. Whence it is clear that the argument in question does away with motion and even with all becoming: whatever is standing will always stand and what is sitting will always sit. I.e., if it is sitting it will never stand up, for it is obviously impossible that anything should stand up that is incapable of standing up. Since the conclusion is untenable it becomes clear that there is a difference between potency and actuality, and those theories that identify them are trying to abolish a distinction of no little importance.

Consequently it is possible that something may be capable of being and yet not be, or capable of not being and yet be; and the distinction applies also to other 'kinds of predicate' (*katêgoria*): e.g., it is possible to be capable of walking and yet not walk, and to be capable of not walking and yet walk. The capability (*dynaton*) of anything means that there is nothing impossible in its having the 'actual expression' (*energeia*) of that whereof it is said to have the capacity (*dynamis*). I mean, for example, that if something is capable of sitting and conditions are such as to allow it to sit, then there is nothing impossible in its actually beginning to sit; and the same interpretation applies to its capability of being moved or producing motion, or standing or causing to stand, or being or becoming, or not being or not becoming.

vi. *The nature of actuality*

Now that we have dealt with potency in its relation to motion, let us examine the nature and characteristics of actuality. By 'potential' we mean not only what consists in setting something else in motion or being set in motion by something else (whether this be interpreted generally or strictly), but analysis will show that there are further meanings too, and we have given some attention to these in the course of our discussion.

'Actuality' means the existence of something in a different sense from that which we express by the term 'potency.' We say, for instance, that potentially Hermes is in a carver's block of wood, or the half-line in the whole, because in both cases the thing in question can be separated out. And we call someone a student who has developed an ability of studious contemplation, even if he is not contemplating at the moment. Now consider actuality. What we mean by it will be clear from an 'inductive inspection' (*epagôgê*) of instances; which is to say, that instead of stopping to define all our terms we shall understand the matter analogically, like this: as what builds is to what is capable of building, so the waking is to the sleeping, and so one seeing is to one who can see but has his eyes shut, and so the thing shaped from some material is to the material, and so the finished product is to the unwrought stuff. Let 'actual' be defined by the one member of this antithesis and 'potential' by the other. For different things are not all said to exist 'actually' in the same sense but only by analogy: i.e., as one thing is *in* another or *to* another, so a third thing is *in* or *to* a fourth— where the relation may be either that of motion to potency or that of 'individual thinghood' (*ousia*) to a certain kind of matter. . . .

viii. On the priority of the actual

From the distinctions made [in our Lexicon] as to the meaning of priority it becomes evident that actuality is prior to potentiality. And by potentiality I mean not only what we have defined as "a principle of change in something other than the thing changed or in that same thing under the aspect of otherness"; but more broadly any initiating principle of motion or of rest. *Nature* falls within the same genus as potency taken in this sense, for it too is an initiating source of motion—not involving otherness to be sure, but working in a given thing quâ that thing itself. To potency, thus defined, actuality is always prior, both logically and in terms of 'specific thinghood' (*ousia*); temporally it is prior in one respect and not prior in another.

(1) That actuality is logically prior is clear enough: for it is only through its ability to be actualized that the potential exists even as potential. I mean, to call something a potential builder implies that it is capable of actually building; to say 'capable of seeing' or 'capable of being seen' implies a possibility that the thing in question will actually see or be seen. The same type of definition holds good in other such cases; whence it follows that the definition and knowledge of the actual must [logically] precede the definition and knowledge of the potential.

(2) In terms of *time* the question of priority may be explained thus: the actual is prior to the corresponding potential of the same type (*eidos*) but not prior to the potential that corresponds to it numerically. What I mean is that on the one hand the [spermatic] matter, the seed, and the faculty of sight, which in a potential sense are the man, the corn, and the seeing, but not yet actually, must be prior in time to the individual man, corn, and seeing [which they produce]. But prior in time to themselves, in turn, are other actualities [of the same type] out of which the potencies were generated. For the actually existent is always produced from the potentially existent by the agency of something actually existent:

e.g., man by man, and cultured man by cultured man. There is always some first producer of motion, and that first mover already exists in actuality. . . . This explains why it is agreed that no one can possibly be a builder without ever having built, or a harper without ever having played the harp. For one learns to play the harp only by playing it; and so with all such cases. . . .

(3) Actuality is also prior in respect of 'specific thinghood' (*ousia*): first, because things that are posterior in 'the order of development' (*genesis*) are prior in 'determinate form' (*eidos*) and 'specific whatness' (*ousia*); e.g., the adult is prior in 'specificity of whatness' (*ousia*) to the child, and man to the semen, inasmuch as the first of each pair has already its determinate form and the other has not. Secondly, because everything 'in process of development' (*gignomenon*) moves toward an 'initiating principle' (*archê*) which is its goal. For the initiating principle is that for the sake of which a process of becoming takes place, and this is always the 'end, or goal' (*telos*). Now the end of anything is its 'full actualization' (*energeia*), and it is for the sake of this that the potency [or capability] is acquired; e.g., animals do not see in order that they may have sight, but they have sight in order that they may see. Similarly, men possess the art of building in order that they may build, and 'contemplative science' in order that they may contemplate. They do not contemplate in order to have the power of contemplating, except in the case of learners, and these do not really contemplate, or at best they do so in a limited sense and without full seriousness.

In some cases the exercise of the faculty is the ultimate [step]. Thus in the case of sight the ultimate [step] is seeing, and sight produces nothing more than this; while in other cases something is produced—e.g., from the art of building comes not only the building activity but a house. In the former type of situation the act itself, though not a product, is nevertheless an end; in the latter type it is at any rate more of an end than the potency is, inasmuch as the act of building is 'in' the thing built in the sense that it begins and occurs simultaneously with [the beginning and existence of] the house.

Accordingly, wherever the result is something more than the simple exercise of the faculty, the actualization (*energeia*) resides in what is produced; e.g., the act of building [finds its actualization] in the thing built, the act of weaving in the thing woven, and so on; the motion, in short, [finding its actualization] in the thing that is moved [into existence]. But where there is no product over and beyond the 'process of actualizing' (*energeia*), the actualization resides in the subject: e.g., seeing [is actualization] in the organ of sight, contemplation in the contemplative thinker, and life and hence happiness in the soul—happiness being a particular kind of life.

From this it is evident that the 'specific whatness' (*ousia*) or form (*eidos*) is [what defines] the actuality. Whence it logically follows that actuality is prior in 'essential specificity' (*ousia*) to potentiality. And from the standpoint of time, as we have already said, one actuality is always preceded by another, all the way back to the eternal Prime Mover.

There is a still more profound sense in which the actual is prior to the potential with respect to essential specificity—namely, inasmuch as the eternal is prior in this respect to the perishable, and nothing eternal exists as a mere potency. This may be demonstrated as follows. Every potentiality is at one and the same time a potentiality of the opposite; for, granted that what is *not* capable of happening to a subject will certainly not happen to it, still what *is* capable of happening may yet fail to actualize. What is capable of being, therefore, is capable both of being and of not being; which is to say, the one identical thing is capable both of being and of not being. But that which is capable of not being may possibly *not be*, and that which may possibly not be is something perishable —either absolutely perishable, which means with respect to its essential specificity, or perishable with respect to some more special aspect of being, e.g., with respect to place or quantity or quality. Therefore, nothing which is absolutely imperishable is absolutely potential—although it may very well, of course, be potential in some particular respect such as quality or place. Consequently, everything imperishable exists as [fully] actual.

Again, nothing which exists of necessity exists as a mere potency; and things which exist of necessity are the primary things, for if they did not exist nothing would exist.

The necessary, like the imperishable, cannot have merely potential existence; and the most primary things are necessary, in the sense that if they did not exist nothing would exist. This argument applies to motion, too, if there be any that is eternal. For if anything has eternal motion it cannot be merely potentially in motion —except with respect to its whence and whither, since our argument does not preclude that the moving thing should have a 'stuff' (*hylê*) [which allows of these]. Consequently the sun and stars and the entire heaven are perpetually in a state of [full] actuality, and there is no fear that they will ever come to a stop—a fear which troubles some of the natural philosophers. The celestial bodies never tire in their activity: because motion does not involve for them, as it does for perishable things, the potentiality of the opposite (which arises only when the essential specificity of the motion resides in its material source, i.e., in its potency rather than in its actuality), and it is only this [having the potentiality of the opposite] that makes the continuity of motion laborious.

Imperishable things are imitated (*mimêsthai*) by things in [a natural condition of] change (*metabolê*), like earth and fire; these likewise being always in a state of actuality, since they have their motion by and in themselves. As distinguished from other potencies (which, as the foregoing distinctions have shown, admit of opposite results, since whatever acts rationally, if it can cause motion to occur in a certain way can also cause it *not* to occur in that way), the *non*-rational potencies that we have been speaking of can produce opposite results only by their presence and absence.

It follows that if any such natures (*physis*) or 'whatnesses' (*ousia*) existed as those who use apriori reasoning declare the Forms (*idea*) to be, there would have to be something that is more essentially knowledge than knowledge itself, and more essentially motion than motion itself; that is to say, there would have to be actualities for which actual knowledge and motion are but potentialities.

At any rate, it is now clear that actuality is prior both to potency and to every 'initiating principle' of change.

ix. *Good and bad actualities and potencies*

A good actuality is both better and more estimable than the corresponding good potency, as may be seen from the following considerations. Everything that we describe as 'capable' is capable of opposite results: e.g., when we declare some [organ] to be capable of being well, we mean that the same [organ] at that very moment is also capable of being ill; for there is one and the same potentiality of health and disease, or of rest and motion, or of building and demolishing, or of being built and being demolished. Thus the capacity for two contraries is present in a thing at one and the same time. Two opposite actualities, on the other hand, like health and disease, cannot be present in a thing at the same time. Therefore while one of these, and one only, can be good, the potency [which admits of either of them] is equally good and bad, or neither. Consequently the actuality is better.

Contrariwise, in the case of bad things the end, or actuality, must be worse than the potency; since this too follows from the argument that whatever is capable must be capable of both contraries alike.

THE ETERNAL UNMOVED MOVER

[In the first chapter of this Book Aristotle distinguishes three kinds of *ousia*: (1) the perceptible-perishable (plants, animals, and any other terrestrial things), (2) the perceptible-eternal (the celestial bodies), (3) the nonperceptible-immutable (the forms of things, i.e., their intelligible meanings and relations). This triadic distinction is assumed in the discussion that follows.]

vi. That there is an actual Eternal Mover

OF THE THREE KINDS of 'essential specificity' (*ousia*) that there were shown to be—two 'of the order of nature' (*physikos*) and one immutable (*a-kinêtos*)—our next step is to discuss this third kind, and to demonstrate the existence of a 'specific essence' (*ousia*) that is eternal and immutable. Specific essences are the primary kind of Being, so that if they are perishable everything is perishable.

Motion [in general] cannot come into existence or pass away; in other words, it has always existed. The same is true of time; for if time ever *was not,* the word 'before' has no meaning, and if time ever *will not be,* the word 'after' has no meaning.[1] Time, then, must be continuous in the same way that motion is, for time is either identical with motion or an attribute of it. But the only continuous motion is spatial motion, and the only continuous spatial motion is circular.[2]

Where something is *capable* of making or moving a thing with-

[1] Cf. *Nat. Sci.*, Bk. VIII, Chap. i; esp. pp. 49–50: the argument that time can have no beginning or end because time consists of 'nows' and a 'now' can neither be nor be conceived except as a before and an after.
[2] Cf. *Nat. Sci.*, Bk. VIII, Chap. ix, p. 62.

out actually doing so, no motion results; for there can be a potency that does not actualize. It is not a sufficient principle of explanation, then, to postulate eternal essences (*ousia*) as the advocates of Forms do, unless we postulate them as including an 'initiating principle' (*archê*) of change. And even this qualification would not be enough, nor would it be enough to postulate another kind of 'essential nature' (*ousia*) besides the Forms, for unless it were 'actually functioning' (*energeein*) there would be no motion. But even for a thing to actually function is not enough if its essential nature were but a potency; for as the potential may fail to exist, eternal motion would not thereby be assured. There must, accordingly, be an initiating principle of the kind we are seeking whose 'essential nature' (*ousia*) involves actuality (*energeia*). Furthermore, as such essential natures [3] must be eternal if anything is eternal, and accordingly are without admixture of the 'material component' (*hylê*), it follows on this ground too that they are actuality.

There is a difficulty, however: it being argued that because everything that actually functions is capable of functioning while not everything capable of functioning actually functions, potency must be prior [to actuality]. But if this were true, then (since what *can* exist nevertheless *may not* exist) there might quite well be nothing in existence at all.

The theories of the 'religious philosophers' (*theologos*) who derive everything from 'Night' and of the 'natural philosophers' (*physikos*) who say that "all things were together" [4] lead to the same impossible result: for how could motion have arisen out of these situations unless some reason-why were actually functioning?

[3] The plural is introduced to include not only God or Mind but also the celestial spheres.
[4] The *theologos* principally meant is Hesiod: see *Works and Days*, l. 17; and *Theogony*, ll. 116 ff. The formula "all things were together" refers to Anaxagoras' doctrine that the original state of things was an utterly chaotic jumble of the qualities that constitute our world of experience, and that Creation therefore was a cosmic process of differentiating and separating out.

Wood will not operate on itself, carpentry must operate upon it; nor will the earth nor the menstrual fluid operate on themselves, but the seeds and semen respectively must operate upon them.

Accordingly there are certain thinkers, among them Plato and Leucippus, who postulate an eternal actuality, on the ground that there is always motion. But the why and the what of such motion they do not explain—i.e., the reason of its having this or that character. For nothing is moved fortuitously, there must always be something that accounts for it: as, for example, we see things being operated on in one way by their own natures and in a different way by some outer force or by mind or whatever else. . . .

vii. *God as unmoved and self-contemplative*

Since our own explanation is a possible one, and since if it is not true we shall have to explain things as originating out of Night, or out of an original togetherness of everything, or out of not-being, our difficulties would appear to be solved, and we may agree that there is something which is eternally moved with an unceasing motion which is circular—as indeed not only theory but plain fact also proves. It follows from this that the 'first heaven' [5] is eternal. Hence there must be something [eternal] that moves it. Now whatever operates [i.e., produces motion] while itself in motion is intermediate, not ultimate. There must therefore be something which operates without being in motion—something eternal which is at once 'something substantial' (*ousia*) and 'in actual operation' (*energeia*).

How it operates may be explained as follows. An object of desire and an object of thought 'produce motion' [6] without being moved. The primary [i.e., ultimate] objects of desire and of thought are the same. For it is the apparent good that is the object of appetite and the real good that is the 'object of rational deliberation' (*boul-*

[5] The outermost sphere, containing the fixed stars.

[6] 'Operate' and 'produce motion' are translations of the active form of the verb *kinein*. 'Be in motion' and 'be moved' are translations of its passive form.

êton). We desire because of our opinions rather than form opinions because of our desires; which shows that thinking (*noêsis*) is the 'initiating principle.' Now thought is moved by what is thinkable, and one of the two columns of contraries [7] is intrinsically more thinkable than the other. In this more thinkable column *ousia* stands first, particularly such *ousia* as exists without qualification and as fully actual.

Can 'that for whose sake' [i.e., the telic determining factor] be itself something motionless? A distinction will show that it can. That for whose sake anything occurs may be good *for* something, or it may be [simply and entirely] that at which [the action or occurrence] aims. In the latter sense, not in the former, it can be something immutable; *it produces motion through being loved;* whereas other things produce motion through being in motion themselves. Now if anything is moved it is capable of being otherwise than it is. In so far, then, as a thing's actuality consists in motion—even though it be the primary form of motion, which is spherical,—then, in respect of that motion, the thing can be otherwise than it is, i.e., in respect of place, not of essential whatness (*ousia*). But since there must be Something which, existing in full actuality, produces motion without being moved, that Something cannot be otherwise than it is *in any respect*. For the primary kind of change is 'spatial movement' (*phora*), and the primary kind of spatial movement is circular; which is the kind that the Something in question produces. Consequently this Something must necessarily exist; and with respect to its necessity [8] it is good, and in this sense it is an initiating principle.

---

[7] For the best known Pythagorean list of contraries see *Nat. Sci.*, Bk. I, p. 7. In *Metaph.* IV, 2 (1004 b, pp. 27 ff.) Aristotle evidently refers to a list of his own, headed by the antitheses Being vs. Not-being and One vs. Many. There, however, he speaks of *ousia* as composed (συγκεῖσθαι) of contraries; here as heading the positive column.

[8] "Three different meanings of 'necessary' are to be distinguished: (1) what is forcibly imposed upon us contrary to impulse, (2) that without which there can be no good, and (3) that which cannot be otherwise but is necessary without qualification."—Aristotle's gloss.

Such, then, is the Initiating Principle upon which the phenomena of sky and earth depend. It enjoys such a life as we may enjoy in our best moments, and it lives perpetually in that state (as we cannot do), for actuality in that state is pleasure as well.[9] Now thought (*noêsis*) in its intrinsic nature deals with what is intrinsically best, and where thought is most completely present its object is most completely present. [Therefore] thought [in the most complete sense] *thinks itself,* [because] it participates in the object it is thinking of. That is to say, [perfect] thought apprehends and thinks its object in such a way that the thought and its object become one, and the thought [thus] becomes its own object. For in all thought there is receptivity to the object of thought—i.e., to its 'specific whatness' (*ousia*). And thought is fully active in so far as it possesses [that object in its essential specificity].[10] Hence, to be active rather than to be receptive would seem to be the divine aspect of thought, and its 'contemplative activity' (*theoria*) is at once its best and its most highly pleasurable state. If, then, God is perpetually in that condition of contemplative activity to which we occasionally attain, it is wonderful enough; if in an even higher condition, it is still more wonderful. And this is indeed the case. Life, too, belongs to God. For the actuality of thought is what constitutes life, and God is that actuality—in the intrinsic and best and eternal sense. We declare, then, that God is a living being of the highest kind and eternal; so that life and continuous eternal duration belong to God—*are* God, in fact. . . .

It is clear from the foregoing argument that there is some 'Essential Individuality' (*ousia*) that is eternal and immutable and distinct from perceptible things. Moreover, this Individuality [can be] demonstrated to have no magnitude, [which implies that] it

---

[9] "[Indeed, actuality as such yields pleasure,] as is shown by the fact that waking, perception, and thinking are most highly pleasurable, while hopes and memories derive their pleasant character from them."—Aristotle's gloss.

[10] Cf. *Psychology*, Bk. III, Chap. iv; p. 145. To know an object is for thought and the intelligible form of the object to become one.

is without parts and indivisible. For magnitude must be either finite or infinite: and the Individuality in question cannot be finite inasmuch as it produces motion throughout infinite time and nothing finite has infinite potentiality; nor can it be infinite, because an infinite magnitude cannot exist. Furthermore, this Individuality must be unaffected by anything and unalterable; because [to be affected would mean that it was causally posterior to some kind of motion] but all other kinds of motion are posterior to spatial motion [and, as we have shown, spatial motion is causally posterior to the Prime Mover].

ix. *The Divine Mind as self-thinking*

Our account of [Supreme] Mind (*nous*) raises certain problems; for while we may agree that it is the most divine of all phenomena, the question of what further attributes it must have in order to be divine involves difficulties. If Mind thinks of nothing, how could it have any majesty, being in the condition of one who sleeps? If, on the other hand, Mind thinks of something other than Itself, so that Its thinking is governed by the nature of that something else, then Its 'specific essence' (*ousia*) would lie not in Its thinking but in Its *capacity* to think, and this would not be the most excellent sort of specificity (*ousia*) for what is most estimable is the act of thinking [and not the mere capacity].

In any case, whether its specific essence consists in the 'faculty of thought' (*nous*) or the 'act of thinking' (*noêsis*), *what* does It think of? Either of Itself or of something else; and if of something else, then either of the same thing perpetually or of different things at different times. And does it make any difference, or does it not, whether It thinks only of what is excellent or of anything that occurs to It? For are there not some things that it would be absurd to suppose that It thinks of? Evidently, then, what It thinks of is what is most divine and most worthy of esteem. And in this It is unchanging, because any change would be for the worse, and would be a kind of motion, [which, as we have already shown, cannot exist in the Prime Mover].

In short, if [Divine] Mind were not an actual thinking but only a capacity, (1) it would be reasonable to suppose that the continuity of its thinking must be laborious; and (2) there would be something else more excellent than Mind—namely, the object of which it thinks—inasmuch as thought and the act of thinking [considered as potentialities] might perfectly well belong even to one who was thinking of something utterly bad. Therefore, if this consequence is to be avoided (as it ought to be, for it is better not to see some things than to see them), the Highest Good cannot be 'thought [in general]' (*noêsis*). Rather, if it is really the supreme good, it is that which *thinks Itself*, and Its thinking (*noêsis*) is a thinking of thinking.

The objection might be raised that [such species of thinking as] as knowledge, perception, opinion, and understanding always pertain to something other than themselves, and to themselves only incidentally. Further it may be objected that as the act of thinking and the thought-of object are logically distinguishable, since the *meaning* of 'think' and the *meaning* of 'be thought' are obviously different, we must specify to which of these aspects we are ascribing goodness [in the case of the Divine Mind which thinks Itself]. Our reply [to both objections] is that in certain cases the knowledge is its own object. In the productive sciences the object of inquiry (if we disregard the material) is the essence of the thing that is being produced; but in the contemplative sciences it is the meaning (*logos*), which involves the act of thought itself. That is to say, in cases where what is thought of contains no matter, mind (*nous*) and its object are not distinct but identical, and the thinking (*noêsis*) is one with what is thought of.

It remains to inquire whether the object of [divine] Thought is composite; for if it were, the Divine Thinking would undergo change in passing from one part of its entirety to another. Our answer is that whatever has no matter is indivisible. Whereas the human mind—which is to say the mind of composite beings [containing matter as well as form]—does not possess its entire good at any one moment, but requires a certain period, a certain wholeness of time, in which to attain to its supreme good, which is other than itself; [divine] Thought, on the other hand, is the [absolutely simple and unified] thought of Itself throughout all eternity.

Zoology

Zoology[1]

i. Right attitude of the zoologist
(The Parts of Animals: I. v)

OF THINGS (*ousia*) which hold together by nature there are two kinds: those that are unborn, imperishable, and eternal, and those that are subject to generation and decay. The former, although of highest worth and even divine, are less accessible to our investigation, inasmuch as the findings of sense-experience throw very little light on the questions which we most desire to answer about them. It is much easier to learn about things that perish—i.e., plants and animals—because we live in their midst, and anyone who cares to take the trouble can acquire abundant information about them. . . . In any case, having discussed elsewhere the apparent nature of divine objects, our present task is to speak about the nature of animals. So far as possible we will omit no species of animal from consideration, however mean its condition. For even animals that are not attractive to sense offer, to the contemplative vision, the immeasurable joy of discovering creative nature at work in them. It would be strangely paradoxical if we enjoyed studying mere likenesses of nature, because of the painter's or carver's art that they embody, while ignoring the even greater delight of studying nature's own works where we are able to discern the formative factors. So we should not childishly refuse

---

[1] Under the heading of "Zoology" I have brought together a few representative passages from three of Aristotle's writings: *Description of Animals* (*Historia Animalium*), *The Parts of Animals*, and *The Generation of Animals.*—TR.

to study the meaner animals, for in all works of nature there is something of the marvellous. A story is told of Heraclitus, that when some visitors desired to see him but hesitated when they found him in the kitchen warming himself by the fire, he bade them: "Come in, don't be afraid! for here, too, are gods." In like manner, boldly and without distaste, we ought to pursue the investigation of every sort of animal, for every one of them will reveal to us something both of nature and of beauty. I say beauty, because in nature it is purpose, not haphazard, that predominates; and the purpose which directs and permeates her works is one type of the beautiful. . . .

Whatever part or structure happens to be under discussion is not important in itself, as a material thing, but only in relation to the whole conformation of which it is a part. Just as the real interest of architecture lies not in the bricks, mortar, and timber, but in the whole house, so the study of nature is properly concerned not with the material parts (which have no independent existence) but with the 'precise character' (*ousia*) of the composite whole. . . .

For as each part of the body, like any other instrument, serves a purpose, and that purpose is some specific action, so the body as a whole must exist for the sake of some organic action. As the saw [an instrument] exists for the sake of the sawing—its proper function—and not sawing for the sake of the saw, so the body exists somehow for the sake of the soul [i.e., the vital function of the entire body], whereas the parts of the body exist for the various subordinate functions to which they are severally adapted.

ii. Parts of animals: simple and composite

(*Description of Animals: I. i*)

The parts of animals are of two kinds. Those are simple [or uniform] which can be divided into smaller parts like themselves, as flesh into pieces of flesh. Those are composite [or non-uniform], which cannot be divided into like parts, as the hand cannot be divided into hands nor the face into faces. . . . All non-uniform parts are composed of uniform parts, as the hand, for example, is composed of flesh, sinews, and bone.

Nearly all the parts exhibit contrasting qualities with respect to such variables as color and shape, some being more and others less affected in certain ways—'more and less' connoting not only size but whatever other properties admit of excess and deficiency. Some animals, for instance, have a soft skin, others a scaly one; some have a long beak or bill, others a short one; some have many feathers, others few. Some animals, again, have parts entirely lacking in others: e.g., some have spurs, others not; some a crest, others not. In short, the main parts which constitute the bulk of the body are either the same [in different species of animal], or differ only with respect to some contrast of excess and deficiency—for so we can interpret any case of more and less—or else they are related in neither of the above ways but analogically. Instances of analogy are found in the relation of a bone to a spiny structure, of nail to hoof, hand to claw, and scale of fish to feather of bird: for as a feather is to birds so a scale is to fish. . . .

Some animals make sounds, others are silent. Of the former some have a voice; and of these some are able to carry on conversation, while others are inarticulate. Some animals are noisy, others quiet; some are musical, others unmusical. Their singing and chattering are always especially marked in connection with mating. . . .

There are likewise many differences of disposition (*êthos*) among animals. Some, like the ox, are gentle, sluggish, and not given to ferocity; others, like the boar, are violent, ferocious, and untamable. Some are prudent and timid, like the stag and the hare; others are treacherous and crafty, like the snake; others are noble, courageous, and aristocratic, like the lion; still others are brave, wild, and crafty, like the wolf. . . . But the only animal capable of deliberation is man. For although many other animals

have the ability to remember and to learn through experience, no
animal except man is able to recall the past at will.

iii. *Touch and action*

(*Description of Animals: I. iii*)

The only sense common to all animals is touch. . . . It resides
mainly in the simple [uniform] parts of the body, such as the flesh,
and particularly (in the case of blooded animals) in places where
there is blood. Other animals have the sense of touch in parts
analogous to those containing blood—but in any case in the uniform parts.

The powers of action, on the contrary, are located in the composite parts: e.g., mastication of food in the mouth, locomotion
in the feet or wings or analogous members.

iv. *The skeletal and vascular structures*

(*The Parts of Animals: II. ix*)

The skeletal structure is similar to the arrangement of blood-
vessels, in that each of them is a continuous system of branches
leading out from a center. There is no case of a bone existing off
by itself: each one exists either as part of a virtually continuous
system or as attached to that system in some way; whereby Nature
can use adjoining bones either as though they formed a single
continuous bone or, in the bending of joints, as two distinct pieces.
Similarly there is no blood-vessel existing off by itself: they are
all parts of a single system. If there were an isolated bone it could
not perform the function for which bones exist: being unconnected
and separate it would not serve for bending or straightening a limb,
and in fact it would even cause injury, like a thorn or arrow lodged
in the flesh. Similarly if there were a blood-vessel off by itself, unconnected with the source (*archê*) [of blood supply], it would be
unable to preserve its own blood; for when blood can no longer

draw warmth from its central source of supply it coagulates and takes on the appearance of putrefaction. The source of the blood-vessels is the heart, and the corresponding source from which in a bony creature the entire system of bones takes its beginning is the so-called backbone, which runs without a break the entire length of an animal's body and holds it straight. But inasmuch as an animal is obliged to bend while in motion, the backbone despite its unity is divided into segments which are the vertebrae.

From the backbone the various limbs extend, in such animals as have any, by a system of connections in which the extremities of each bone fit on to the adjacent ones, sometimes by the one being hollow and the next one rounded, sometimes by their both being hollow and joined together by a cross-ligament, a sort of connecting bolt, to permit bending and straightening, for without such an arrangement this type of movement would be either quite impossible or at any rate extremely awkward. A third kind of connecting arrangement is where two adjacent bones are alike in shape, bound together by sinews, and padded with pieces of cartilage in between, to prevent their rubbing against each other.

Surrounding the bones are the fleshy parts of the body, attached to them by thin fibrous threads, and it is for the sake of these fleshy parts that the bones exist. In the same way that modelers in moulding an animal out of clay or some other soft material start with a hard firm core and then fashion the figure around it, so Nature works in forming an animal body out of flesh. Thus all the fleshy parts, with one exception, have a supporting bone structure. It is what enables certain parts to make bending movements, while to stationary parts it serves as a protection—as illustrated by the ribs, which by enclosing the chest protect the organs in the region of the heart. The one exception is the belly, which in all animals is boneless. This is in order that the swelling which inevitably takes place after a meal may not be hindered, and, in females, that there may be no interferences with the growth of the foetus which takes place there.

v. Male and female roles in generation

(The Generation of Animals: I. xxi-xxii)

The next question to be investigated is how the male contributes to generation—that is, in what sense the semen produced by the male is a 'determining factor' (aition) of the offspring. Does the semen become an actual part of the embryo in the sense that it mingles with the material supplied by the female; or does it contribute nothing of a material sort, but only its power (dynamis) and motion (kinêsis)? The latter alternative seems to be the right one, supported by reasoning and by factual evidence alike.

The semen is the active, productive factor; while the residue of fluid in the female [i.e., what has not been outwardly discharged in menstruation] is that which is acted upon and receives a form (morphê).[2] Now it appears, if we look at the matter broadly, that whenever a product is formed out of two factors, an active and a passive, the active factor does not become a physical part of the product; and the same principle holds good, more broadly still, where the relation is between what sets in motion and what receives motion, for the former never becomes an actual part of the latter.[3] Now the female quâ female is passive, whereas the male quâ male is active in that the 'initiating principle' (archê) of the motion [of generation] comes from him. Accordingly if we regard male and female as falling under these higher categories—the one as active and motion-giving, the other as passive and motion-receiving—we can see that there is no other sense in which the offspring comes from them jointly than that in which a bedstead comes into being from both the carpenter and the wood, or a ball from the wax and the form (eidos). It seems evident, then, that nothing need really pass out of the male in the process of genera-

---

[2] This and the preceding sentence stand in reverse order in the Bekker text.
[3] E.g., the marble (the passive, material factor) becomes an actual part of the statue, but the sculptor (the active, productive factor) does not. Analogously God makes and acts upon the world without becoming a physical part of it. Cf. Mctaphysics, XII. vii, especially p. 100.

tion; or at any rate that what passes out contributes to the embryo not as a phyical constituent but as that which imparts motion (*kinêsis*) and form (*eidos*), analogously to the way in which a cure is effected by the medical art.

vi. Man compared with the other animals
(Description of Animals: VIII. i)

While certain traits in men differ only in degree from those in animals—man exhibiting more of one trait and certain animals more of another—there are also traits in man to which the corresponding traits in animals are related only by the principle of analogy. For as men exhibit art and wisdom and intelligence, animals possess other kinds of natural ability which serve much the same purpose. This view of the matter is confirmed by considering human children: for in them can be seen the indications and seeds of their future dispositions, yet their psychic traits at that age are virtually the same as those of the lower animals. Accordingly it is not unreasonable to regard animals as exhibiting traits analogous to those in man, even where no identity or similarity is apparent. Nature passes from lifeless things up to animal life by such gradual degrees that the continuity obscures boundaries and puzzles us how to classify intermediate forms.

Psychology

Psychology

BOOK I

GENERAL DISCUSSION OF THE SOUL

i. The subject-matter of psychology

BECAUSE ALL KNOWLEDGE is in our estimation a thing of beauty and worth, and because this is more particularly true of those types of knowledge which are more exact in themselves or which refer to more excellent or more remarkable objects; on both these grounds we are justified in ranking psychology, or a study of the soul (*psychê*), among the first of our interests. Moreover, it is commonly agreed that a knowledge of this subject contributes greatly to the general discovery of truth, especially in the domain of nature; for the soul is, as it were, the 'moving principle' (*archê*) of animal life. Our aim is to discover and understand, first the nature (*physis*) and essence (*ousia*) of the soul, and next its various properties, some of which are held to be attributes (*pathos*) peculiar to the soul itself, others to belong to the 'whole animal' (*zoön*) [1] by virtue of the soul's presence in it.

To arrive at any 'trustworthy conviction' (*pistis*) about the soul is one of the hardest tasks with which we are ever confronted. As we are faced here with the same problem as in many other fields of investigation—the problem of discovering a thing's 'essential

[1] The soul is merely a part—the living, motivating part—of the whole animal.

nature' (*ousia*) and 'what it really is' (*ti esti*)—it might be supposed that there is some single procedure (*methodos*) applicable to all the objects whose essential natures we may wish to ascertain, just as there is a single way of demonstrating each derivative property. If such were the case, it would be our task to discover the procedure in question. If, on the contrary, there is no universal procedure for finding a thing's 'real nature' (*ti esti*), we are faced with an even harder task; for we shall then have to determine with respect to each particular subject what method (*tropos*) is to be pursued. Moreover, even if it is obvious that the method is to be a certain kind of demonstration (*apodeixis*) or 'logical division' (*diairesis*) or something equally familiar, we are still beset with difficulties and liable to error when we look for the proper starting-point of our inquiry; for the starting-points of different sciences differ, as may be seen by comparing the science of numbers with the science of plane figures.

Our first task must doubtless be to determine under which of the 'highest classes' (*genos*) of things the soul falls, and what it essentially is: whether it is a particular substance, a quality, a quantity, or some one of the other types of predicate already distinguished; and also (a point of extreme importance) whether it belongs to the class of potential existents or is rather a kind of actuality. We must consider too whether souls are divisible or indivisible, and whether they are entirely homogeneous; and if not homogeneous, then whether their differences are differences of genus or merely of species: for current discussions and investigations about the soul apparently are restricted to the human soul. Nor should we overlook the question whether soul, like animal, has a single 'definitive meaning' (*logos*), or whether on the contrary we must give a separate definition for each kind of soul—as we should have to do for horse, dog, man, and deity if 'animal in general' were taken to be either non-existent or logically posterior to these. The same question, as a matter of fact, may be raised about any other general notion.

Again, supposing that there is not a plurality of souls but merely a plurality of parts [of one all-embracing soul], it may be asked whether our investigation should start with soul in its entirety or with its particular parts; for the natural divisions between the parts would not be easy to determine. Also there would be the question whether we ought to start with the parts themselves or with their 'active employment' (*ergon*): [2] e.g., with mind or the act of thinking. And taking the latter alternative, there is the further question whether we should start with the correlative objects—with the objects perceived and thought rather than with the faculties of perception and intellect.

Not only, it seems, does knowledge of a thing's essential nature help us to see the causes of its incidental properties—as in mathematics an understanding of straight and curved, line and plane, helps us to perceive the equality between the angles of a triangle and a certain number of right angles—but conversely as well, an acquaintance with a thing's incidental properties greatly promotes an understanding of its essential nature. For we are best qualified to speak of a thing's essential nature when we are able to give an account of all or most of its properties as they are directly experienced. To determine a thing's real nature is the 'first step' (*archê*) of any demonstration; hence definitions that neither tell, nor even facilitate a conjecture about, a thing's incidental properties are void of content and evidently framed merely 'for purposes of disputation' (*dialektikos*).

A further problem respecting the attributes of the soul is whether they all belong to body and soul together or whether any of them are peculiar to the soul alone—a difficult question but unavoidable. Apparently in a majority of cases, such as anger, courage, desire, and all sensation, the soul neither acts nor is acted upon apart from the body. Thinking is perhaps the most likely exception; yet if thinking consists in a succession of mental im-

---

[2] In *Nic. Eth.*, Bk. I, Chap. i, however, *ergon* is used for the result of a process as distinguished from the process itself. See p. 157.

ages, or at least is impossible without such images, it is plain that even thinking cannot be carried on independently of the body. If we can discover any functions or other characteristics peculiar to the soul alone, we may regard the soul as capable of existing apart from the body; while if it possesses no such functions or characteristics of its own, separate existence will be impossible to it. In the latter case the soul will be comparable to the straightness of a line. The line, quâ straight, has many properties, such as that of touching a bronze sphere at a point; but this does not mean that straightness by itself will have such a property. For, in fact, straightness never exists by itself, but is always found existing as an aspect of body. Similarly we may take it that the affections of the soul—angry passion and gentleness, fear, pity, courage, and even joy, love, and hate—always involve body; for their occurrence is accompanied by some specific affection of the body. This is shown by the fact that violent and striking things may happen to us without our being either frightened or irritated; while at other times, when the body is already perturbed and in a condition like that of anger, our emotions may be aroused by faint and trifling occurrences. Even better evidence is found in the fact that men sometimes fall into a state of terror without anything terrible having occurred. This being so, it is evident that *the affections of the soul are simply meanings (logos) subsisting in matter,* and ought therefore to be defined accordingly: anger, for instance, as a certain way in which a body, or some organ or faculty of a body, is moved by such and such a cause with reference to such and such an end.

A study of the soul, then, at least in the aspects of it above mentioned, falls within the province of the natural scientist. But the natural scientist interprets the soul differently from the dialectical philosopher. Anger, for example, would be defined by the philosopher as a desire for retaliation or the like, by the natural scientist as a ferment of the blood or warm fluid about the heart. The one stresses the 'significant form' (*eidos kai logos*), the other the material basis. While the 'real meaning' (*logos*) of a thing consists in its form (*eidos*), this meaning must be embodied in a particular kind of matter if the thing is to have existence. Thus the meaning of a house might be stated as 'a shelter to ward off disaster from wind, rain, and heat'; another person, however, might describe it in terms of stones, bricks, and timber; while yet a third might declare it to be a certain 'form, or plan' (*eidos*) at once embodied in the materials and conducing to certain ends. Which of these is the true natural scientist—he who treats only of the material while ignoring the 'meaning of the whole' (*logos*), or he who treats of this meaning alone? Presumably it is rather he whose inquiry embraces both aspects. What, then, of the other two?[3] As a matter of fact, there is probably no one who deals [with matter exclusively]—i.e., with such attributes of matter as cannot be separated from, nor even abstracted in thought from, their material basis. The natural scientist, for his part, treats of all the active functionings and passive affections that are the properties of determinate sorts of bodies and materials.[4] Properties of a less general kind he leaves to others, who may chance to be specialists in a particular line—carpenters, for instance, or physicians. Properties which, while inseparable from bodies in general, are not treated of as affections of this or that particular body but are reached by abstraction, fall within the province of the mathematician; while properties that are treated of in abstraction from all bodies whatever constitute the subject-matter of basic philosophy.

But let us return to our main line of argument. At the point of digression we were saying that the affections of the soul, such as 'angry passion' (*thymos*) and fear, are inseparable from the physical basis of animal life to which they belong; and we have

[3] I.e., is there any legitimate field of investigation to which either of the two one-sided interpretations of things—as mere materials or as pure forms —is appropriate?

[4] Which, being determinate, are distinguishable in thought from the bare general concept of matter.

shown that in this respect they differ from mathematical entities like lines and planes.

iv. The soul not in motion except incidentally

. . . There is, as we have seen,[5] an incidental sense in which the soul can be regarded as partaking of the motion which it produces—viz., that the body in which it resides may move from place to place by its agency. In any other sense, however, spatial movement is impossible to it.

A more plausible argument that the soul is in motion might be based on such considerations as the following. We speak of the soul as being pained or pleased, confident or afraid; as raging or as perceiving or thinking. All these states are regarded as motions, which might lead us to infer that the soul itself is in motion. This, however, is no necessary inference. Though we grant that thinking and being pained or pleased are motions (each of them being an actual process) and that these motions are produced by the soul; and though we might explain anger or fear, for instance, as a certain motion of the heart, and thinking as a motion either of this or of some other organ (regardless of whether these motions are to be accounted changes of place or changes of quality, and ignoring the question of their specific natures and causes); yet, even then, to speak of the soul as being angry is much as if we were to speak of it as weaving a fabric or building a house. We might better leave off saying that the soul pities or learns or thinks, and regard rather the man as carrying on these activities by means of the soul—in the sense not that the motion takes place in the soul, but that the soul is either its terminal or its starting-point: sensation (aesthêsis), for instance, being a motion from external objects to the soul, while recollection (ana-mnêsis) starts out from the soul and terminates in motions or arrestations of the sense-organs.

Mind (nous), on the other hand, would seem to arise in the

[5] The reference is to Chap. iii, omitted from the present edition.

soul as a substance that is self-existing and imperishable; for it can be destroyed, if at all, only by the dimness of old age. But, as a matter of fact, what really occurs in old age is probably like what occurs in the sense-organs. If an old man could procure the proper sort of eye, he would see as well as a young man. Old age, then, is marked by certain affections not of the soul itself but of its vehicle, the body; resembling in this respect intoxication and disease. Similarly, although the mind's actual thinking and intuiting may be weakened by the decay of some inner organ of the body, the mind itself is unaffected. Thinking, loving, and hating are affections not of the mind but of the organism possessing a mind—so far as it does possess one. That is why, when the organism decays, there is an end to memory and love; for these belong not to the mind itself, but to the synthesis of mind and body, which has perished. Mind itself, by reason of its more divine nature, we may suppose to be imperishable.

From these considerations it is clear that the soul is incapable of being moved; and since it cannot be moved at all, it obviously cannot be [as many have supposed] self-moving. . . .

v. Is the soul composed of material elements?

. . . We must next examine the theory that the soul is composed of the [four] elements (*stoicheion*).[6] This theory, which is an attempt to explain how the soul can perceive and be cognizant of the various sorts of objects, involves a number of paradoxes. It is based on the supposition that like can be known only by like; which would mean that the soul must be the same as the objects that it knows. It can know not only the elements, however, but a great many, if not an infinite number of things besides—i.e., the things that are compounded of the elements. Granted that the theory in question explains how the soul can know and perceive the elements of composite things, how are we to explain its knowledge and perception of the composite things themselves—of God,

[6] This was the theory of Empedocles.

man, flesh, bone, or any other such compound? None of these is merely the totality of elements that compose it; it is those elements brought together in a determinate ratio and arrangement, as Empedocles himself says of bone:

> Bounteous Earth, in the melting-pot of her broad bosom,
> Won two parts from the bright moisture, four from the
>   firegod;
> And with eight parts all told,[7] created the white bones.

Consequently nothing would be gained by the presence of [the four] elements in the soul unless they were combined in the same order and arrangement as in the outer world. For while each element would know its like, there would be nothing to know bone or man, unless these specific complexes were also present in the soul. The impossibility of this is obvious; for who would suppose for a moment that a stone or a man might be present in the soul? The same argument could be applied to good and its opposite, as well as to any other composite entity. . . .

From the foregoing discussion it is plain, first, that the soul's ability to know does not prove that it is composed of the [four] elements; secondly, that it is wrong and untrue to regard the soul as in motion. . . .

---

[7] It may be conjectured that she contributed two parts from her own substance.

psyche – soul

BOOK II

THE SOUL AND ITS FACULTIES

i. Definition of soul

TAKING leave of the theories about the soul that have been handed down by our predecessors, let us make virtually a fresh start by trying to determine what the soul is and how in its most general aspect it is to be defined.

There is a certain type of entity to which we give the name 'thing' (*ousia*), and by this word we may mean either: (1) matter, which in itself has not the character of a 'this' or (2) the shape and essential form by which we distinguish this thing from that, or (3) the whole, which comprises these two aspects. By matter we mean potentiality, by form actuality; and of the latter there are in turn two kinds, illustrated by the possession of knowledge as distinguished from its active exercise.

The most generally recognized class of things is that of bodies —especially natural bodies, which are the originals of all others. Some natural bodies possess life, others do not; life signifying the power of self-nourishment, and of growth and decay. Accordingly, every natural body possessing life must be not only a 'specific thing' (*ousia*) but one comprising both matter and form. But because body thus possesses a certain attribute, namely life, it is not on that account to be identified with the soul; for body is not itself an attribute but simply the subject and the material basis of attributes. Soul, therefore, must be a specific thing in the sense that it is the form (*eidos*) of a natural body endowed with the capacity of life. Specific thinghood in this sense is actuality (*entelecheia*);

and soul, therefore, is the actuality of body as just defined. Further, as the word actuality has two senses, illustrated respectively by the possession and exercise of knowledge, it is evident that soul is actuality in the former of these senses; for sleep as well as waking is a state of the soul, and while waking is analogous to the exercise of knowledge, sleep is analogous to its mere possession. Moreover, since the possession of knowledge must precede its exercise, the soul may be defined as *the initial actuality of a natural body endowed with the capacity of life.*

This definition of soul is applicable to whatever body possesses organs. The term organs is here extended to include the parts of plants; for these, in spite of their rudimentary structure, exhibit certain analogies to animal organs: the leaf, for instance, serves as protective covering for the pericarp, and the pericarp for the fruit; while again, the roots are analogous to mouths, since like them they ingest food. Hence if we require a general definition applicable to every type of soul, we may define the soul as *the initial actuality of a natural body possessing organs.* The question whether soul and body are identical, therefore, is as superfluous as to ask whether wax and the shape imprinted on it are identical, or, in general whether the material of a thing is identical with the thing of which it is the material. 'Is' and 'one' have various meanings, but in their most legitimate meaning they connote the fully actual character of a thing.

We have now stated in a broad way what soul is: it is the 'essential whatness' (*ousia*) of a thing in the sense of its 'definitive meaning' (*logos*); the 'essential and enduring character' (*ti ên einai*) of a body possessing the capacity of life. Suppose, for example, that an instrument such as an axe were a natural body. Its character of being an axe would then be its 'whatness, or essential thinghood' (*ousia*), and therefore its 'soul'; if this were taken away it would no longer be an axe except in name. But in point of fact the axe is merely a man-made instrument, not the kind of body whose definitive nature may be called a soul; for soul is ascribed only to a particular kind of natural body which has within itself the 'power of producing' (*archê*) movement and rest.

We must further consider our definition of soul with reference to the parts of a living body. If the eye were an independent organism, sight would be its soul, for it is in terms of sight that the essential whatness of the eye must be defined. The eye is the 'material condition' (*hylê*) of seeing, and if its power of sight were removed it would no longer be an eye—except in name, like an eye carved in stone or sketched. What is thus true of a bodily organ must be no less true of the whole organism; for a particular mode of perceptual awareness stands in the same relation to its particular organ as our whole conscious life stands to the whole sentient body as such. . . .

ii. Soul in relation to life

As it is by starting from confused but familiar truths that we attain to truths that are clear and logically more intelligible, this is the procedure that we must try to follow in resuming our inquiry about the soul. It is not enough that the formula by which we define a thing should give, as most definitions do, only the fact; it should explicitly include the reason for the fact as well. What is ordinarily stated in a definition is merely a sort of conclusion; as when, in reply to the question, "What is quadrature?" we define it as the construction of a square of equal area to a given oblong rectangle. Such a definition expresses merely the conclusion of the implicit syllogism; whereas if we define quadrature as the discovery of the line that is a mean proportional between two adjacent sides of the oblong rectangle we then exhibit the ground (*aition*) [1] of our definition.

Accordingly we shall start our inquiry with the observation

[1] The formula, $a:b::b:c$, or $b^2 = ac$, which is the mathematical expression of the length of the sides of any square and rectangle that are equal to each other in area, is the 'formal determinant' of the corresponding geometrical construction.

that what differentiates the animate from the inanimate is possession of life.[2] Now the word life connotes several meanings—intelligence (*nous*), sentience (*aesthêsis*), spatial movement and rest, and the processes of nutrition, growth and decay; and if life in any of these senses is present in a thing we call that thing alive. Hence even plants are regarded as alive, since they evidently possess an intrinsic power which governs their growth and contraction in contrary directions at once. For plants do not grow upwards exclusively, but so long as they both have and can absorb nourishment, and thus can continue to live, they grow both upwards and downwards, and indeed in all directions at once. Although in mortal creatures this aspect of life is the precondition of all others, it can exist independently of them, as is evident when we reflect that in the case of plants it is the only faculty (*dynamis*) of soul that they possess.

It is by virtue of this faculty [of nourishment, growth, and decline] that things live; but it is 'the capacity for receiving sensations' (*aesthêsis*) that chiefly distinguishes animal life. For even such creatures as do not move or change their place, if only they be sentient, are called not merely living creatures but animals. . . .

iii. *Levels of soul*

Of the powers of the soul just enumerated—i.e., nutrition, appetition, sensation, locomotion, and intelligence—some organisms, as we have said, possess all, others some, still others only one. Plants have only the faculty of nutrition. There are other organisms that possess sensation as well; and sensation involves appetency, under which term are included desire (*epithymia*), 'violent feeling' (*thymos*), and volition (*boulêsis*). All animals possess at least one sense, namely touch; possession of sense implies both a capacity for pleasure and pain and the existence of pleasant and painful objects, and these in turn imply desire, since desire

---

[2] Not a circular definition; for what 'animate' *means* is possessing a soul (Latin, *anima*), not possessing life. The etymology in Greek is parallel.

is a propensity for what is pleasurable. Moreover, animals possess a sense for nourishment; and this is touch. It is by the qualities that touch apprehends—the dry, the moist, the hot, and the cold —that all living things are nourished. Other qualities, such as sound, color, and odor, which are related to touch only indirectly (*kata symbebêkos*), contribute nothing to nourishment; while flavor, [which does contribute to nourishment], falls within the class of tactile objects. As hunger and thirst are forms of desire, the one for what is hot and dry, the other for what is cold and moist, flavor may be considered the sauce that gives relish to these qualities. Details, however, can wait; for the present it is enough to say that all animals endowed with a sense of touch possess appetition also. . . . None of the other senses exists without the sense of touch; touch, however, can exist without the others, as in the case of certain animals that enjoy neither sight nor hearing nor smell.

Again, the sentient faculty never exists without the nutritive; but the nutritive may exist without the sentient, as in the case of plants. Of organisms that possess sensation, some have a power of locomotion, others not.[3] Finally, there is a small fraction of living things that possess understanding (*dianoia*) and 'reasoning power' (*logismos*). All mortal beings that possess reasoning power possess also the other faculties of soul; but not all those with the other faculties possess the power to reason: some must live by the 'power of imagination' (*phantasia*) alone, and some lack even that. Of the 'power of rational apperception' (*theorêtikos nous*) we shall speak elsewhere.[4] At any rate, these illustrations may serve to show that the most appropriate definition of the soul consists in a description of its several [aspects or faculties].

[3] This sentence and the preceding one have been interchanged from the Bekker edition.
[4] Bk. III, Chap. iv–viii.

iv. *Further characteristics of soul*

. . . The nutritive aspect of soul belongs to all living things, being at once the most primitive and most universal of the soul's several faculties, and the condition of life in all creatures. Its functions are reproduction and assimilation of food. Reproduction is the most natural of functions in such organisms as are normally developed and not defective nor spontaneously generated.[5] Creatures produce others of their kind, animals producing animals and plants producing plants, in order that they may share, so far as their several natures allow, in the eternal and divine. That is the ideal for which all creatures strive, and which determines their behavior, so far as their behavior is natural.[6] But since mortal things cannot share continuously in the eternal and divine (because nothing that perishes can preserve its identity nor remain numerically one), they partake of eternity and divinity in the one way that is open to them, and with unequal success; achieving immortality not in themselves, but vicariously through their offspring, which, though distinct individuals, are one with them in kind.

The soul is the 'determining principle' (*aitia kai archê*) of the living body. But these two words, 'determining' and 'principle,' have a variety of meanings. Soul is a determining factor in three explicitly recognized respects: as the originator of motion, as the end [or ideal guide of conduct], and as the 'essential nature' (*ousia*) of the living body. That the soul has this last characteristic is evident when we consider that the existence of anything is determined by its essential nature, and that in living things, whose existence consists in being alive, the soul is the 'determining principle' of their life. Besides, [the soul, as we have previously

---

[5] The minute organisms present in decaying bodies were among those explained by 'spontaneous generation' (*genesis automatos*).

[6] What was probably intended as a gloss is inserted in the Greek text at this point: "It is in a double sense that we may speak of an ideal, or telic, determinant. We may mean either the state of affairs for the sake of which, or the person for the sake of whom, an action is performed."

declared, is actuality, and] actuality may be considered the 'essential meaning' (*logos*) of whatever exists in a potential state.

Second, the soul is also a determining factor in the telic sense. Nature, like mind, acts with reference to a purpose (*heneka tou*), and this purpose is its end (*telos*). In animals the soul is such an end. That it should be so is according to nature; for every physical part of a living body, whether animal or plant, is the soul's instrument. Evidently, then, all such parts are for the sake of the soul, which is their natural end.[7]

Third, the soul is also the cause of an organism's movements from place to place; although not all organisms, to be sure, have the power of such movement. But 'qualitative change' (*alloiôsis*) and growth are also caused by the soul; for sensation, which is regarded as a kind of qualitative change, is not present in anything that lacks soul. The same holds true of growth and decay; for nothing undergoes natural growth and decay except such things as take nourishment, and nothing takes nourishment unless it possesses life, [which is to say, soul].

Empedocles, in dealing with the growth of plants, falls into error when he proceeds to explain that they take root downwards because the earth in them has a natural tendency in this direction, and that they foliate upwards because of an upward tendency in the fire that they contain. He is wrong in his interpretation of up and down. Up and down are not the same for each individual as for the universe. On the contrary, if we differentiate and identify organs according to their functions, the roots of plants will correspond to the heads of animals. Besides, what of the force that holds together the fire and earth within a plant, which thus exert a pull in opposite directions? If there is nothing to counteract them they will be torn asunder; and if there is, this will be their soul, the cause of their nourishment and growth. . . .

Nutrition involves three factors: that which is nourished, that

---

[7] There is a repetition in the text at this point of Aristotle's earlier gloss on the two meanings of 'telic determinant.' See above, footnote 6.

wherewith it is nourished, and that which performs the nutritive
act. The act of nourishment is performed by the 'rudimentary
soul' (*prôtê psychê*); that which is nourished is the body, and
that wherewith it is nourished is food. But as it is more just to
call things after the ends they subserve, and as the end subserved
by the soul is reproduction of its kind, the rudimentary soul may
be called reproductive. The wherewithal of nourishment may be
understood in two senses, as both hand and rudder may be considered the means by which we steer: the one as at once receiving
and producing movement, the other as only receiving it. Similarly,
all food must be capable of digestion, and digestion is produced
by the vital heat;[8] which explains why everything with a soul
has warmth. . . .

v. The nature of sensation

These points settled, let us next speak of sensation (*aesthêsis*)
in the broadest sense of the word. Sensation, as we have said
consists in being moved and acted upon; and it is commonly re
garded as a sort of qualitative change. There are some who add
that all change is an action of like upon like. To what extent this
principle can be accepted we have explained in our general discussion of activity and passivity.[9]

It may be wondered why sensation does not arise in the sense-
organs themselves. These are known to contain fire and earth and
the other elements, which either in themselves or through their

---

[8] The vital heat is like the hand, at once receiving and producing movement; while food merely receives the 'movement' of being broken up and
assimilated.

[9] In Bk. I, Chap. vii, of his treatise *De Generatione et Corruptione* Aristotle
offers two arguments against an extreme interpretation of the principle that
like acts on like: (1) If two things are in every respect exactly alike, there
is no more reason that one of them should act on the other than that the other
should act on it. (2) If like tends to act upon like *quâ* like, then (since a thing
is like itself) everything would be constantly producing movement in itself,
so that there would be nothing stable in the universe. But what acts and what
is acted upon must, he adds, have a *generic* identity: body can be directly
affected only by body, flavor by flavor, color by color.

attributes are the objects of sense-experience: why, then, can they not produce sensations without the presence of external objects? The answer must be that sensation is present in them not actually but only potentially: in the same way that combustible objects obviously cannot catch fire of themselves without anything to ignite them, for if they could they would not need the application of already existing fire to set them ablaze.[10] Sensation thus has two meanings: we attribute seeing and hearing to what has the capacity to see and hear, though perhaps momentarily asleep, no less than to what is actually seeing and hearing at the moment. This indicates the twofold meaning of sensation, as potential and actual; and 'to be sentient' likewise has both these meanings.

Provisionally we may speak as if being moved or acted upon were identical with the corresponding 'active operation' (*energeia*); for movement is active operation after a fashion, but incomplete, as has been explained elsewhere. Now whatever is moved or acted upon implies the functioning of an active agent. Hence in being acted upon a thing is in one sense like the active agent, in another unlike. To the extent that it is being acted upon it is unlike; to the extent that it has been acted upon [and thereby been made active] it is like. . . .

Potentiality, in turn, has been shown to have two meanings: the one according to which we speak of a boy as able to become a general, the other according to which we speak of an already grown man as able to do so; and the case is similar with what is potentially sentient. . . .

vi. The kinds of sensible object

In treating of each of the senses we must start with their objects. The term *sensible object* may mean any one of three things, two

---

[10] It was known, of course, that fire could be struck from flint and produced by other kinds of friction, but this was believed to be due to the presence of the fire-element in the flint or rubbed object.

of which we should call perceptible *per se*, the third only indirectly or incidentally. Of the first two sorts of sensible object, the one is peculiar to a single sense, the other common to all the senses. By an object peculiar to a particular sense I mean one that cannot be perceived by any other sense, and in respect of which no deception is possible. Thus color is an object peculiar to sight, sound to hearing, and flavor to taste; while touch, on the other hand, has objects of several different kinds. Each sense judges of the objects peculiar to it, and is never deceived as to the existence of the color or sound that it perceives, although it may, of course, be deceived as to the nature or location of the colored or audible object. So much, then, for our discussion of the objects peculiar to the several senses.

Common sensibles include movement, rest, number, figure, and magnitude; for these are not objects peculiar to this or that sense, but are common to all. There are movements, for example, perceptible to touch as well as sight.

Finally, what we have called an *incidentally sensible object* may be illustrated by the case of seeing a white object which is Diares' son. We perceive Diares' son 'indirectly, or incidentally' (*kata symbebêkos*), because the character of being Diares' son is related in an incidental way to what we perceive directly. The senses themselves are not affected by an indirectly sensible object of this sort. Of the two classes of directly sensible objects, it is the objects peculiar to this or that sense that are sensible in the strict meaning of the word; and it is to them that the 'essential structure' (*ousia*) of each sense is naturally adapted.

xii. Sense and sense-organ

With reference to sensation in general, we must understand by 'sense' (*aesthêsis*) that which can receive the sensible forms of things without their matter, as wax receives the imprint of a signet-ring without receiving the iron or gold of which it is made. It is stamped by something golden or brazen, but not quâ gold or bronze. Similarly, a thing that possesses color or flavor or sound affects the sense belonging to the appropriate organ; not, however, quâ individual substance, but as possessing a certain quality and a certain 'proportionate arrangement of parts' (*logos*).

By 'sense-organ' we mean primarily that in which there is a capacity for receiving sense-impressions in the way just described. But while the sense and its organ are thus one in fact, they are logically distinguishable; for whereas the sentient organ is characterized by spatial extension, the sense, i.e., the capacity for receiving sense-impressions, is not itself extended, but is a power (*dynamis*) deriving from a certain ratio (*logos*) in the physical organ. This explains why excesses in the sensible objects will destroy the sense-organs. If the movement in the sense-organ becomes too violent, the ratio (which, as we have seen, constitutes the sense) is dissolved, just as we destroy harmony and tone by plucking too rudely at the strings of a lyre. It explains, too, why plants are not sentient, even though they possess a certain element of soul and are in some degree affected (in respect of temperature, for instance) by tangible objects in their environment. The reason is that they have in them no 'state of tension between opposite qualities' (*mesotês*), and hence no principle capable of receiving the disembodied forms of sensible qualities; when they are affected it is by the matter as well.

The question might be raised whether a thing unable to smell can be in any way acted upon by odors, a thing unable to see by colors, and so on. Our reply must be that as an odor is what is smelt, its effect, if any, can only be to produce the experience of smelling. Hence nothing that cannot smell is ever acted upon by an odor; and the same reasoning may be applied to the other senses. Moreover, even that which does have the power of smell is affected only by such sensible objects as are specifically objects of smell. This is further shown by the following consideration. Organic bodies themselves, [as distinguished from their senses], are not affected by light and darkness, odor and sound, but only by the physical vehicles of such qualities. It is not the noise of thunder but the attendant commotion of air that splits the tree-trunk.

It may be retorted, however, that unless bodies are acted upon by tangibles and by flavors, it is impossible to explain by what agency inanimate things are acted upon and caused to undergo qualitative change. Shall we accept this argument and extend it to the objects of the other senses as well? No, we ought perhaps rather to conclude that not all bodies are affected by odor and sound, and that those which are so affected—e.g., air, which as it is sometimes fragrant must be acted upon by odor—do not preserve a determinate character. In what respect, then, is smelling to be distinguished from merely being acted upon by an odor? Our answer must be that smelling is simultaneously an act of perceiving, whereas air, when acted upon by an odor, does not itself perceive the odor but is merely thereby made perceptible to sense.

BOOK III

MIND AS RELATED TO SENSATION AND DESIRE

i. How the common sensibles are perceived

. . . UNLESS THERE exists some [fifth] element or some property different from those possessed by the [four] elements that we know, our catalogue of the senses [as sight, hearing, smell, taste, and touch] is complete.[1] Neither can there be a special sense-organ for the common sensibles such as movement and rest, figure and magnitude, number and unity; but all of these are perceived indirectly (*kata symbebêkos*) as a result of the functioning of the particular senses. All of the common sensibles are perceived through movement (*kinêsis*): magnitude, for instance, and therefore figure, which is a species of magnitude; while an object at rest is perceived as something not moving. Number is perceived by the negation of continuity, and also by the special senses, from the fact that each of them perceives unity, [which is the basis of number]. Clearly, then, the common sensibles such as movement cannot be objects private to some particular sense. For if they were, we should perceive them in the same way that we now perceive by sight what is sweet. When a given object is at once visible and sweet, and when on seeing it as visible we recognize it as something sweet, this is because we possess an independent sense for the perception of each of these qualities. If, then, [the common sensibles were objects of a particular sense] [2]

[1] The present chapter begins with a passage, here omitted, in which Aristotle demonstrates *a priori* that there can be no sixth sense.

[2] Interpreting εἰ δὲ μὴ (425a, 24) as referring to δῆλον (20).

we should perceive them only indirectly, in much the same way
that we perceive Cleon's son; whom we recognize not because
he is Cleon's son but because he is a light-colored object, which
from the standpoint of being Cleon's son is incidental. It is not
in this fashion that we perceive the common sensibles, but by a
'central sense, or general sensibility,' [3] which acts directly upon its
object. They are not, therefore, dependent on the action of a particular sense; otherwise we should never perceive them except in
the way we perceive Cleon's son.

It is only 'incidentally' that we can speak of the senses as perceiving each other's proper objects: they do so not in so far as
they are distinct but in so far as they form a unity—i.e., when
there is a simultaneous perception of different qualities in one
object, as bile is at once bitter and yellow. This explains why we
may mistake a thing, because it happens to be yellow, for bile.

But why, it may be asked, have we several senses instead of
one? Presumably it is to prevent our overlooking the common
sensibles, such as movement, magnitude, and number, which follow upon the sensibles of special sorts. For if sight were the only
sense and whiteness its only object, we should tend to overlook
the abstract properties of a thing: magnitude and whiteness, being
invariably conjoined, would be indistinguishable. In point of fact,
however, since the common sensibles are joined also with other
objects than visible ones, they are recognized as obviously distinct
from these.

ii. Objects appropriate to the several senses

Since we perceive that we see and hear, it must be either by
sight that we are cognizant of sight, or by some other sense. Let

---

[3] *Aesthêsis koinê:* not a sixth sense distinct from the other five, but a 'common sense' in the original meaning of that expression: i.e., a faculty of grasp-
ing the various types of sense-data as a single whole; of 'apperceiving' the
undivided nature of the object. Since the nineteenth century, however, 'common sense' has come to mean rather a faculty of holding unexamined opinions
of a somewhat practical nature.

us grant that sight is perceived by the same sense as perceives the color which is the immediate object of sight. Then, unless we are to assume that there are two distinct sense-faculties by which we perceive color, we must conclude that the one sense, sight, perceives itself. This is further supported by the consideration that if sight were perceived by some sense other than itself, either there would be an infinite regress [of senses perceived by other senses] or else somewhere in the series there would have to be a sense that perceived itself. Hence we may as well postulate such a sense in the first place.

But there is a difficulty. What we see is color, or something possessing color. Now since seeing is the same as perceiving by sight, it may be argued that if this sight is in turn an object of sight it will necessarily be colored. In reply we may say that to perceive by sight does not have a single invariable meaning. Even when we 'see nothing' we are in a manner seeing, for it is by sight that we are cognizant of darkness as something different from light. Besides, there is a respect in which it is true that the sense of sight is colored—in that what enters the eye is the sensible object divested of its matter.[4] This is the reason why sensations and images remain in the eye after the sensible objects are gone.

The activity of a sensible object is identical with that of the sense that perceives it, although the sense and its object are in their natures distinct. Consider, for instance, the relation of sound to hearing when both are active: for of course a man may have a sense of hearing and yet not hear, just as an object may possess sound without actually sounding. But when that which can sound does sound and that which can hear does hear, then the actual sound and the actual hearing—the phonation and the audition, so to speak—coincide. . . .

As the activity of the object is identical with that of the corresponding faculty of sense, although abstractly they are different, it follows that hearing and sound, so far as they are actual, must per-

[4] I.e., the color itself enters the eye, although the colored object does not.

sist or perish together. The same is true of flavor and taste, and of each other pair of sense-correlatives. Considered merely as potencies, on the other hand, the object and the sense exhibit no such necessary relation. The earlier natural philosophers were wrong in supposing that without sight there could be neither white nor black, and without taste no flavor. Their tenet is partly true and partly false. Sense and sensible object are ambiguous terms, connoting both potency and actuality; with respect to the latter meaning the statement holds true, with respect to the former it does not. Our predecessors too often failed to discriminate the different meanings implicit in their subject-matter.

If, then, there is a respect in which 'vocal sound' (*phonê*) and hearing are one and the same, and if concord (*symphonia*) is a species of vocal sound, and if concord consists in proportion (*logos*), it follows that hearing must also consist in a kind of proportion. This is the reason why hearing ceases when the pitch is too high or too low. In the same way, taste is nullified by excessive flavors, sight by extreme brilliancy or faintness of colors, smell by excessively strong odors, whether too cloying or too pungent. Such phenomena prove that sensation consists in a kind of due proportion. Moreover, this principle explains why it is that pure and unmixed qualities, such as the flavors acid, sweet, and salt, become pleasurable when combined in a suitable proportion; for they do. Generally speaking, too, a blend or concord of sounds is more pleasant to the ear than a high or low pitch alone; and moderate [or mixed] temperatures are more pleasing to the sense of touch. To conclude, then: sensation consists in due proportion; while excess in the object causes pain and destroys the operation of the sense.

Each sense has its own type of sense-object. Residing in its own sense-organ it discriminates the specific differences of the sense-objects proper to it. Thus sight discriminates between white and black, taste between sweet and bitter, and so on. But we can also discriminate between white and sweet, and in fact between any two sensible qualities; by what means, then, do we perceive generic differences such as these? It must be by sense, for all such qualities are objects of sense. Certainly flesh cannot be the ultimate organ of sense, for if it were we could discriminate sense-objects only by physical contact with them. Nor is it possible to discriminate between white and sweet by means of a different sense for each of them; there must be some one sense to which both of the compared qualities are discernibly present. Otherwise it would be like trying to establish a difference between two objects on the ground that you perceived one of them and I the other. Objects can be differentiated only where there is a single faculty to discriminate between them. In the case of white and sweet too, since these are recognized to be distinct, there must be a single faculty to affirm the distinction, and hence a single faculty which thinks and perceives them both. We may conclude from this that different things cannot be discriminated by a separate organ for each. . . .

iii. Perception distinguished from thought and imagination

There are two distinctive characteristics by which we principally define soul: (1) its power of causing movement; (2) thinking, judging, and perceiving. 'Abstract thinking' (noein) and 'typically human intelligence' (phronein) may thus be grouped along with perceiving, because in them, as in it, the soul discriminates and apprehends certain aspects of what exists. The ancients went so far as to identify intelligence (phronein) with perception. Thus Empedocles says, "It is in respect of what is present to the mind that man's wisdom (mêtis) is increased"; and again, "Thus they have an ever shifting array of thoughts." [5] Homer, too, says much the same thing in the passage beginning, "Such is the mind of man." All of them, in fact, treat thinking (noein) as a bodily process of the same order as perceiving; and declare that like can only be

[5] Evidently Aristotle interprets this second quotation from Empedocles to mean that since thought 'moves' it must be dependent on bodily movements and therein akin to sense-perception. The context of the words from Homer (Odyssey, XVIII, 136) supplies a similar meaning.

understood, as it can only be perceived, by like—a doctrine explained in our opening lectures.[6] They ought at the same time, however, to have considered the problem of error, which is a state intimately affinitive to animal life and in which the soul persists most of the time. On their premises they would have had either to accept the truth of whatever is presented to the mind, as some of them in fact do, or, abandoning the tenet that like is known only by like, to explain error as contact with what is unlike.[7] Yet error, like knowledge, is with respect to each of two contraries one and the same.[8]

Perception, then, is clearly not identical with intelligence; for all animals share in the one, and only a few in the other. As for 'thinking' in the narrower sense (*noein*)—which includes both right and wrong thinking, while right thinking in turn includes sagacity (*phronêsis*), understanding (*epistêmê*), and sound opinion (*doxa*), and wrong thinking the opposites of these—this too is distinguishable from perception. Perception, with respect to the objects of the sense directly involved, is always true,[9] and moreover is found in all animals; while thinking may be either true or false, and is limited to animals possessing 'articulate reason' (*logos*).

[Where does imagination (*phantasia*) fit into this scheme? Our

[6] The doctrine is referred to, but hardly explained, in Bk. I, Chap. ii, in a passage omitted from the present edition.

[7] The three propositions—(*p*) "Thought and perception are entirely caused by material processes"; (*q*) "Thought and perception may be erroneous"— i.e., *unlike* the material entities and processes to which they refer and by which, according to the postulate expressed by *p*, they are caused; (*r*) "A cause must be like its effect"—constitute an antilogism. All three of them cannot be simultaneously true; the truth of any two of them implies a denial of the third.

[8] To mistake beauty for ugliness is the same kind of error as to mistake ugliness for beauty, for the error in either case consists in an insufficiency of the aesthetic judgment. But on the materialistic hypothesis, the two errors will be opposite in character: the one will be a state of mind caused by ugliness but opposite to it in character, the other will be a state of mind caused by beauty but opposite to *it* in character. Aristotle's own theory, on the other hand, postulates a state of mind that is neither beautiful nor ugly, but is a 'mean' between them, in the sense of being potentially either.

[9] Cf. Bk. II, Chap. vi, p. 134.

answer must be that] [10] it is distinct from perception and thought (*dianoia*) alike, although it neither occurs without sensation nor is itself absent from any act of 'rational belief' (*hypolêpsis*). Yet [while 'rational belief' thus resembles thinking (*noêsis*) in its dependence on imagination], the two are not identical. So far as we are merely thinking, we have the power to imagine things whenever we please, seeing them in our mind's eye—as is most strikingly shown by the case of those who practice visualizing their ideas under mnemonic headings. But believing does not lie in our power, for we are up against the question of truth and falsity. Besides, when we believe that something is dreadful and alarming we at once feel the appropriate emotion, and so too with what we believe to be auspicious; whereas with regard to what is merely imagined we are no more affected than when we behold a picture of dreadful or reassuring objects. There are different forms of 'rational belief' (*hypolêpsis*): knowledge (*epistêmê*), 'sound opinion' (*doxa*), 'prudent counsel, or sagacity' (*phronêsis*), and their opposites. We shall elaborate these distinctions in another discourse.[11] But let us now postpone further inquiry about thinking until after we have determined the nature of imagination; for thinking, besides being quite different from sensation, appears to involve imagination and belief. . . .[12]

Whatever is in motion can produce motion in other objects. Imagination is held to be a sort of motion which presupposes sense-perception, inasmuch as it arises only in percipient beings and has the same content as what is perceived. Perceptions can cause motion, and when they do the motion thus produced must resemble the original perceptions. The resultant motion [of imagination]

---

[10] The bracketed words are an explication of the meaning of γάρ. Imagination is not taken up directly until the next paragraph.

[11] The reference is probably to Book VI of the *Nicomachean Ethics*, although the grouping there is different.

[12] In the omitted passage Aristotle demonstrates that imagination cannot be identical with either (1) sensation, or (2) opinion (*doxa*), or (3) sensation and opinion combined.

cannot exist apart from perception and percipient beings; it entails a variety of effects, both active and passive, in its possessor; and lastly, it is of such a nature as to admit of both truth and falsity.

This last characteristic may be explained as follows. So long as each sense merely perceives its own special objects, its perception is true, or subject to a minimum of falsity. But when we take the further step of perceiving these special sensibles as attributes belonging to certain actual things, we reach the stage at which deception becomes possible. The percipient cannot be mistaken as to the fact that he perceives white, but he may well be mistaken as to whether the white object is this thing or that. Finally, there is a third stage, where in perceiving the objects that are connected in this way with the special sensibles, we perceive also certain attributes of a common nature accompanying them: I mean, for example, movement and magnitude, which are indirectly connected with the original sensibles. It is in respect of such attributes that illusion is preëminently possible.

Now the motion that results from perceptual activity will differ according as it arises from one or another of these three types of perception. A resultant motion of the first type will be true so long as the bare sensation continues; while one that corresponds to the second or third type will admit of error whether the perception continues or not, and especially when the perceived object is far away. Accordingly, if imagination answers to the description just given, and has no other characteristics than those mentioned,[13] it follows that imagination must be this motion that results from the process of perception.

Since the motions that constitute imagination linger on [in the sense-organs] and resemble actual sensations, animals frequently act under their influence: if brutes, because they lack intellect (*nous*); if men, because their intellect is sometimes veiled by passion, disease, or sleep.

---

[13] Hicks suggests that the characteristics meant are dependence on sensation, presence in living beings, and fallibility. *Op. cit.*, his note on 428 b, 30.

Let this suffice as an account of the nature and causal basis of imagination.

iv. Mind: its receptive aspect

Coming now to that aspect or faculty of the soul whereby it knows (*gignôskein*) and 'takes counsel' (*phronein*), and putting aside the question of whether this aspect can be separated from the rest of the soul actually or only in thought, we must investigate both its distinguishing characteristics and the way in which its thinking (*noein*) occurs.

If thinking is analogous to perceiving it will be a process wherein [the intellectual aspect of the soul] is acted upon by an object capable of being thought; or at any rate, something similar to that. It follows that this aspect of the soul, although itself impassive, must be capable of receiving the form of the intelligible object: that is to say, it must be at once potentially like its object and actually distinct from it. In short, as the faculty of sense is related to sensible objects, so thought (*nous*) must be related to intelligible objects. And since everything is a possible object of thought, Anaxagoras was right in declaring that this aspect of the soul, in order to have authority over the things it knows, must be unmixed with any of them; for its functioning is hindered and impaired by the intrusion of anything alien. Accordingly, the intellectual faculty, like the sensitive, has no other intrinsic nature than that of being a certain capacity; from which it follows that 'mind' (*nous*), as we may call this aspect of the soul—I mean its thinking and judging aspect—has no actual existence before it thinks. This is another reason why we cannot properly regard it as containing an alloy of anything physical; for if it did, it would have had to take on particular qualities, such as coldness and warmth, and perhaps would even, like the sensitive faculty, have acquired a special organ of its own. But in fact nothing of the sort occurs. Hence [the Platonists] are justified in calling the soul the place of forms (*eidos*); although it should be recognized that this description applies not to the entire soul but only to its intellective aspect, and that the forms do not reside there actually but only potentially.

That the intellect does not become blunted in the same way that the senses do is evident from the nature of the senses and their organs. Over-excitation by its object deprives a sense of the power to perceive: we cannot hear after too loud a noise, nor see nor smell after colors and odors of unusual intensity. Mind, on the contrary, when it has been reflecting on objects of an unusually rational character, is thereafter not worse but all the better equipped to deal with lesser matters. This is because the faculty of sensation is dependent upon the body, whereas mind is separable from it.

When the mind has actualized itself with respect to each set of its potential objects—as in the case of a true savant, who has achieved entire control over his mind—then, although it is still to be regarded as a capacity, it is no longer the same kind of capacity as before it had learnt or discovered its knowledge; for it has now become able to think *itself*. . . .

If it is true that the mind is something simple and impassive and that it has, in Anaxagoras' words, nothing in common with anything else, and if to think is to be acted upon, the question may be raised how in that case the mind can possibly think. For we assume that one thing can act upon another only so far as both have some element or aspect in common. A second objection might be raised against our doctrine that mind can know itself. For if mind can thus know itself by its own unaided power, and if the objects of its knowledge must be one and the same in kind; it will follow either that all the objects of mind contain a portion of mind in themselves, or else that the mind's own character contains an admixture of the character possessed by its objects, by virtue of which they are known.

[Regarding the former of these criticisms,] we may refer to our preceding analysis of what is meant by 'being acted upon in virtue of a common element'; where we pointed out that the mind is 'potentially,' so to speak, identical with its objects, but is not actually identical with any of them until it thinks [them]: just as figures may be regarded as existing potentially on a writing-tablet which contains as yet no actual writing. This is precisely the case with mind.

[To the second criticism it may be replied that] mind is intellectually knowable in the same way as its objects are. For where the objects are not such as possess 'physical substance' (*hylê*), the thinking and the thought-of object are identical in any case. That is to say, all 'contemplative knowledge' (*epistêmê theôrêtikê*) is identical with its object. This suggests, by the way, the question why our thinking is not uninterrupted.[14] Where, on the contrary, the objects of thought are themselves material, it is only potentially [i.e., in their formal aspect] that they are identical with thought. Consequently, since mind is the power of becoming these objects without their matter, it follows that the objects themselves do not contain mind, and yet that the mind itself may be an object of its own thinking.

v. Mind: its active, independent aspect

Since each general class of things in nature, like nature itself, has (1) a material basis, i.e., an original capacity of becoming any of the things included within the class, and also (2) a creative (*poiêtikos*) cause that makes the things actual—cf. the relation of art to its material—this same pair of distinct factors must likewise be present in the soul. In its passive aspect, described above, mind is capable [of experiencing and therein] of becoming all things; but it has also another aspect in which it [wills or] 'makes' all things, therein manifesting a 'determinate character' (*hexis*)—like light, which may be regarded as making potential colors into actual ones. In this latter aspect mind is separable [from body], impassive, and unmixed; for it is essentially an activity, and whatever

[14] I.e., if the abstract objects of thought are indestructible and if thought is identical with them, how can thought ever cease to be? Aristotle touches on this question briefly in the next chapter.

acts is superior to what is acted upon, the 'moving principle' (*archê*) to the matter.[15]

Mind is not intermittent in its activity. Its true nature becomes apparent, however, only when it is separated [from the lower functions], and is revealed as our only deathless and eternal part, without which nothing thinks. But we have no recollection of the activity of mind in a pure state; [16] for when mind is in that state it is not affected by impressions; while conversely, the impressionable side of mind is perishable.

vi. How error is possible

In cases where thinking cannot err its objects are unanalyzable wholes; but where both truth and falsity are possible there has been a previous synthesis of the objects of thought into a sort of unity. As "where neckless heads of many creatures sprouted forth" and were afterwards, Empedocles tells us, combined by Love, so objects of thought are first cognized separately and then joined— e.g. the ideas of the incommensurable and the diagonal. If such thinking refers to past or future, time becomes an element in the synthesis. Falsehood always presupposes a synthesis; for even if we declare white to be not white, the idea of 'not-white' is made an element in such a synthesis.[17] Such statements can also be regarded as cases of disjunction. At any rate, the question of true or false applies not only to the assertion that Cleon is fair, but also to the assertion that he was or will be fair. The unifying agency is in every case the mind. . . .

Every proposition (*phasis*), as is perhaps most evident in the case of an affirmation (*kataphasis*), predicates something of something, and therein becomes either true or false. But this does not

[15] I omit two sentences here, as evidently misplaced, and as recurring four paragraphs later.—Tr.

[16] Before birth, for instance, as taught by the Platonists and Pythagoreans. I have altered the position of these clauses.—Tr.

[17] Probably this is offered as an answer to the objection that an erroneous denial, since it contains only one positive term, cannot depend upon a prior mental synthesis.

hold good for all acts of mind. When the mind asserts the 'whatness' (*ti esti*) of a thing—i.e., its 'constitutive and enduring essence' (*ti ên einai*)—it is not making a predicative judgment, and hence cannot err. Just as sight is infallible in its awareness that a certain visible datum is white, although perhaps deceived in taking this white datum for a man, so it is likewise with immaterial entities.

vii. The process of cognition

Actual knowledge is identical with the known object. In individuals potential knowledge is prior in time to actual knowledge; but this priority does not hold true universally,[18] for whatever comes into existence must come from something that already actually exists. [In the case of individuals, at any rate,] what obviously occurs is that a sense-faculty which is already potentially sentient is made actively sentient by the presence of a sensible object, without being thereby affected or qualitatively altered. It follows that the motion of perceiving through the senses is a somewhat special kind of motion. For whereas we have defined motion to be a 'self-realizing activity' (*energeia*) of what is still imperfect, there is also an absolute and quite distinct sense in which we can speak of the activity of a perfected thing.

Sensation is thus analogous to the bare formulation or immediate intellectual apprehension of a proposition; and when its object is pleasant or painful the soul's pursuit or avoidance of it is a sort of affirmation or negation. Indeed, to feel pleasure and pain is nothing else than to respond with our general sensibility [19] to good and evil as such, and this is what constitutes desire and avoidance. The faculties of desire and avoidance are, in actual fact, identical both with each other and with the sensitive faculty, although there is a logical distinction between them.

In the thinking soul images may take the place of sensations, and it is these images that the soul pursues and avoids when affirming

---

[18] I.e., in the universe as a whole.
[19] Lit., "with the sensitive 'mean' (*mesotês*)."

or denying good or evil. . . . The thinking faculty thinks its ideas (*eidos*) in terms of images (*phantasma*). Not only do sensations determine for the mind its objects of pursuit and avoidance, but independently of sensations, when the mind is wholly preoccupied with its mental images, it may likewise be moved to action. We may, for example, perceive a lighted beacon, and then, observing by our 'central sense' that it is in motion, take it to mean that the enemy is coming. But at other times we base our reasoning on the images and thoughts within the soul, building our deliberations about the future on these images now present. And when we declare an object of sense-experience to be pleasurable or painful, our subsequent thoughts about it eventuate in pursuit or avoidance, or, generally speaking, in action.

There are also ideas that involve no action, such as truth and falsity. They belong in the same 'generic category' (*genos*) as good and evil, but differ in that they are absolute while these are relative to the persons concerned.

How the soul discriminates between [the qualities appropriate to the different senses, such as] sweet and hot, has already been explained and may be recapitulated as follows. There is an aspect of the soul that at once unifies and delimits [its several faculties]. The several faculties, besides being similarly related to their respective objects, have thus an actual connection within the soul; and their relation to each other is the same as that of the corresponding sensible qualities to each other. This is equally true whether we are comparing qualities falling under different genera [like sweet and hot] or contraries [belonging to the same genus] like white and black. . . .[20]

---

[20] Cf., however, Chap. ii, p. 140, where it is declared that comparisons of this latter kind are the function of the particular sense that perceives the compared qualities. That was evidently an earlier and tentative hypothesis. Aristotle's mature theory, stated in the present chapter, is that the 'central sense' or 'general sensibility' comes into play not only in discriminating between heterogeneous qualities like sweet and hot but also in discriminating and comparing opposite qualities belonging to a single genus. The last two

How we conceive the so-called abstract objects may be illustrated by the way in which we conceive the snub-nosed. Quâ
snub-nosed we are not conceiving it abstractly; but quâ concave
shape (supposing we were really to think of it in that aspect) we
should be conceiving it in abstraction from the flesh in which the
concavity is embodied. Similarly, when we conceive mathematical
objects we conceive them as separate from matter, although in
fact they are not separate. And in every case the mind is identical
with the objects that it is actively engaged in thinking about. How,
then, is it possible for the mind, not being itself independent of
spatial conditions, to conceive what is independent? We shall re-
serve this question for a later discussion.

ix. The faculty of locomotion

The soul in animals is defined in terms of two faculties: the
power of discrimination, which is the work of thought and of sense-
perception, and the power of locomotion. Having sufficiently discussed sensation and thought, let us consider next what it is in the
soul that causes movement: whether it is some part of the soul that
can be logically or even spatially distinguished from the rest, or
whether it is the whole soul; and if it is only a part, whether it is
a peculiar part distinct from those usually recognized and here
enumerated, or whether it is some one of these. . . . The motion
of growth and decay, as it is found in all animals, must evidently
have its source in the generative and nutritive powers which all
possess. [Other animal motions such as] breathing and exhaling,
sleeping and waking, present such difficulties that they may best
be postponed until later.[21] For the present let us consider only
locomotion and ask what it is that produces progressive movements
in animals.

---

paragraphs have been rearranged from the text, for the sake of better co-
herence.

[21] See the *Parva Naturalia*: Essays iii, "On Sleeping and Waking," and viii,
"On Respiration."

Clearly it is neither (1) the nutritive . . . nor (2) the sensitive faculty. . . .[22] Nor (3) is it the power of reasoning, or as we call it the mind (*nous*); for the mind in its speculative character does not exercise itself upon questions of what is to be done, nor make any assertion regarding what is to be avoided or pursued, whereas the movement of which we are speaking always involves avoidance or pursuit of something. Even though it may be intellectually aware of an object to be avoided or pursued, the mind does not thereby prompt us to the appropriate action. Frequently, it will contemplate something dreadful or something pleasant without inducing fear; the only effect being a quickened heart-beat, or, in the case of what is pleasant, some other bodily motion. Moreover, even when our reason (*nous*) commands and our understanding (*dianoia*) bids us shun or pursue a thing, action does not necessarily follow—as we may see in the conduct of one who is incontinent. And as a more general analogy, we observe that one who has a knowledge of medicine does not necessarily practice it: showing that there must be some factor which, though not itself knowledge, may determine action in accordance with knowledge. Lastly, (4) the movement of which we are speaking is not accounted for wholly in terms of desire. Continent men, though prompted by desire and appetite, do not yield to their inclinations, but follow reason.

x. The source of animal locomotion

At any rate, it is apparently these two, 'appetency or desire' (*orexis*) and thought (*nous*), that are the motive causes [in animals]. Imagination (*phantasia*) may be regarded as a species of thought. [It must, of course, be included in any explanation of animal movement, for] men often follow their fancies to the neglect of what they know, and in the other animals there is no thinking (*noêsis*) or calculating (*logismos*), but only imagination.

---

[22] Omitting a short passage in which Aristotle demonstrates that neither the nutritive nor the sensitive faculty can be the source of locomotion.

Locomotion, then, is produced by a combination of these two factors, thought and appetency. By thought we here mean practical thought, which calculates the means to an end; it differs from speculative thought in that it is motivated by a purpose. Appetency, too, is in every case directed to some end: the thing desired is the starting-point of the operation of the 'practical intellect' (*praktikos nous*), while the last stage of this is the starting-point of action. Hence there is good reason to regard these two, appetency and practical thought, as the factors productive of animal movement. The cause of movement is an object desired; and when thought causes movement, it is because a desired object was what started the thought itself. Likewise when imagination prompts us to action, it never does so apart from appetency.

Thus at bottom there is a single cause of movement, and this is the appetitive faculty; for if both appetency and thought were causes, this could only be by virtue of some characteristic that they shared. But the fact of the matter seems to be that thought without appetency does not produce movement; for when movement is produced by deliberate calculation it is produced in accordance with a 'conscious wish' (*boulêsis*), which is a form of appetency. But appetency can also move us contrary to reason; for concupiscence (*epithymia*) does this, and concupiscence is a species of appetency. Thought is universally right, while appetite and imagination may be either right or wrong. Hence, while it is always the object of appetency that causes movement, this object may be either the real good or the merely apparent good. Nor will every kind of good serve, but only such good as can be realized in action; and in order to be realizable in action a thing must be capable of being other than it actually is. . . .

When impulses conflict it is because reason and the appetites are opposed, and this opposition occurs in those animals which have a sense of time. Thought bids us resist because of the future, while appetite (*epithymia*) regards only the present: the immediate pleasure seems to be absolutely pleasant and absolutely good simply because we do not see the future. Hence, while the moving cause will be of a single kind—i.e., the faculty of appetency considered in its essential character, and beyond that the object of appetency, which though not itself in motion causes motion by being thought of or imagined—there is actually a considerable number of moving causes.

Movement involves three factors: (1) a cause of the movement, (2) an instrument by means of which the movement is produced, and (3) a thing moved. The determining factor of the movement may be interpreted in a twofold sense: either as an unmoved [i.e., unchanging] principle of motion, or as something which, being in motion itself, imparts its motion to another thing. [In the case of animal movement] the determining factor in the former sense [i.e., the unchanging principle of motion] is the practical good. The moving cause that imparts its own motion is the appetitive faculty, for the animal becomes active to just the extent that desire is active within it, and desire in process of realization is a kind of motion. The thing moved is the animal. The instrument which desire employs in producing movement is of a bodily nature, and must accordingly be investigated when we come to deal with the functions common to body and soul. At this point we need only observe summarily that [the instrument of] organic movement is located where beginning and end coincide. An example of this is the joints, in which the convex ball and the concave socket mark an end and a beginning respectively; and that is why the one of them remains at rest while the other is moving—the two being logically distinct but physically inseparable. All physical motion is caused by pushing and pulling; hence there must be in the moving things a fixed point, like the hub of a wheel, in which the movement originates.

Restating our position very generally, then: to just the extent that an animal is capable of desire, it is capable of self-movement. Capacity for desire presupposes imagination, and all imagination is either rational or sensuous. The latter variety is shared by man with the other animals. . . .

The Nicomachean Ethics

The Nicomachean Ethics

BOOK I

THE AIM OF MAN

i. Definition of the good

EVERY ART (*techn̂ê*) and every 'scientific investigation' (*methodos*), as well as every action (*praxis*) and 'purposive choice' (*proairesis*), appears to aim at some good; hence the good has rightly been declared to be that at which all things aim. A difference is observable, to be sure, among the several ends: some of them are activities (*energeia*), while others are products (*ergon*) over and above the activities that produce them. Wherever there are certain ends over and above the actions themselves, it is the nature of such products to be better than the activities.

As actions and arts and sciences (*epistêmê*) are of many kinds, there must be a corresponding diversity of ends (*telos*): health, for example, is the aim of medicine, ships of ship-building, victory of military strategy, and wealth of domestic economics. Where several such arts fall under some one faculty (*dynamis*) [1]—as bridle-making and the other arts concerned with horses' equipment fall under horsemanship, while this in turn along with all other military matters falls under the head of strategy, and similarly in the case of other arts—the aim of the master art is always more

---

[1] An 'art or technique' (*techn̂ê*) may be regarded as a capability of action, and is accordingly sometimes referred to by Aristotle as a *dynamis*.

choiceworthy (*hairetos*) than the aims of its subordinate arts, inasmuch as these are pursued for its sake. And this holds equally good whether the end in view is just the activity itself or something distinct from the activity, as in the case of the sciences above mentioned.

ii. Primacy of statecraft

If in all our conduct, then, there is some end that we wish on its own account, choosing everything else as a means to it; if, that is to say, we do not choose everything as a means to something else (for at that rate we should go on *ad infinitum*, and our desire would be left empty and vain); then clearly this one end must be the good—even, indeed, the highest good. Will not a knowledge of it, then, have an important influence on our lives? Will it not better enable us to hit the right mark, like archers who have a definite target to aim at? If so, we must try to comprehend, in outline at least, what that highest end is, and to which of the sciences or arts it belongs.

Evidently the art or science in question must be the most absolute and most authoritative of all. Statecraft (*politikê*) answers best to this description; for it prescribes which of the sciences are to have a place in the state, and which of them are to be studied by the different classes of citizens, and up to what point; and we find that even the most highly esteemed of the arts (*dynamis*) are subordinated to it, e.g. military strategy, domestic economics, and oratory (*rhetorikê*). So then, since statecraft employs all the other sciences, prescribing also what the citizens are to do and what they are to refrain from doing, its aim must embrace the aims of all the others; whence it follows that the aim of statecraft is man's proper good. Even supposing the chief good to be eventually the same for the individual as for the state, that of the state is evidently of greater and more fundamental importance both to attain and to preserve. The securing of even one individual's good is cause for rejoicing, but to secure the good of a nation (*ethnos*) or of a city-state (*polis*) is nobler and more divine. This, then, is the aim of our present inquiry, which is in a sense the study of statecraft.

iii. *Two observations on the study of ethics*

Our discussion will be adequate if we are content with as much precision as is appropriate to the subject-matter; for the same degree of exactitude ought no more to be expected in all kinds of reasoning than in all kinds of handicraft. Excellence and justice, the things with which statecraft deals, involve so much disagreement and uncertainty that they come to be looked on as mere conventions, having no natural foundation. The good involves a similar uncertainty, inasmuch as good things often prove detrimental: there are examples of people destroyed by wealth, of others destroyed by courage. In such matters, then, and starting from such premises as we do, we must be content with a rough approximation to the truth; for when we are dealing with and starting out from what holds good only 'as a general rule,' the conclusions that we reach will have the same character. Let each of the views put forward be accepted in this spirit, for it is the mark of an educated mind to seek only so much exactness in each type of inquiry as may be allowed by the nature of the subject-matter. It is equally wrong to accept probable reasoning from a mathematician and to demand strict demonstrations from an orator.

A man judges well and is called a good judge of the things about which he knows. If he has been educated in a particular subject he is a good judge of that subject; if his education has been well-rounded he is a good judge in general. Hence no very young man is qualified to attend lectures on statecraft; for he is inexperienced in the affairs of life, and these form the data and subject-matter of statecraft. Moreover, so long as he tends to be swayed by his feelings he will listen vainly and without profit, for the purport of these [lectures] is not purely theoretical but practical. Nor does it make any difference whether his immaturity is a matter of years or of character: the defect is not a matter of time, but consists in the fact that his life and all his pursuits are under the control of his passions. Men of this sort, as is evident from the case of those we call incontinent, do not turn their knowledge to any account in practice; but those whose desires and actions are controlled by reason will derive much profit from a knowledge of these matters.

So much, then, for our prefatory remarks about the student, the manner of inquiry, and the aim.

iv. The good as happiness

To resume, then: since all knowledge and all purpose aims at some good, what is it that we declare to be the aim of statecraft; or, in other words, what is the highest of all realizable goods? As to its name there is pretty general agreement: the majority of men, as well as the cultured few, speak of it as happiness (*eudaimonia*); and they would maintain that to live well and to do well are the same thing as to be happy. They differ, however, as to what happiness is, and the mass of mankind give a different account of it from philosophers. The former take it to be something palpable and obvious, like pleasure or wealth or fame; they differ, too, among themselves, nor is the same man always of one mind about it: when ill he identifies it with health, when poor with wealth; then growing aware of his ignorance about the whole matter he feels admiration for anyone who proclaims some grand ideal above his comprehension. And to add to the confusion, there have been some philosophers who held that besides the various particular good things there is an absolute good which is the cause of all particular goods. As it would hardly be worth while to examine all the opinions that have been entertained, we shall confine our attention to those that are most popular or that appear to have some rational foundation.

One point not to be overlooked is the difference between arguments that start from first principles and arguments that lead up to first principles. Plato very wisely used to raise this question, and to ask whether the right way is from or toward first principles—

as in the race-course there is a difference between running from
the judges to the boundary-line and running back again. Granted
that we must start with what is known, this may be interpreted in
a double sense: as what is familiar to us or as what is intelligible
in itself. Our own method, at any rate, must be to start with what
is familiar to us. That is why a sound moral training is required
before a man can listen intelligently to discussions about excellence
and justice, and generally speaking, about statecraft. For in this
field we must take as our 'first principles' plain facts; if these are
sufficiently evident we shall not insist upon the whys and where-
fores. Such principles are in the possession of, or at any rate readily
accessible to, the man with a sound moral training. As for the man
who neither possesses nor can acquire them, let him hear the words
of Hesiod: [2]

> Best is he who makes his own discoveries;
> Good is he who listens to the wise;
> But he who, knowing not, rejects another's wisdom
>   Is a plain fool.

v. Conflicting views of happiness

Let us now resume our discussion from the point at which we
digressed. What is happiness, or the chief good? If it is permissible
to judge from men's actual lives, we may say that the mass of them,
being vulgarians, identify it with pleasure, which is the reason why
they aim at nothing higher than a life of enjoyment. For there
are three outstanding types of life: the one just mentioned, the
political, and, thirdly, the contemplative. 'The mass of men' (hoi
polloi) reveal their utter slavishness by preferring a life fit only
for cattle; yet their views have a certain plausibility from the fact
that many of those in high places share the tastes of Sardanapalus.[3]
Men of superior refinement and active disposition, on the other

---

[2] Works and Days, ll. 293–297.
[3] An ancient Assyrian king to whom is attributed the saying, "Eat, drink,
and be merry: nothing else is worth a snap of the fingers."

hand, identify happiness with honor, this being more or less the aim of a statesman's life. It is evidently too superficial, however, to be the good that we are seeking; for it appears to depend rather on him who bestows than on him who receives it, while we may suspect the chief good to be something peculiarly a man's own, which he is not easily deprived of. Besides, men seem to pursue honor primarily in order to assure themselves of their own merit; at any rate, apart from personal acquaintances, it is by those of sound judgment that they seek to be appreciated, and on the score of virtue (*aretê*). Clearly, then, they imply that virtue is superior to honor: and so, perhaps, we should regard this rather than honor as the end and aim of the statesman's life. Yet even about virtue there is a certain incompleteness; for it is supposed that a man may possess it while asleep or during lifelong inactivity, or even while suffering the greatest disasters and misfortunes; and surely no one would call such a man happy, unless for the sake of a paradox. But we need not further pursue this subject, which has been sufficiently treated of in current discussions. Thirdly, there is the contemplative life, which we shall examine at a later point.

As for the life of money-making, it is something unnatural.[4] Wealth is clearly not the good that we are seeking, for it is merely useful as a means to something else. Even the objects above mentioned come closer to possessing intrinsic goodness than wealth does, for they at least are cherished on their own account. But not even they, it seems, can be the chief good, although much labor has been lost in attempting to prove them so. With this observation we may close the present subject.

vi. Criticism of the Platonic doctrine of archetypes

Perhaps we ought now to consider the notion of a universal good and the difficulties that it involves; although such an inquiry is a little embarrassing because those who have introduced the theory

---

[4] Lit., 'violent'—i.e., doing violence to nature. Grant translates: "But the life of gain is in a way compulsory."

of forms (*eidos*) are friends.[5] Nevertheless it would appear to be the better course, and indeed the only right one, if we lay claim to the title of philosophers, to sacrifice in the interests of truth even what lies closest to us. Both are dear, but it is a sacred duty to put truth first.

(1) Those who have supplied us with the theory of forms did not themselves postulate archetypes (*idea*) for classes whose members they described as prior and posterior to one another;[6] and for this reason they did not provide for an archetype of numbers. The term good, however, is predicated alike in the categories of substance, of quality, and of relation; and of these, substance, being absolute, is prior by nature to what is merely relative (this being an offshoot or 'logical accident' of substance); consequently there can be, on their own showing, no common archetype of good.

(2) Again, the term 'good' is used in as many different senses as we use the verb 'is.' We apply it as predicate in the category of substance, as when we say that God and reason are good; in the category of quality, as applied to the virtues; of quantity, as applied to the moderate and due amount; of relation, as applied to what is useful; of time, as applied to what is opportune; of place, as applied to an abode; and so on. Clearly, then, the good cannot be something at once universally present in all cases and single. It could be so only if it were applied as predicate not in all the categories but in a single one only.

(3) Again, as there is a single science for all the things that fall under any one form, there would have to be a single science of all types of good. As a matter of fact, however, there are many sciences

---

[5] See Introduction, pp. xvi; xxix–xxx.

[6] I.e., related in such a way that one implies another without being in turn implied by it. In Aristotle's doctrine, 4 implies 3, because without the smaller number the larger could not exist, but 3 does not in the same way imply 4. Similarly, he held, 'substance, or thinghood' (*ousia*) is prior to quality and relation, because a quality must be a quality of some substance, and a relation can subsist only between substances; whereas although a substance never, to be sure, exists without qualities and relations, they are not a part of its essential nature, but are superadded to it.

even of the goods that fall under one category: what is opportune, for example, in war is a question of strategy, in disease of medicine; and what is the due amount in the matter of food is a question of medicine, but in the matter of exercise a question of gymnastic.

(4) As still a further objection we might ask just what they mean by the expression 'as such.' [7] The same definition applies to 'man as such' or 'ideal man' as to 'man': in so far as both of them mean *man* there is no difference between them. Neither, then, will there be any difference in respect of goodness between the 'good as such' or 'ideal good' and simply the good. The good is not made more real by being eternal, any more than a white thing becomes more truly white by reason of lasting a long time.

There seems to be more plausibility in the account given by the Pythagoreans, who give unity a place in their column of goods; [8] and even Speusippus seems to follow them in this. But these points will be discussed elsewhere.

Objection may be taken to the foregoing remarks on the ground that the theory of the Platonists does not refer to all goods indiscriminately, and that only those that are pursued and welcomed for their own sake are called good by reference to a single 'form' of good, while those that tend in any way to produce or preserve these, or to prevent their opposites, are called good only vicariously and in a different sense. Clearly, then, goods must be spoken of in two ways, some being good in themselves and others by reason of these. Let us then separate from the things that are merely useful those that are good in themselves, and inquire whether even they are called good by reference to a single archetype. To begin

[7] *Auto-(h)ekastos:* "the ideal so-and-so"—Rackham; "the absolute"— Grant and Peters; "thing-in-itself or thing in the abstract"—Hatch.

[8] This refers to the Pythagorean doctrine of opposites, which interprets reality in terms of ten pairs of opposing principles: see p. 7, n. 2. Apparently the passage means (as Stewart suggests) that the Pythagoreans do not, like the Platonists, make the good an abstract unity separate from things; according to their doctrine unity is only one of many sorts of good thing—i.e., to be a united whole is only one of many ways of being good. On this interpretation, the passage is best regarded as a gloss to Objection 2 above.

with, what sort of things are called good in themselves? Are they not those things which are sought after even apart from any consequences they might entail—e.g., wisdom, sight, and certain pleasures and honors? For although we sometimes strive after these things as means to something else, still anyone would class them among the things good in themselves. Or shall we say that only the archetype (*idea*) of goodness is good in itself? If so, then this 'form' (*eidos*) will be empty of any content. If, on the contrary, not only goodness but also the specific good things above mentioned belong to the class of things good in themselves, then we must be able to show that the logical meaning of good is the same in all of them, as that of whiteness is the same in snow and in white lead. But as a matter of fact the meanings of honor, of wisdom, and of pleasure are different even in respect of their goodness. Hence it follows that good is not some element common to all of these several things and implying a single archetype.

In what sense, then, are different things called good? They can hardly have received the same name purely by chance. Do we call them all good because they have been derived from a single good, or because they aim at a single good? Perhaps it is rather by a kind of analogy: e.g., as sight is good in the body, so reason is good in the soul, and so other things are good in other connections.[9] But we may as well dismiss this question for the present: a more detailed discussion would belong more properly to another branch of philosophy.

(5) For the same reason we may dismiss the question of an archetype; for even if we grant that there is a unitary good which is possessed in common by all good things while at the same time it is separable from them and capable of an independent existence, clearly it will not be anything that man can attain to or realize in action; and this is the sort of good we are now seeking. However,

---

[9] I.e., different things are called good not because they share an identical element, but because they are analogous to one another in that each of them contributes in *some* manner to the welfare of *some* other thing.

it might be argued that to know the ideal good is worth while as an aid in securing those goods whose attainment and practical realization is possible; on the ground that having it as a pattern we shall know better what things are specifically good for us, and that by this knowledge we shall be enabled to achieve them. While this argument has some plausibility, it appears to be at variance with the procedure of the sciences; for although all of them aim at some good and strive to make progress toward it,[10] they make no attempt to know about the ideal good. Surely if such knowledge were as useful as it is claimed to be, we would scarcely expect to find all the experts both ignorant of it and indifferent to it. Finally, it is hard to see just how a knowledge of this 'good in itself' is going to help a weaver or carpenter in the practice of his craft, or how anyone by contemplating the pure archetype will thereby become a better physician or a better general. This is evidently not the way in which a physician studies health. He studies the health of man, or rather of some particular man; for it is individuals that he has to cure.

So much, then, for the theories of the Platonists.

vii. Functional definition of man's highest good

Returning now to the good that we are seeking, let us inquire into its nature. Evidently it is different in different actions and arts (*techné*): it is not the same thing in medicine as in strategy, and so on. What definition of good will apply to all the arts? Let us say it is that for the sake of which all else is done. In medicine this is health, in the art of war victory, in building it is a house, and in each of the arts something different, although in every case, wherever there is action and choice involved, it is a certain end; because it is always for the sake of a certain end that all else is done. If, then, there is one end and aim of all our actions, this will be the realizable good; if there are several such ends, these

[10] Lit., "make up their deficiency [with respect to it]."

jointly will be our realizable goods. Thus in a roundabout way the discussion has been brought back to the same point as before; [11] which we must now try to explain more clearly.

As there is evidently a plurality of ends, and as some of these are chosen only as means to ulterior ends (e.g., wealth, flutes, and instruments in general), it is clear that not all ends are final (*teleios*). But the supreme good must of course be something final. Accordingly, if there is only one final end, this will be the good that we are seeking; and if there is more than one such end, the most complete and final of them will be this good. Now we call what is pursued as an end in itself more final than what is pursued as a means to something else; and what is never chosen as a means we call more final than what is chosen both as an end in itself and as a means; in fact, when a thing is chosen always as an end in itself and never as a means we call it absolutely final. Happiness (*eudaimonia*) seems, more than anything else, to answer to this description: for it is something we choose always for its own sake and never for the sake of something else; while honor, pleasure, reason, and all the virtues, though chosen partly for themselves (for we might choose any one of them without heeding the result), are chosen also for the sake of the happiness which we suppose they will bring us. Happiness, on the other hand, is never chosen for the sake of any of these, nor indeed as a means to anything else at all.

We seem to arrive at the same conclusion if we start from the notion of self-sufficiency (*autarkeia*); for the final good is admittedly self-sufficient. To be self-sufficient we do not mean that an individual must live in isolation. Parents, children, wife, as well as friends and fellow-citizens generally, are all permissible; for man is by nature political.[12] To be sure, some limit has to be set to such relationships, for if they are extended to embrace ancestors, de-

---

[11] Cf. the beginning of Chap. ii.
[12] *Politikos:* "born for citizenship"—Ross.

scendants, and friends of friends, we should go on *ad infinitum.*
But this point will be considered later on; [13] provisionally we may
attribute self-sufficiency to that which taken by itself makes life
choiceworthy and lacking in nothing. Such a thing we conceive
happiness to be. Moreover, we regard happiness as the most
choiceworthy of all things; nor does this mean that it is merely one
good thing among others, for if that were the case it is plain that
the addition of even the least of those other goods would increase
its desirability; since the addition would create a larger amount of
good, and of two goods the greater is always to be preferred. Evidently, then, happiness is something final and self-sufficient, and
is the end and aim of all that we do.

But perhaps it will be objected that to call happiness the supreme good is a mere truism, and that a clearer account of it is
still needed. We can give this best, probably, if we ascertain the
proper function (*ergon*) of man. Just as the excellence and good
performance of a flute-player, a sculptor, or any kind of artist,
and generally speaking of anyone who has a function or business
to perform, lies always in that function, so man's good would seem
to lie in the function of man, if he has one. But can we suppose
that while a carpenter and a cobbler each has a function and mode
of activity of his own, man quâ man has none, but has been left by
nature functionless? Surely it is more likely that as his several
members, eye and hand and foot, can be shown to have each its
own function, so man too must have a function over and above
the special functions of his various members. What will such a
function be? Not merely to live, of course: he shares that even
with plants, whereas we are seeking something peculiar to himself. We must exclude, therefore, the life of nutrition and growth.
Next comes sentient life, but this again is had in common with the
horse, the ox, and in fact all animals whatever. There remains only
the 'practical' [14] life of his rational nature; and this has two aspects,

---

[13] In Bk. IX, Chap. x; omitted from the present edition.
[14] *Praktikos.* Aristotle generally uses this word with an ethical significance,

one of which is rational in the sense that it obeys a 'rational principle' (*logos*), the other in the sense that it possesses and exercises reason (*logos*). To avoid ambiguity let us specify that by 'rational' we mean the 'exercise or activity' (*energeia*), not the mere possession, of reason; for it is the former that would seem more properly entitled to the name. Thus we conclude that man's function is an activity of the soul in conformity with, or at any rate involving the use of, 'rational principle' (*logos*).

An individual and a superior individual who belong to the same class (*genos*) we regard as sharing the same function: a harpist and a good harpist, for instance, are essentially the same. This holds true of any class of individuals whatever; for superior excellence with respect to a function is nothing but an amplification of that selfsame function: e.g., the function of a harpist is to play the harp, while that of a good harpist is to play it well. This being so, if we take man's proper function to be a certain kind of life, viz. an activity and conduct of the soul that involves reason, and if it is the part of a good man to perform such activities well and nobly, and if a function is well performed when it is performed in accordance with its own proper excellence; we may conclude that the good of man is an activity of the soul in accordance with *happiness* virtue, or, if there be more than one virtue, in accordance with the best and most perfect (*teleios*) of them. And we must add, in a complete (*teleios*) life. For one swallow does not make a spring, nor does one fine day; and similarly one day or brief period of happiness does not make a man happy (*eudaimôn*) and blessed (*makarios*).

So much, then, for a rough outline of the good: the proper procedure being, we may suppose, to sketch an outline first and afterwards to fill in the details. When a good outline has been made, almost anyone presumably can expand it and fill it out; and time

---

as connoting purposive activity, of which man alone is capable. Cf. Kant's use of the word (Germ. *praktisch*) in the title of his work on ethics, *Critique of Practical Reason*. 'Rational' is a translation of *logon echôn*, 'having reason.'

is a good inventor and collaborator in this work. It is in just such a way that progress has been made in the various 'human techniques' (*techné*); for filling in the gaps is something anybody can do.

But in all this we must bear constantly in mind our previous warning: not to expect the same degree of precision in all fields, but only so much as belongs to a given subject-matter and is appropriate to a particular 'type of inquiry' (*methodos*). Both the carpenter and the geometer investigate the right angle, but in different ways: the one wants only such an approximation to it as will serve his work; the other, being concerned with truth, seeks to determine its essence or essential attributes. And so in other subjects we must follow a like procedure, lest we be so much taken up with side issues that we pass over the matter in hand. Similarly we ought not in all cases to demand the 'reason why' (*aitia*); sometimes it is enough to point out the bare fact. This is true, for instance, in the case of 'first principles' (*arché*); for a bare fact must always be the ultimate starting-point (*arché*) of any inquiry. First principles may be arrived at in a variety of ways: some by induction, some by direct perception, some by a kind of habituation, and others in other ways. In each case we should try to apprehend them in whatever way is proper to them, and we should take care to define them clearly, because they will have a considerable influence upon the subsequent course of our inquiry. A good beginning [15] is more than half of the whole inquiry, and once established clears up many of its difficulties.

viii. Confirmation by popular beliefs

It is important to consider our ethical 'first principle' not merely as a conclusion drawn from certain premises, but also in its relation to popular opinion; for all data harmonize with a true principle,

---

[15] A pun on the word *arché*, which means in general 'beginning,' but which Aristotle has been using in the more special sense of 'first principle.' Cf. the adage, "Well begun is half done."

but with a false one they are soon found to be discordant. Now it has been customary to divide good things into three classes: external goods on the one hand, and on the other goods of the soul and goods of the body; and those of the soul we call good in the highest sense, and in the fullest degree. 'Conscious actions' (*praxis*), i.e. 'active expressions of our nature' (*energeia*), we take, of course, as belonging to the soul; and thus our account is confirmed by the doctrine referred to, which is of long standing and has been generally accepted by students of philosophy. . . .

We are in agreement also with those who identify happiness with virtue or with some particular virtue; for our phrase 'activity in accordance with virtue' is the same as what they call virtue. It makes quite a difference, however, whether we conceive the supreme good as the mere possession (*hexis*) of virtue or as its employment (*energeia*)—i.e., as a state of character or as its active expression in conduct. For a state of character may be present without yielding any good result, as in a man who is asleep or in some other way inactive; but this is not true of its active expression, which must show itself in action, indeed in good action. As at the Olympic games it is not merely the fairest and strongest that receive the victory wreath, but those who compete (since the victors will of course be found among the competitors), so in life too those who carry off the finest prizes are those who manifest their excellence in their deeds.

Moreover, the life of those active in virtue is intrinsically pleasant. For besides the fact that pleasure is something belonging to the soul, each man takes pleasure in what he is said to love—the horse-lover in horses, the lover of sights in public spectacles, and similarly the lover of justice in just acts, and more generally, the lover of virtue in virtuous acts. And while most men take pleasure in things which, as they are not truly pleasant by nature, create warring factions in the soul, the lovers of what is noble take pleasure in things that are truly pleasant in themselves. Virtuous actions are things of this kind; hence they are pleasant for such men, as well as pleasant intrinsically. The life of such men, therefore, requires no adventitious pleasures, but finds its own pleasure within itself. This is further shown by the fact that a man who does not enjoy doing noble actions is not a good man at all: surely no one would call a man just who did not enjoy performing just actions, nor generous who did not enjoy performing generous actions, and so on. On this ground too, then, actions in conformity with virtue must be intrinsically pleasant. And certainly they are good as well as noble, and both in the highest degree, if the judgment of the good man is any criterion; for he will judge them as we have said. It follows, therefore, that happiness is at once the best and noblest and pleasantest of things, and that these attributes are not separable as the inscription at Delos pretends:

> Perfect justice is noblest, health is best,
> But to gain one's heart's desire is pleasantest.

For our best activities possess all of these attributes; and it is in our best activities, or in the best one of them, that we say happiness consists.

Nevertheless, happiness plainly requires external goods as well; for it is impossible, or at least not easy, to act nobly without the proper equipment. There are many actions that can only be performed through such instruments as friends, wealth, or political influence; and there are some things, again, the lack of which must mar felicity, such as good birth, fine children, and personal comeliness: for the man who is repulsive in appearance, or ill-born, or solitary and childless does not meet the requirements of a happy man, and still less does one who has worthless children and friends, or who has lost good ones by death. As we have said, then, happiness seems to require the addition of external prosperity, and this has led some to identify it with 'good fortune' (*eutychia*), just as others have made the opposite mistake of identifying it with virtue.

ix. Sources of happiness

For the same reason there are many who wonder whether happiness is attained by learning, or by habituation or some other kind of training, or whether it comes by some divine dispensation, or even by chance (*tyché*). Well, certainly if the gods do give any gifts to men we may reasonably suppose that happiness is god-given; indeed, of all human blessings it is the most likely to be so, inasmuch as it is the best of them all. While this question no doubt belongs more properly to another branch of inquiry, we remark here that even if happiness is not god-sent but comes as a result of virtue or some kind of learning or training, still it is evidently one of the most divine things in the world, because that which is the reward as well as the end and aim of virtuous conduct must evidently be of supreme excellence, something divine and most blessed. If this is the case, happiness must further be something that can be generally shared; for with the exception of those whose capacity for virtue has been stunted or maimed, everyone will have the ability, by study and diligence, to acquire it. And if it is better that happiness should be acquired in this way than by chance, we may reasonably suppose that it happens so; because everything in nature is arranged in the best way possible—just as in the case of man-made products, and of every kind of causation, especially the highest. It would be altogether wrong that what is greatest and noblest in the world should be left to the dispensation of chance.

Our present difficulty is cleared up by our previous definition of happiness, as a certain activity of the soul in accordance with virtue; whereas all other sorts of good are either necessary conditions of, or coöperative with and naturally useful instruments of this. Such a conclusion, moreover, agrees with the proposition we laid down at the outset: that the end of statecraft is the best of all ends, and that the principal concern of statecraft is to make the citizens of a certain character—namely, good and disposed to perform noble actions.

Naturally, therefore, we do not call an ox or a horse or any other brute happy, since none of them is able to participate in conduct of this kind. For the same reason a child is not happy, since at his age he too is incapable of such conduct. Or if we do call a child happy, it is in the sense of predicting for him a happy future. Happiness, as we have said, involves not only a completeness of virtue but also a complete lifetime for its fulfillment. Life brings many vicissitudes and chance happenings, and it may be that one who is now prosperous will suffer great misfortunes in his old age, as is told of Priam in the Trojan legends; and a man who is thus buffeted by fortune and comes to a miserable end can scarcely be called happy.

x. Happiness and the vicissitudes of fortune

Are we, then, to call no one happy while he lives? Must we, as Solon advises, wait to see his end? And if we accept this verdict, are we to interpret it as meaning that a man actually becomes happy only after he is dead? Would not this be downright absurd, especially for us who define happiness as a kind of vital activity? Or if we reject this interpretation, and suppose Solon to mean rather that it is only after death, when beyond the reach of further evil and calamity that a man can safely be said to have been happy during his life, there is still a possible objection that may be offered. For many hold that both good and evil may in a certain sense befall a dead man (just as they may befall a living man even when he is unconscious of them)—e.g., honors and disgraces, and the prosperity or misfortune of his children and the rest of his descendants. And this presents a further problem: suppose a man to have lived to a happy old age, and to have ended as he lived, there are still plenty of reverses that may befall his descendants—some of them will perhaps lead a good life and be dealt with by fortune as they deserve, others not. (It is clear, too, that

a man's relationship to his descendants admits of various degrees.)
It would be odd, then, if the dead man were to change along with
the fortunes of his descendants, becoming happy and miserable
by turns; although, to be sure, it would be equally odd if the fortunes of his descendants did not affect him at all, even for a brief
time.

But let us go back to our earlier question,[16] which may perhaps clear up the one we are raising at present. Suppose we agree
that we must look to the end of a man's life, and only then call
him happy, .not because he then *is* happy but because we can
only then know him to have been so: is it not paradoxical to
have refused to call him happy during just the period when happiness was present to him? On the other hand, we are naturally
loath to apply the term to living men, considering the vicissitudes
to which they are liable. Happiness, we argue, must be something that endures without any essential change, whereas a living
individual may experience many turns of fortune's wheel. Obviously if we judge by his changing fortunes we shall have to
call the same man now happy now wretched, thereby regarding
the happy man as a kind of chameleon and his happiness as built
on no secure foundation; yet it surely cannot be right to regard
a man's happiness as wholly dependent on his fortunes. True good
and evil are not of this character; rather, as we have said, although
good fortune is a necessary adjunct to a complete human life, it
is virtuous activities that constitute happiness, and the opposite
sort of activities that constitute its opposite.

The foregoing difficulty [that happiness can be judged of only
in retrospect] confirms, as a matter of fact, our theory. For none
of man's functions is so permanent as his virtuous activities—
indeed, many believe them to be more abiding even than a knowledge of the sciences; and of his virtuous activities those are the
most abiding which are of highest worth, for it is with them that
anyone blessed with supreme happiness is most fully and most

---

[16] I.e., whether we are to call no one happy while he still lives.

continuously occupied, and hence never oblivious of. The happy man, then, will possess this attribute of permanence or stability about which we have been inquiring, and will keep it all his life; because at all times and in preference to everything else he will be engaged in virtuous action and contemplation, and he will bear the changes of fortune as nobly and in every respect as decorously as possible, inasmuch as he is truly good and 'four-square beyond reproach.' [17]

But the dispensations of fortune (*tyché*) are many, some great, others small. Small ones do not appreciably turn the scales of life, but a multitude of great ones, if they are of the nature of blessings, will make life happier; for they add to life a grace of their own, provided that a man makes noble and good use of them. If, however, they are of an evil kind, they will crush and maim happiness, in that they bring pain and thereby hinder many of our natural activities. Yet true nobility shines out even here, if a multitude of great misfortunes be borne with calmness—not, to be sure, with the calmness of insensibility, but of nobility and greatness of soul.

If, as we have declared, it is our activities that give life its character, then no happy man can become miserable, inasmuch as he will never do what is hateful or base. For we hold that the truly good and wise man will bear with dignity whatever fortune sends, and will always make the best of his circumstances, as a good general makes the most effective use of the forces at his command, and a good shoemaker makes the best shoes out of the leather that is available, and so in the case of the other crafts. On this interpretation, the happy man can never become miserable—although of course he will not be blessed with happiness in the full sense of the word if he meets with such a fate as Priam's. At all events, he is not variable and always changing; for no ordinary misfortunes but only a multitude of great ones will dislodge him from his happy state, and should this occur he will not readily recover

---

[17] A quotation from Simonides.

his happiness in a short time, but only, if at all, after a long period has run its course, during which he has achieved distinctions of a high order.

Is there any objection, then, to our defining a happy man as one whose activities are an expression of complete virtue, and who at the same time enjoys a sufficiency of worldly goods, not just for some limited period, but for his entire lifetime? Or perhaps we had better add the proviso that he shall be destined to go on living in this manner, and die as he has lived; for, whereas the future is obscure to us, we conceive happiness to be an end, something altogether and in every respect final and complete. Granting all this, we may declare those living men to be 'blessed with supreme happiness' (*makarios*) in whom these conditions have been and are continuing to be fulfilled. Their blessedness, however, is of a human order.[18]

So much for our discussion of this question.

xiii. Derivation of the two kinds of human excellence

Since happiness is a certain activity of the soul in accordance with perfect virtue, we must next examine the nature of virtue (*aretê*). Not only will such an inquiry perhaps clarify the problem of happiness; it will also be of vital concern to the true student of statecraft, whose aim is to make his fellow-citizens good and law-abiding. The Cretan and Spartan law-givers, as well as such others as may have resembled them, exemplify this aim. And clearly, if such an inquiry has to do with statecraft, it will be in keeping with our original purpose to pursue it.

It goes without saying that the virtue we are to study is human virtue, just as the good that we have been inquiring about is a human good, and the happiness a human happiness. By human virtue we mean virtue not of the body but of the soul, and by happiness too we mean an activity of the soul. This being the

---

[18] As distinguished from the blessedness of the gods, to whom the word *makarios* is more properly applied.

case, it is no less evident that the student of statecraft must have some knowledge of the soul, than that a physician who is to heal the eye or the whole body must have some knowledge of these organs; more so, indeed, in proportion as statecraft is superior to and more honorable than medicine. Now all physicians who are educated take much pains to know about the body. Hence as students of statecraft, too, we must inquire into the nature of the soul; but we must do so with reference to our own distinctive aim and only to the extent that it requires, for to go into minuter detail would be more laborious than is warranted by our subject-matter.

We may adopt here certain doctrines about the soul that have been adequately stated in our public discourses: [19] as that the soul may be distinguished into two parts, one of which is irrational while the other possesses reason. Whether these two parts are actually distinct like the parts of the body or any other divisible thing, or are distinct only in a logical sense, like convex and concave in the circumference of a circle, is immaterial to our present inquiry.

Of the irrational part, again, one division is apparently of a vegetative nature and common to all living things: I mean that which is the cause of nutrition and growth. It is more reasonable to postulate a vital faculty of this sort, present in all things that take nourishment, even when in an embryo stage, and retained by the full-grown organism, than to assume a special nutritive faculty in the latter. Hence we may say that the excellence belonging to this part of the soul is common to all species, and not specifically human: a point that is further confirmed by the popular view that this part of the soul is most active during sleep. For it is during sleep that the distinction between good men and bad is least apparent; whence the saying that for half their lives the happy are no better off than the wretched. This, indeed, is natural enough, for sleep is an inactivity of the soul in those re-

[19] Or possibly: "in my published essays."

spects in which the soul is called good or bad. (It is true, however, that to a slight degree certain bodily movements penetrate to the soul; which is the reason why good men's dreams are superior to those of the average person.) But enough of this subject: let us dismiss the nutritive principle, since it has by nature no share in human excellence.

There seems to be a second part of the soul, which though irrational yet in some way partakes of reason. For while we praise the rational principle and the part of the soul that manifests it in the case of the continent and incontinent man alike, on the ground that it exhorts them rightly and urges them to do what is best; yet we find within these men another element different in nature from the rational element, and struggling against and resisting it. Just as ataxic limbs, when we choose to move them to the right, turn on the contrary to the left, so it is with the soul: the impulses of the incontinent man run counter to his ruling part. The only difference is that in the case of the body we see what it is that goes astray, while in the soul we do not. Nevertheless the comparison will doubtless suffice to show that there is in the soul something besides the rational element, opposing and running counter to it. (In what sense the two elements are distinct is immaterial.) But this other element, as we have said, seems also to have some share in a rational principle: at any rate, in the continent man it submits to reason, while in the man who is at once temperate and courageous it is presumably all the more obedient; for in him it speaks on all matters harmoniously with the voice of reason.

Evidently, then, the irrational part of the soul is twofold. There is the vegetative element, which has no share in reason, and there is the concupiscent (*epithymêtikos*), or rather the appetitive (*orektikos*) element, which does in a sense partake of reason, in that it is amenable and obedient to it: i.e., it is rational in the sense that we speak of 'having *logos* of' [paying heed to] father and friends, not in the sense of 'having *logos* of' [having a rational understanding of] mathematical truths. That this irrational element is in some way amenable to reason is shown by our practice of giving admonishment, and by rebuke and exhortation generally. If on this account it is deemed more correct to regard this element as also possessing reason, then the rational part of the soul, in turn, will have two subdivisions: the one being rational in the strict sense as actually possessing reason, the other merely in the sense that a child obeys its father.

Virtue, too, is differentiated in accordance with this division of the soul: for we call some of the virtues intellectual and others moral: wisdom, understanding, and sagacity being among the former, liberality and temperance among the latter. In speaking of a man's character we do not say that he is wise or intelligent, but that he is gentle or temperate; yet we praise the wise man too for the disposition he has developed within himself, and praiseworthy dispositions we call virtues.

BOOK II

MORAL VIRTUE

i. How moral virtue is acquired

VIRTUE, or excellence (*aretê*), then, being of two kinds, intellectual and moral, intellectual excellence owes its birth and its growth mainly to teaching, and so requires experience and time, while moral excellence is the product of habit (*êthos*), and in fact has derived its name, *êthikos,* by a slight variation from that word. Hence it is plain that none of the moral virtues is implanted in us by nature, for no natural property can be changed by habit. A stone, for instance, which has the natural property of falling, can never be habituated to rise, even though we made innumerable attempts to train it by throwing it into the air; nor can fire be habituated to move downwards, nor can anything else that has a natural property of behaving in one way be habituated to behave differently. The virtues, then, are not engendered in us either by nature or in opposition to nature: rather nature gives us the capacity for receiving them, and this capacity is developed through habit.

Moreover, in the case of our natural endowments we first receive a certain power, to which we later give expression by acting in a certain way. The senses offer an illustration of this: they are not acquired as a result of seeing and hearing; on the contrary, instead of being acquired by practice they had first to be possessed before they could be used. The virtues, on the other hand, are acquired by first giving them expression in actual practice, and this is true of the arts as well. To learn an art (*technê*) it is first necessary to perform those actions that pertain to it: e.g., we become builders by building, and harpists by playing the harp. Similarly we become just by performing just actions, temperate by temperate actions, brave by brave actions. This is confirmed by what goes on in our city-states, where it is by training that legislators make people good; at any rate that is the aim of legislation, and if it is not achieved the legislation is a failure. By such legislation a good constitution is distinguished from a bad.

From the same causes and by the same means that a moral virtue is produced it may also be destroyed. This is equally true of the arts. It is by playing the harp that both good and bad harpists are produced, and so of builders and the rest; for men become good or bad builders according as they practise building well or badly. If this were not so, they would require no instruction, but would all have been born good or bad at their trades. So too in the case of the virtues. It is by our actual conduct in our intercourse with other men that we become just or unjust, and it is by our conduct in dangerous situations, accustoming ourselves there to feel fear or confidence, that we become cowardly or brave. So, too, with our appetites and angry impulses: it is by behaving in one way or another on the appropriate occasions that we become either temperate and gentle or profligate and irascible. In short, a particular kind of 'moral disposition' (*hexis*) is produced by a corresponding kind of activities. That is why we ought to take care that our activities are of the right sort, inasmuch as our moral dispositions will vary in accordance with them. It is no small matter, then, what habits we form even from early youth; rather this is of great, indeed of paramount importance.

ii. On right method

Since our present inquiry has not, like the others, a merely speculative aim (i.e., we are inquiring not merely in order to know what virtue is, but in order to become good, for otherwise the knowledge would avail us nothing), we must investigate the subject of 'moral actions' (*praxis*) and inquire how they are to be performed; for they, as we have said, determine the kind of 'moral dispositions' (*hexis*) that will be produced. That we are to be guided by 'right principle' (*orthos logos*) is generally admitted, and may be taken as our present starting-point; although we shall have to discuss later [1] what this 'right principle' is and how it is related to the other virtues.

But before proceeding further let us acknowledge that in matters of conduct our theories must be stated inexactly and in outline; for, as we remarked at the outset, we are to demand only so much of any theory as may be appropriate to its subject-matter, and in matters of conduct and expediency there are no fixed laws, any more than in matters of health. And if our general theory is thus inexact, its application to particular cases will be all the more so; for these do not come under the head of any specific art or system of rules, but the agent himself must consider on each occasion what the situation requires, just as in medicine or navigation.

Yet while our present theory is thus necessarily inexact, we must do what we can to help it out. First of all, then, let us observe that the virtues we have been discussing [2] are destroyed equally by deficiency or by excess. We may see this illustrated in the analogous case of bodily strength and health (for in illustrating what is immaterial we must have recourse to material analogies): strength is as much destroyed by an excess as by a deficiency of bodily exercise, health by too much as by too little food; but both are produced, developed, and preserved by a moderate amount. So with temperance, courage, and the other virtues: the man who flees and fears everything and never stands his ground is a coward, while he who fears nothing at all and is ready to face everything is rash. Similarly, the man who partakes of every pleasure and abstains from none is a profligate, while he who boorishly

[1] See Bk. VI, Chap. xiii, pp. 230–231.
[2] I.e., moral virtues, as distinguished from intellectual.

shuns all pleasures may be called insensible. Thus temperance and courage are destroyed by excess and deficiency but are preserved by moderation.

Not only are the virtues produced and developed by the same actions and situations as those by which they may also be destroyed; but the resulting conduct, in turn, will find expression in terms of these same situations and actions. We may see this in the case of more readily observable qualities like strength; for strength is produced by eating a great deal of food and doing a great deal of hard work, and it is the strong man, in turn, who is best able to perform these actions. So, too, with the virtues: by abstaining from pleasures we become temperate, and when temperance has been acquired we are best able to abstain. And in the case of courage, similarly, it is by habituating ourselves to despise and stand up to danger that we become brave, and after we have become brave we are able to face dangers all the more readily.

iii. *Pleasure and pain as tests of virtue*

The best index to our dispositions (*hexis*) is found in the pleasure or pain that accompanies our actions. A man who abstains from bodily indulgence and finds enjoyment in doing so is temperate, but he who abstains reluctantly is licentious (*akolastos*); and he who faces danger gladly, or at any rate without pain, is brave, while he who does it with pain is a coward. Thus pleasure and pain are matters that deeply concern the question of moral virtue. This is evident, first, from the fact that it is pleasure which prompts us to base deeds, and pain which deters us from noble ones; and therefore men ought, as Plato observes,[3] to be trained from youth to find pleasure and pain in the right objects—which is just what we mean by a sound education.

Again, each particular virtue is a matter of actions and feelings, and these are in every case accompanied by pleasure or pain—

---

[3] *The Laws*, Bk. II, pp. 653A, ff.

a further proof that pleasures and pains are the concern of virtue.

Again, punishment is inflicted through the medium of pains, by reason of their curative property; and a cure must naturally be the opposite of the disease to which it is applied.[4]

Again, as we have said before, every disposition of the soul realizes its nature through being related to and concerned with those things that influence it for better or worse. But it is through pleasures and pains that our dispositions are corrupted—i.e., through pursuit or avoidance of pleasures and pains of the wrong sort, or at the wrong time, or in the wrong manner, or wrongly in some other specific respect. This is why some people [5] go so far as to define the virtues as states of quietude without feeling; but they make a mistake when they use these terms in an absolute sense instead of qualifying them by adding, 'in the right or wrong manner,' 'at the right or wrong time,' etc.

We may conclude, therefore, that virtue of a moral sort makes us do what is best in matters of pleasure and pain, while vice has the opposite effect. And the following considerations offer further evidence of the same point.

There are three sorts of thing that move us to choice, and three

---

[4] Whence it follows that the original disease must have been pleasure: a third proof that moral virtue (which is presumably the end of punishment) is concerned with pleasures and pains. Andronicus' paraphrase throws light on this passage:—"This truth is further evident from the punishments which are inflicted in states. Lawgivers cause trouble to fall upon such as take pleasure in vicious courses, and thus try to induce them to hate what is evil, and to find their pleasure rather in a virtuous life. Thus it is, by the moral discipline which they inculcate, that lawgivers instill into men's minds the pleasure which is consequent upon virtue. Legal punishments thus fill a position analogous to medical remedies toward those who are diseased in their social relations. Just as the diseases are opposed to the remedies which cure them (if, for instance, we see a physician employing a cold method of cure, we know at once that the disease has been brought on by heat), so also we know from the painful nature of punishments that the vices which those punishments are designed to cure, arise from pleasure." (Hatch's translation, *op. cit.*, of the paraphrase attributed, perhaps erroneously, to Andronicus of Rhodes; concerning whom, see Introduction, p. xxii).

[5] Probably the Cynics. Afterwards this notion of virtue became a part of the Stoic doctrine.

that move us to avoidance: on the one hand, the 'nobly beautiful' (*kalos*), the advantageous, and the pleasant (*hêdys*); on the other their opposites, the basely ugly, the injurious, and the painful. The good man is apt to go right and the bad man to go wrong about all of these, but especially about pleasure: for pleasure is experienced by men and animals alike; also it is an accompaniment of all objects of choice; and, as a matter of fact, even the nobly beautiful and the advantageous may be regarded as in a sense pleasant.

Again, a love of pleasure has been fostered in all of us from infancy, and thus has become so thoroughly engrained in our lives that it can hardly be eradicated.[6] And even in the judging of actions we all of us tend, to a greater or less degree, to make pleasure and pain our standard. Here, then, is still another reason why pleasure and pain are matters with which our whole inquiry must be concerned; for the actions we perform depend a good deal on whether we are pleased and pained in the right or the wrong way.

Moreover, it is harder, as Heraclitus says, to fight against pleasure than against wrath; and virtue, like art, is always concerned with what is harder, for good actions are made all the better by being hard to achieve. Here, then, is still another reason why the whole subject both of moral virtue and of statecraft is bound up with the question of pleasures and pains; for if a man employs these well he will be good, if badly bad.

Hence we may take it as established: (1) that moral virtue has somehow to do with pleasures and pains; (2) that the same actions that have produced it will also develop it, or, if performed differently, will destroy it; and (3) that it finds eventual expression in activities of the same kind as those by which it was produced.

[6] Grant supposes this metaphor to have been suggested by the passage in Book IV of Plato's *Republic* (429 D), where the effects of right education are compared to a dye with which the mind is to be imbued so deeply that pleasure and pain will be unable to eradicate it. If so, Aristotle has reversed the original analogy.

iv. Virtue and virtuous action

At this point the question might be raised, what we mean by saying that men become just and temperate only by doing just and temperate acts; for if men do just and temperate acts they must be just and temperate already—in the same way that if a man writes sentences or plays music he must already be literate or a musician.

In reply we may first of all challenge the validity of this objection even with respect to the arts. A man may possibly form sentences by chance, or at another's prompting; he will be literate, however, only if he does this in a literate way—that is, through having a literate man's knowledge of what he is about. But in any case the virtues are not entirely like the arts in this respect. In the arts the outward result is something good in itself, and its quality therefore is all that matters; but in the case of the virtues the character of a man's acts does not mean that he has acted justly or temperately, unless he is also in a certain state of mind during their performance. To act justly or temperately a man must, first of all, know what he is doing; secondly, he must choose it, and choose it for its own sake; thirdly, it must be the expression of a firm and stable character. Of these conditions only the first is included among the prerequisites of the various arts; whereas for the attainment of virtue knowledge alone is of little avail, and the other two conditions, which can only come as a result of repeatedly behaving in a just and temperate manner, are of great, indeed of supreme importance. Thus while acts are called just or temperate when they are such as a just or temperate man would perform, the agent is called just or temperate only when he does them in the spirit of a just or temperate man.

Hence we are correct in asserting that a man becomes just by doing just acts and temperate by doing temperate acts, and that without doing them he has no prospect of ever becoming good. But most men, instead of following this advice, take refuge in theories, and suppose that by philosophizing they will be improved —like a sick man who listens attentively to his physician but disobeys his orders. Bare philosophizing will no more produce health in the soul than a course in medical theory will produce health in the body.

v. *The genus of moral virtue*

Our next task is to inquire just what virtue is. Every state of the soul is one of three things: a feeling (*pathos*), an 'ability or faculty' (*dynamis*), or a 'developed disposition, i.e., a state of character' (*hexis*). By 'feelings' I mean appetite, anger, fear, confidence, envy, joy, 'friendly affection' (*philia*), hatred, longing, emulation, pity, and in general whatever is accompanied by pleasure or pain; by 'faculties' I mean the capacities by which we are said to be capable of any of these feelings—the ability, for instance, to feel anger or pity or pain; and by 'dispositions' I mean the possession of a certain attitude, whether good or bad, with reference to the passions—e.g., we are badly disposed with respect to anger if our angry feelings are either too violent or too slack, well disposed if they are moderate, and similarly in the case of the other feelings.

Now the virtues and vices cannot be feelings. For, in the first place, we are called good or bad in respect of our virtues or vices, whereas we are not called so in respect of our feelings. Then too, we are praised and blamed for our virtues and vices, but not for our feelings: it is not simply for being frightened or angry that a man is praised, nor is it for that alone that he is blamed, but for being so in a particular way. Furthermore, fear and anger are not the result of 'deliberate choice' (*proairesis*), but the virtues are a kind of choice, or at any rate are impossible without it. Finally, in the case of feelings we are said to be 'impelled,' while in the case of virtues and vices we are not said to be impelled but to be 'disposed' in a certain way.

The same considerations show that the virtues cannot be faculties: we are not called good or bad for being merely *capable* of feeling, nor are we praised or blamed for this. And further, while faculties are given to us by nature, we are not made good or bad by nature—a point already treated of.[7]

Consequently, as the virtues are neither feelings nor faculties, the only thing that remains for them to be is dispositions; and therein we have stated what virtue is in respect of its genus.

vi. Differentia of moral virtue: doctrine of the mean

But to say that virtue is a disposition is not enough; we must specify what kind of a disposition it is.

The 'virtue or excellence' (*aretê*) of anything must be acknowledged to have a twofold effect on the thing to which it belongs: it renders the thing itself good, and causes it to perform its function well. The excellence of the eye, for instance, makes both the eye and its work good, for it is by the excellence of the eye that we see well. Likewise the proper excellence of horse at once makes a particular horse what he should be, and also makes him good at running and at carrying his rider and at facing the enemy. Hence, if this is universally true, the virtue or proper excellence of man will be just that 'formed disposition' (*hexis*) which both makes him good and enables him to perform his function (*ergon*) well. We have already indicated how this is accomplished; but we may clarify the matter by examining wherein the nature of virtue consists.

Of everything that is both continuous and divisible it is possible to take a greater, a less, or an equal amount; [8] and this may be true either objectively with respect to the thing in question or else relatively to ourselves. By 'equal' (*ison*) I mean that which is a mean (*meson*) between excess and deficiency. By the objective mean I denote that which is equidistant from both extremes,

---

[7] In Chap. i of the present Book.
[8] These three words, *pleion, elatton, ison,* carry also secondary connotations: 'too great,' 'too little,' 'fair.'

and this will always be the same for everybody. By the mean that is relative to ourselves I denote that which is neither too much nor too little,[9] and this is not one and the same for everybody. For instance, if ten is many and two is few, then six is the mean considered in terms of the object; for it exceeds and is exceeded by the same amount, and is therefore the mean of an arithmetical proportion. But the mean considered relatively to ourselves cannot be determined so simply: if ten pounds of food is too much for a certain man to eat and two pounds is too little, it does not follow that the trainer will prescribe six pounds, for this may be too much or too little for the man in question—too little for Milo,[10] too much for the novice at athletics. This is equally true of running and wrestling.

So it is that an expert in any field avoids excess and deficiency, and seeks and chooses the mean—that is, not the objective mean, but the mean relatively to ourselves. If, then, every sort of skill (*epistêmê*) perfects its work in this way, by observing the mean and bringing its work up to this standard (which is the reason why people say of a good work of art that nothing could be either taken from it or added to it, implying that excellence is destroyed by excess or deficiency but is preserved by adherence to the mean; and good artists, we say, observe this standard in their work), and if furthermore virtue, like nature, is more exact and better than any art, it follows that virtue will have the property of aiming at the mean. I am speaking, of course, of moral virtue, for it is moral virtue that has to do with feelings and actions, and it is in respect of these that excess, deficiency, and moderation are possible. That is to say, we can feel fear, confidence, desire, anger, pity, and in general pleasure and pain, either too much or too little, and in either case not well; but to feel them at the right times, with reference to the right objects, toward the right people,

---

[9] The verbal forms, connoting 'to superabound' and 'to fall short [of a goal or standard]' are used here.

[10] A famous wrestler.

with the right motive, and in the right manner, is to strike the
mean, and therein to follow the best course—a mark of virtue.
And in the same way our outward acts admit of excess, deficiency,
and the proper mean. Now virtue has to do with feelings and also
with outward acts; in both of these excess and deficiency are regarded as faults and are blamed, while the mean amount is both
praised and regarded as right—palpable signs of virtue. Virtue,
then, is a kind of moderation (*mesotês*), in that it aims at the
mean (*meson*). This conclusion is further confirmed by the fact
that while there are numerous ways in which we can go wrong
(for evil, according to the Pythagorean figure of speech, belongs
to the class of the unlimited, good to that of the limited), there
is only one way of going right. That is why the one is easy, the
other hard—easy to miss the mark, but hard to hit it. And this
offers further evidence that excess and deficiency are characteristic of vice while hitting the mean is characteristic of virtue: "for
good is simple, badness manifold."

We may conclude, then, that virtue is an habitual disposition
with respect to choice, the characteristic quality of which is moderation judged relatively to ourselves according to a determinate
principle, i.e. according to such a principle as a man of insight
would use. The quality of moderation belongs to virtue in a double sense: as falling between two vices, the one of which consists
in excess, the other in deficiency; and also in the sense that while
these vices respectively fall short of and exceed the proper standard
both of feelings and of actions, virtue both finds and chooses the
mean. Hence, in respect of its essence and according to the definition of its basic nature, virtue is a state of moderation; but regarded
in its relation to what is best and right it is an extreme.

intellectual virtue

Accordingly it is not every action nor every feeling to which
the principle of the mean is applicable. There are some whose
very names imply badness: e.g., malevolence, shamelessness, envy,
and among actions, adultery, theft, and murder. These and everything else like them are condemned as being bad in themselves

and not merely when in excess or deficiency. To do right in performing them is therefore impossible; their performance is always wrong. Rightness or wrongness in any of them (e.g., in adultery) does not depend on the rightness or wrongness of person and occasion and manner, but on the bare fact of doing it at all. It would be absurd to distinguish moderation, excess, and deficiency in action that is unjust or cowardly or profligate; for we should then have moderation of excess and deficiency, excess of excess, and deficiency of deficiency. The truth of the matter is that just as there can be no excess and deficiency of temperance and courage (for the proper mean is, in its own way, an extreme), so these opposite kinds of conduct likewise do not admit of moderation, excess, and deficiency; they are always wrong, no matter how they are done. . . .

vii. Species of the moral mean

But to make general statements like these is not enough; we must next apply them to particular virtues and vices. For while general statements cover more ground, they have less content of truth than particular propositions. Conduct has to do with particulars; it is important, therefore, that our statements when tested by them should be found to hold good. Let us take our particular virtues and vices from the following table.

In respect of fear and confidence, observance of the mean is called courage. Of the people who go to excess, those who exceed in fearlessness are given no name (as often happens), but those who exceed in confidence are rash; while those who exceed in fear and are deficient in confidence, are craven.

In respect of pleasures and pains—not all of them, however, and to a less extent in the case of pains—the mean is temperance, excess is profligacy. But persons deficient in respect of pleasures, as they are not often found, have received no name: let us call them 'insensible.'

In respect of the giving and taking of money, the mean is generosity, excess and deficiency are prodigality and stinginess. These two vices both exceed and fall short at once, but in contrary ways: the prodigal man exceeds in spending and falls short in taking, while the stingy man exceeds in taking but falls short in spending.[11]

There are also certain other dispositions in respect of money: a mean which is magnificence (the magnificent man differs from the merely generous man, in that he deals with large sums, the other with small), an excess which is bad taste and vulgar display, and a deficiency which is niggardliness. This pair of contrary vices differs from the corresponding pair of vices opposed to generosity; the manner of difference to be explained later.

In one's attitude toward public opinion, the mean is proper pride (*megalopsychia*), excess may be called vanity, and deficiency—pettiness (*mikropsychia*). And just as generosity was said to be related to magnificence, differing only in the smallness of the sums with which it deals, so too there is a virtue related to magnanimity and differing only in being concerned with small rather than great honors. It is possible to desire the right amount of honor, or more than the right amount, or less; and the man who carries this desire to excess is called ambitious, while he who is deficient in it is called unambitious, and he who is intermediate between these has no name. The corresponding dispositions too are nameless, except that of the ambitious man, which is called ambition. Hence it is that persons who occupy the extremes lay claim to the middle place: in fact, we ourselves refer to the moderate man sometimes as ambitious, sometimes as unambitious; and sometimes it is the ambitious man that we praise, sometimes the unambitious. The reason for this will be explained later; for the present let us speak of the remaining states of character according to the plan already proposed.

Excess and deficiency and moderation are found also in respect

[11] Aristotle's gloss, incorporated in the Greek text: "For the present it is our purpose to give merely an outline or summary; afterwards [from Bk. III, Chap. vi, to the end of Bk. IV] these states will be defined with more accuracy."

of anger. Although the dispositions have no well-recognized names, yet as the man who occupies the intermediate state is called gentle, we may give his character the name of gentleness; and of those who occupy the extremes, let the one who exceeds be called irascible, and his vice irascibility, while the deficient man may be called apathetic and his vice apathy.

There are also three other respects, mutually related yet distinct, in which one may observe a mean. All of them have to do with intercourse in speech and action, but they differ in that one is concerned with the truth of intercourse, the other two with its pleasantness; and of these latter, one has to do with pleasantness in matters of amusement, the other with pleasantness in any situations that life may offer. We must accordingly include these in our account, in order to see more plainly how in all things moderation is praiseworthy, while going to extremes is neither praiseworthy nor right, but an object of censure. Incidentally, most of these qualities too are without names; which means that we must undertake, here as elsewhere, to coin names ourselves, so that our discourse may be clear and easy to follow.

In respect of truth, then, the moderate man may be called a truthful sort of person, and his moderation truthfulness. Pretence which takes the form of exaggeration is boastfulness, and its possessor is a boaster; in the form of understatement it is self-depreciation [12] and its possessor self-depreciatory.

In respect of pleasantness in amusing others, the moderate man may be called witty and the corresponding disposition wittiness; excess may be called buffoonery, and its possessor a buffoon, while the man who falls short may be called boorish, and his disposition boorishness.

In respect of pleasantness in the other affairs of life, he who is pleasant in the right way is friendly and his moderation is friend-

---

[12] *Eirôneia:* refers to the attitude of mock modesty, or ironical self-depreciation, by which Socrates was wont to provoke his opponents to make positive statements.

liness; he who exceeds is obsequious if he has no ulterior motive, or a flatterer if he is looking to his own advantage; and he who falls short and in every situation makes himself disagreeable is a peevish and surly sort of person.

In our feelings, too, and in conduct that pertains to them, there are ways of observing the mean. Shame, for instance, is not a virtue, but modesty receives praise. For in these matters also we speak of one man as observing the mean, and of another, viz. the sheepish man whom everything throws out of countenance, as overstepping it; while he who is deficient in this feeling, or entirely lacks it, is called shameless. The term 'modest,' on the other hand, is reserved for him who observes the mean.

Again, 'righteous indignation' (*nemesis*) is the mean state between envy and malice—all of these having to do with the pain and pleasure that are felt at the fortunes of our neighbors. The righteously indignant man is pained by undeserved good fortune; the envious man goes further and is pained by all good fortune; while the malicious man falls so far short of being pained that he actually rejoices [at his neighbors' misfortunes].

But there will be another opportunity to discuss these matters. As for justice, since it has not one simple meaning, we shall, after treating of the other dispositions, distinguish its two kinds and show in what way each of them represents an observance of the mean. After that we shall treat in a similar manner of the rational virtues.

viii. Various relations of extremes and mean

Thus there are three kinds of disposition: two of them vices, marked by excess and deficiency respectively, and one of them, observance of the mean, a virtue. Each of them may be regarded as, in a sense, the opposite of both others; for the extreme states are opposites both of the middle state and of one another, while the middle state is opposite to both the extremes. Just as an amount that is equal to some other amount is greater when compared with a less and less when compared with a greater amount, so it is that moderate dispositions, whether in feelings and in action, are excessive as compared with deficient dispositions and deficient as compared with excessive ones. The brave man, for example, seems rash as compared with a coward and cowardly as compared with a daredevil; likewise the temperate man seems profligate as compared with a man who is insensible to pleasures, and insensible as compared with a profligate; while the generous man seems prodigal as compared with a miser and stingy as compared with a prodigal. For this reason people whose dispositions are at one extreme try to dislodge the moderate man from his position by representing him as an extremist of the opposite sort: the coward calls the brave man rash, the rash man calls him coward, and so in the other cases.

But while all three states are thus opposed to one another, the most marked contrariety is that which subsists between the two extremes, rather than between either of them and the mean; for the extremes are farther from each other than from the mean, just as the great is farther from the small and the small from the great than either one is from the equal. Again, certain extremes bear a kind of resemblance to the mean, as rashness to courage and prodigality to generosity, while between the extremes themselves there is the greatest possible unlikeness. Opposites, moreover, are defined as the things that are farthest away from each other; hence things must be more opposite according as they are farther apart.

In some cases it is the deficiency, in others the excess that is the more opposed to the mean. For example, it is not rashness, which is excess, but cowardice, which is deficiency, that stands the more opposed to courage; while to temperance, on the other hand, it is not insensibility, the deficiency, but profligacy, which is excess, that stands the more opposed. The reasons for this are two. One is the reason drawn from the nature of the subject-matter: since one extreme is in actual fact nearer and more similar to the mean, we choose not this but its contrary to oppose to the mean. Thus, as rashness seems nearer and more similar to courage, cowardice more dissimilar, we tend rather to oppose cowardice to it—for that which is farther away from the mean may be regarded as the more opposed to it. This, then, is one reason, drawn from the nature of the subject-matter. Another may be found in ourselves, in that the things to which we are naturally more attracted appear more opposed to the mean: since we incline naturally toward pleasures, for instance, we are more prone to profligacy than to an orderly way of life. We describe as opposed to the mean those things in which we are more prone to over-indulgence; and thus profligacy, which is excess, is more opposite to the mean than its corresponding deficiency is.

ix. Difficulties of attaining the mean

We have now sufficiently shown that moral virtue consists in observance of a mean, and in what sense this is so: in the sense, namely, of holding a middle position between two vices, one of which involves excess and the other deficiency, and also in the sense of being the kind of a disposition which aims at the middle point both in feelings and in actions. This being the case, it is a hard thing to be good, for it is hard to locate the mean in particular instances, just as to locate the mean point [i.e. the center] of a circle is not a thing that everybody can do, but only the man of science. So, too, anyone can get angry—that is easy—or spend money or give it away; but to do all this to the right person, to the right extent, at the right time, with the right motive, and in the right manner, is not a thing that everyone can do, and is not easy; and that is why good conduct is at once rare and praiseworthy and noble.

Accordingly, whoever aims at the mean should first of all strive to avoid that extreme which is more opposed to it, as in Calypso's advice to "keep the ship well clear of that foaming surf." [13] For of

[13] Odysseus' order to his steersman (Odyssey, xii, 219–220), quoting the advice earlier given by Circe (not Calypso) to steer rather toward the monster Scylla, who will devour only a few of the men, than toward the whirlpool Charybdis, which will engulf them all.

the two extremes one will be more of an evil, the other less; therefore, as it is hard to hit the exact mean, we ought to choose the lesser of the two evils and sail, as the saying goes, in the second best way,[14] and this is accomplished most successfully in the manner stated. But we must bear in mind as well the errors to which we personally are prone. These will be different for different individuals, and each may discover them in his own case by noting the occasions on which he feels pleasure or pain. Having discovered them, let him bend himself in the opposite direction; for by steering wide of error we shall strike a middle course, as warped timber is straightened by bending it backwards. Especially and in all cases we must guard against pleasure and what is pleasant, because we cannot estimate it impartially. Hence we ought to feel toward pleasure as the elders of the people felt toward Helen, and on every occasion repeat their saying; [15] for if we dismiss pleasure thus we are less likely to go wrong.

Such, then, in outline, is the course by which we shall best succeed in hitting the mean. But the task is a hard one, we must admit, especially in particular cases. It is not easy to determine, for instance, how and with whom and on what provocation and how long one ought to be angry; and in fact we sometimes praise those who fall short in this respect, and call them gentle, while sometimes we praise those of harsher temper, calling them manly. We do not, however, censure the man who deviates slightly from goodness, whether on the side of excess or deficiency, but only the man whose error is too considerable to escape notice. To be sure, it is not easy to determine rationally at what point or at what degree of error a man becomes blameworthy; but then, matters that fall within the scope of perception can never be so determined, for they depend upon particular circumstances, and our judgment of them depends upon our perception.

[14] A popular expression, which meant taking to the oars when becalmed.
[15] "She is wondrously like the immortal goddesses to look upon. But be that as it may, let her depart on the ships, rather than be left here as a bane to us and our children after us." (*Iliad*, Bk. III, 158–160.)

So much, then, is clear: that in all departments of conduct it is the intermediate disposition that is laudable; but that we must sometimes incline toward the excess, sometimes toward the deficiency, since in this way we shall most readily hit the mean and thus attain to worthy conduct.

BOOK III

THE WILL

i. Willing and unwilling action

VIRTUE, as we have seen, has to do with feelings (*pathos*) and actions (*praxis*). But it is only when a man feels or acts willingly (*hekousios*) that he deserves praise or blame; feelings or actions that are unwilling (*akousios*)[1] are pardoned or even pitied. To distinguish willing from unwilling conduct, therefore, is presumably incumbent upon students of ethics, and will also be of service to legislators in meting out honors and punishments.

Unwilling actions are generally held to be those that are done either under compulsion or through ignorance. They are done under compulsion if their 'moving principle' (*archê*) comes from without and is of such a nature that the person who is acting or feeling contributes nothing: as, for instance, when someone is driven out of his course by a wind or by pirates.

As for actions performed in order to ward off greater evils or to achieve some noble end—as, for example, if a tyrant were to order us to do something base, threatening the lives of our parents or children, whom he held in his power, unless we would comply—

---

[1] In order to translate *hekousios* and *akousios* it is necessary to violate the canons of good English by using the adjectives 'willing' and 'unwilling' in a passive as well as in an active sense—i.e., as descriptive of actions no less than of agents. English affords the passive adjectives 'voluntary' and 'involuntary,' but these, particularly the latter, do not correspond to the Greek pair. In English we speak of actions as involuntary when they are *not actually* willed; while *akousios* applies only to such involuntary actions as are *contrary* to the agent's will, i.e., as would not have been willed if he could freely have exercised his power of choice.

there is some question whether actions performed in such circumstances should be called willing or unwilling. To jettison a cargo in a storm provides an analogous instance. 'Abstractly considered' (*haplôs*), no one would willingly throw his goods overboard, but any reasonable man would do so if it were a question of saving the lives of himself and his crew. Actions like these are of a mixed nature; yet they are more nearly willing than unwilling actions, for they are accepted as choiceworthy at the moment of performing them. Since the end for which a given action is performed will not be the same on all occasions, the action ought to be judged willing or unwilling with reference to whatever end was actually in view on a particular occasion of its performance. In each of the cases just cited the action is performed willingly, inasmuch as the source (*archê*) of the bodily movements by which it is carried out lies within the agent himself; and when an action thus has its origin in an individual agent it is for that agent to decide whether or not he will perform it. All such actions, therefore, must be regarded as having been performed willingly; although from an abstract point of view they are doubtless against the agent's will, since no one would choose them for themselves.

A further indication that actions of this class are considered 'willing' is our readiness to praise men when, for instance, they submit to disgrace or pain as a means to some great and noble result; although in ordinary circumstances their conduct would meet with reproof, since it is a paltry thing to submit to disgrace without the justification of a high and noble motive. There are other cases in which submission to compulsion though not praised is condoned: when one is induced to do wrong by pressure of circumstances too heavy for any man to bear. Yet even in cases of this kind the plea of compulsion is sometimes inadmissible. We scoff at the idea of Alcmaeon, in Euripides' play, being 'compelled' to murder his mother: a man, we think, should accept torture and death sooner than commit such a crime. If it is sometimes hard to balance the good or evil of our immediate actions with the consequent penalties or gains, it is still harder to abide by our decisions when once made; for in most such cases, although the action to which we are tempted is base, the alternative is prospectively painful. That is why men are praised or blamed according as they resist or yield to compulsion.

What kind of actions, then, should be called compulsory? From an abstract standpoint, any action may be so designated whose cause lies in external circumstances, and to which the individual contributes nothing. If, however, an action that would not willingly have been chosen for its own sake is on a particular occasion regarded as choiceworthy in preference to a given alternative, and if the 'moving principle' of this choice lies within the agent; then such an action must be characterized as abstractly against the agent's will, but willing from the standpoint of existing circumstances and a particular alternative. Yet it will be more nearly akin to willing action; for action (*praxis*) consists in taking particular steps, and here the particular steps are taken willingly. It is not easy, of course, to lay down rules for determining which of two alternatives is to be preferred; for cases differ widely.

It might perhaps be argued that actions done for the sake of what is pleasant or noble are also compulsory, since the pleasant and the noble may be regarded as external principles which constrain us. But such reasoning would make every action compulsory, inasmuch as pleasure and nobility are universal motives of human conduct. Besides, it is painful to act under compulsion and against one's will, whereas from performing pleasant or noble acts we receive pleasure. And lastly, it is absurd to put the blame on external circumstances instead of on ourselves for so readily yielding to their blandishments; or, while taking the credit for our noble deeds, to attribute our base deeds to pleasure. It appears, therefore, that [as we have said] a compulsory action is one whose moving principle is external, and to which the person compelled contributes nothing.

As for actions committed through ignorance, these, while not exactly voluntary (*hekousios*) cannot be called unwilling unless the agent afterward feels sorrow and regret at having done them. If, on the contrary, a man who has acted through ignorance feels not the slightest remorse for what he has done, then although we can scarcely say that he has acted voluntarily, considering that he did not know what he was doing; yet neither has he acted unwillingly, for he feels no sorrow. Of those who act through ignorance, then, he who feels subsequent regret is considered an 'unwilling' agent, whereas he who feels no such regret, since he differs from the former, may be described as an 'involuntary' ('not *hekousios*') agent; for as the cases are dissimilar it is better to give them different names. Still a further distinction must be made between acting *through*, or because of, and acting *in* ignorance. A man's behavior when he is drunk or enraged is considered as attributable to these states rather than to ignorance; yet as he acts without immediate awareness of what he is doing, he may be said to act *in* ignorance.

Wicked men, of course, are ignorant in one sense: viz., of what they ought to do and abstain from doing; and in fact it is just this sort of error that is responsible for injustice and moral badness generally. But an action can hardly be called unwilling on the ground that the agent is ignorant of his true interests. The ignorance that makes an act unwilling is not that which is displayed in 'the choice of ends' (*proairesis*), for such ignorance is the condition of vice. It is not, in other words, ignorance of the universal, for this is held to be blameworthy; but ignorance of particulars, i.e. of the circumstances and prospective effects of the act. These last are the grounds on which we pity and pardon, because he who acts in ignorance of the particular circumstances [that will thwart his end] acts unwillingly.

Perhaps it will be advisable, then, to enumerate and specify these extenuating types of ignorance. They are: ignorance (1) of who it is that is acting, (2) of what is being done, (3) of the person or thing affected; and sometimes also (4) of the instrument—

perhaps some tool—to be employed, (5) of the effect, e.g. saving a life, and (6) of the manner, e.g. gently or violently. No sane person, of course, could be ignorant of all these particulars at once, nor even of (1) the agent: for how could a man fail to know his own identity? But (2) a person might very well be ignorant of what he was doing: as when he pleads, for example, that the words slipped out of his mouth unawares; or, like Aeschylus after revealing the Mysteries, that he did not know the matter was a secret; or, like the man who discharged the catapult, that he let it go off accidentally while only intending to show how it worked. Again, (3) a person might mistake his son for an enemy, as Meropê [2] does; or (4) he might mistake a pointed spear for a foil, or a heavy stone for a pumice-stone; or (5) he might kill a man with a draught intended to save him; or (6) he might deal a blow in a sparring match while intending only a tap. Ignorance, then, is possible with regard to all these particulars of an action, and whoever is ignorant of any one of them may be regarded as acting unwillingly—especially if he is ignorant of the most important of them, i.e. the circumstances in which the act is undertaken and its final effect. But this ignorance makes an action unwilling only on condition that the agent afterward feels sorrow and regret.

As an action is unwilling if done either under compulsion or through ignorance, we may characterize an action as willing when its moving principle lies in the agent, and when the agent is cognizant of the particular circumstances in which the act is performed.

It is a mistake to suppose that actions motivated by 'passionate anger' (*thymos*) or desire (*epithymia*) are performed unwillingly, i.e. that they are altogether beyond the control of our will. For in the first place, (1) animals and even children could not, on such a supposition, be called capable of voluntary action. Moreover, (2) the supposition may mean either of two things: it may mean that none whatever of the actions prompted by desire or passion are

---

[2] A character in a lost play of Euripides.

performed voluntarily; or it may mean that we perform such actions voluntarily and willingly when they are noble, involuntarily and unwillingly when they are base. The second of these interpretations makes a preposterous distinction, considering that both sets of actions have admittedly been motivated in the same way. And as for the first interpretation, it seems illogical to declare both that it is our duty to desire a thing and that we desire it unwillingly, i.e. that we cannot help desiring it. But there are objects toward which it is our duty to feel anger, and others, like health and knowledge, that it is our duty to covet. [Hence we cannot suppose that the feelings in question are altogether beyond the control of our will.] [3] Again, (3) it is recognized that unwilling actions are painful, whereas actions in accordance with desire are pleasant. Finally, (4) what difference is there, in respect of the willingness with which they are performed, between wrong acts committed deliberately and wrong acts done on an angry impulse? Both alike are to be shunned, nor are the non-rational feelings any less a part of human nature [than reason is]; which argues that actions motivated by anger or desire belong [no less than rational actions] to the individual who performs them. Hence it is absurd to class non-rational [actions and feelings] as against or independent of the will.

ii. Purposive choice

Having thus distinguished willing from unwilling action, we have next to discuss 'purposive choice' (*proairesis*); for this is held to be intimately bound up with virtue, and to be a surer criterion of character than action is. . . .

Choice is not the same as wish (*boulêsis*), although they appear to be closely akin. For, in the first place, choice does not apply to impossibilities, and anyone who declared that he 'chose' some-

---

[3] Grant's paraphrase: "There is a feeling of obligation attaching sometimes to these emotions; we *ought* to desire some things and be angry at some. This feeling of 'ought' implies freedom."

thing impossible would be thought a fool; whereas we can wish even for what is impossible, e.g. immortality. Moreover, we may wish for what entails no action on our own part, e.g. for the victory of a certain competing athlete or actor; but no one could be said to choose such things, for we can choose only what we think attainable by our own efforts. Again, wish is directed to the end, choice to the means. Thus we wish to be healthy, and choose the things that will make us so; or we wish, as we say, 'to be happy' (*eudaimonein*), but we cannot properly speaking choose to be happy. Choice, in short, seems always to be directed to what lies within the agent's power.

Similarly, choice must be distinguished from opinion (*doxa*). Anything, it appears, can be a matter of opinion: what is immutable and what is impossible no less than what lies within our control. Moreover we distinguish opinions by their falsity or truth; not, as we distinguish choices, by their moral badness or goodness. Granting, then, as no doubt everyone will, that choice and opinion in general are not identical, we must add that neither is a particular choice identical with the particular opinion [that governs it]. For by choosing what is good or bad we mould our characters, whereas by merely holding opinions we do not. Again, we choose to get or avoid something good or bad; but we opine what a thing is, or whom it will benefit, or in what way: we certainly do not opine to get or avoid anything. Again, we praise choice as being correct, and as aiming at the right object, whereas we praise opinion as being true. . . . Nor are the individuals who make the best choices always those who are best at forming opinions; and conversely there are people who hold excellent opinions but fail, through depravity, to choose what is right. Choice may, of course, be preceded or accompanied by opinion, but that is beside the point. The only question that we are here considering is whether choice is the same thing as an opinion [about what is to be chosen].

If choice, then, is none of the things we have mentioned, what is it, and how is it to be described? An act of choice is evidently voluntary (*hekousios*), yet not all voluntary acts are acts of choice. Choice involves, in addition, reason (*logos*) and thinking (*dianoia*). Perhaps, then, we may define it as voluntary action preceded by deliberation. . . .

iii. Deliberation

As for deliberation (*boulê*) itself, do we deliberate about everything? Can anything whatever be an object of deliberation? Or are there some things about which deliberation is impossible? Presumably we ought to mean by 'object of deliberation' what a reasonable man would deliberate about, not a fool or a madman. On this basis we may declare that no one deliberates, in the first place, about what is immutable, such as the physical universe or the incommensurability of the diagonal and side of a square. Nor again, about things which change always in the same way, such as the solstices or the rising of the sun—regardless of whether their regularity is due to 'mechanical necessity' (*anangkê*) [4] or to 'organic nature' (*physis*) or to some other cause. Nor again, about wholly erratic occurrences, like droughts and rains. Nor about strokes of luck (*tychê*), such as the finding of a treasure. Even among human affairs not everything is a matter for deliberation: no Spartan, for instance, could *deliberate* about the best form of government for the Scythians.[5] For in none of these cases does the matter in question lie within the sphere of our control.

What we do deliberate about are things within our control and attainable by action. Such, indeed, are the only objects left for deliberation; because apart from organic nature, mechanical necessity, and chance, the only remaining causes that are generally recognized are intelligence (*nous*) and human agency generally. [This is not to say that all human affairs are objects of deliberation for everyone;] but rather, that different sorts of men deliberate about

[4] The principal meaning of *anangkê* is "that which cannot be otherwise than it is." *Metaph.*, Bk. V, Chap. v.

[5] This sentence may be misplaced. From its sense it would appear to belong with the third sentence of the next paragraph.

such matters as can be accomplished by themselves. Nor has deliberation any place in realms of knowledge that are exact and have been completely worked out, like calligraphy: we never wonder how we should form the letters of the alphabet. The objects of deliberation are rather such matters as can be brought about by our own agency although not always in a uniform way: e.g., questions of medicine and money-making. We deliberate, too, more about navigation than about gymnastics, because the former of these arts has been less completely systematized. The same principle may be applied to any of the arts or techniques; and in general we deliberate more about these than about the sciences, because we are less sure about them. Deliberation, then, operates with regard to matters that conform roughly to certain rules but whose particular outcome is obscure; i.e., in which there is an element of indeterminateness. When such matters are of great importance, mistrusting our own ability to decide them we invite other persons to share our deliberations.

Moreover, we deliberate not about ends but about means. A physician does not deliberate whether he shall heal, nor an orator whether he shall persuade, nor a statesman whether he shall frame effective laws, nor does a member of any other profession deliberate about his professional aim. Rather, having accepted a certain end, we consider how and by what means it can be attained. If it appears to be attainable by more than one means we then consider which of them is the easiest and best. But if there is only one means of achieving it, we consider how it is to be achieved by that means, and how that means in turn is to be secured, and so on until we reach the first member of the causal series, which in order of discovery is the last. For in deliberating we apparently must use the same method of analytical investigation as in studying a geometrical figure, where the last step of the analysis is the first step in the construction of the figure. All deliberation, in fact, is investigation; although it appears that not all investigation is deliberation, as the case of mathematical investigation shows. And if, in tracing the necessary means to our ends, we come upon an impossibility, we therewith drop the inquiry: e.g., if money is required and none is available; but if the means appear to be possible of execution we begin to act. By 'possible' I mean such as can be accomplished by ourselves; for even if our friends are employed in the task, it is still in a manner accomplished by ourselves, who were its instigators. [Just as in practicing an art or other technique] we must sometimes inquire about the instruments, sometimes about the manner of using them; so in any other matter for deliberation the question is sometimes how to find ways and means, sometimes how to use the means already settled upon. To conclude, then, we may repeat (1) that man is the 'originating principle' (*archê*) of his actions, (2) that deliberation is concerned with things within the subject's own power to accomplish, and (3) that all our actions aim at ends distinct from themselves. Accordingly it is not the end but the means to the end that must be the object of deliberation. Nor is the object of deliberation a particular fact, such as whether this is a loaf of bread or whether this bread is well baked. Such matters fall within the province of sense-perception; and unless we somewhere bring our deliberations to a halt, we shall fall into an infinite regress.

The object of deliberation and the object of choice are identical, except that the object of choice is already determinate, having been decided upon as a consequence of the deliberation. A person ceases to inquire how he should act as soon as he has traced the 'first step' (*archê*) of a proposed course of action back to himself; particularly to the dominant part of himself, i.e., to the part that exercises purposive choice. The process may be illustrated by the analogy of those ancient forms of government described by Homer, in which the king would first decide upon the measures to be adopted and then proclaim his decision to the people.[6]

Since, then, the object of choice is that which both lies within

---

[6] I.e., the king is analogous to that part of the individual soul which exercises purposive choice.

our power and is desired as a result of deliberation, choice itself may be defined as a deliberate desire for what is within our power. Having reached a decision as a result of deliberation, we fix our desire accordingly.

Let this suffice as an outline of the nature of purposive choice, of its objects, and of the fact that it is concerned with means rather than ends.

iv. Wish

Wish (*boulêsis*), on the contrary, as already stated, is concerned with the end. Some declare that the object of wish is the good, others that it is the apparent good. Those who hold the former theory are faced with the consequence that when a man makes a wrong choice, the thing he wishes for cannot be really the object of his wish; since if it were it would be good, whereas *ex hypothesi* it was actually bad. Those, on the other hand, who interpret the object of wish as being the apparent good must accept the consequence that what is to be wished for depends not upon the nature of the object but simply upon how it appears to the individual concerned. Yet to different individuals different or even opposite things appear to be good.

If both of these consequences are inacceptable, we shall doubtless have to conclude that while as a matter of abstract truth it is the good as such that is the object of wish, for the particular individual concerned it is what appears to him to be good. On this basis the true object of wish [i.e. what *ought* to be wished for] will be the object of wish for the 'ideally good man' (*spoudaios*) [i.e. what the ideally good man *actually does* wish for],[1] whereas the inferior man's object of wish may be anything at all. The case

---

[1] *Boulêton*, 'object of wish,' has a double connotation: (1) what *is actually* wished for; (2) what is the proper object of wish, and hence *ought* to be wished for. Only to a modern mind, however, is this likely to appear an equivocation. To Aristotle the opposition between 'is' and 'ought to be' is less sharp; since he assumes that what truly ought to be, while potential with respect to us as imperfect agents, is to be postulated as actually existing in the ideally good man—if and whenever he is to be found.

is similar with respect to the human body: people in good health find those things healthful that are really so, while a different regimen may be more healthful to invalids; and in the same way they will severally find different things to be bitter, sweet, hot, heavy, or the like. The ideally good man, in short, judges rightly of particular cases: in a particular case what is truly good will appear to him such. To the different states of character there correspond different interpretations of the noble and pleasant; and there is perhaps nothing so distinctive of the good man as his ability to form a right judgment of those various interpretations, being himself, as it were, the criterion by which he estimates and judges them. 'Ordinary men' (*hoi polloi*), on the other hand, are likely to be led astray by pleasure, which will seem to them a good even when it is not; with the result that they choose what is pleasant, thinking it to be good, and shun pain as an evil.

v. Responsibility for both good and evil

As the end, then, is the object of wish, and the means to the end are the objects of deliberation and choice, it follows that actions that deal with means must be such as are done by choice, i.e., must be voluntary. Now it is actions expressing particular virtues that have to do with means. Hence virtue depends on ourselves; and so too does vice. For where it is within our power to do, it is within our power to abstain; and conversely, where we can say no, we can also say yes. Accordingly, where action is the honorable course and depends upon ourselves, non-action, the baser alternative, will also depend upon us; and conversely, where inaction is the more decent alternative and is in our power, the baser alternative of action will be in our power also. But if it depends upon us whether we shall do or abstain, and if moral good and evil consist in doing and abstaining, we may conclude that it depends upon ourselves whether we are worthy or worthless individuals. The saying, "None is willingly wicked nor unwillingly happy," appears to be partly false and partly true. No one, to be sure, is unwillingly happy, yet wickedness is voluntary. Were we to deny this, we should have to contradict our former conclusions by denying that man is the moving cause and begetter of his actions as of his children. But if our earlier statements are accepted, and if we cannot trace our actions to any other origin than such as lies within ourselves, then that inner origin must depend upon us and be voluntary.

This conclusion seems to be attested, moreover, both by the private conduct of individuals and by the practice of legislators, who punish and take vengeance on evil-doers—except, of course, such as may have acted under compulsion or through unavoidable ignorance—while they honor those who behave nobly; presumably intending to encourage the latter and deter the former. But surely they would not encourage a man to do what was not within human power, i.e., not voluntary; any more than there would be point in trying to persuade a man not to feel heat or pain or hunger or the like, when he would have to go on doing so in any case.

Even ignorance is not always an excuse: a man is, in fact, punished for his very ignorance if he is thought to be responsible for it. The penalty for an offence committed in drunkenness, for example, is doubled, because here the originating principle of the offence lies within the agent: drunkenness caused his ignorance, but he might have refrained from getting drunk. Again, punishment is meted out to one who breaks a law through ignorance, if the law is one that he ought to have known and could readily have known. The same principle holds good in other cases too, wherever the ignorance in question appears to result from negligence: the offender need not have been ignorant, we argue, had he but taken the trouble to inform himself.

But may not such negligence be ingrained in a man's character? We reply that such a man himself is responsible (*aitios*, adj.), by reason of his slack way of living, for the looseness of his character; just as by acts of cheating, by spending one's time at drinking bouts and the like, one becomes responsible for habits of injustice or profligacy. It is by repeated acts of a certain kind that men acquire a corresponding character. This is shown by the way in which men train themselves for a contest or an enterprise: by actively practicing for it. Consequently, to be ignorant that 'states of character' (*hexis*) are formed by actively practicing the appropriate virtues is to be wanting in ordinary perception.

Moreover, it is absurd to pretend that a man who acts unjustly or self-indulgently does not wish to be unjust or self-indulgent: if he performs knowingly the actions that make him unjust, he therein becomes unjust willingly. Perhaps, to be sure, he can no longer stop being unjust by wishing it; any more than an invalid by wishing can regain his health. Imagine the case of an invalid who has dissipated his health willingly, through rakish living and indifference to the advice of physicians. In the beginning it was in his power to avoid becoming ill, but it is no longer so, now that he has thrown this possibility away. Once you have let fly a stone it is too late to recall it; nevertheless it is you who are responsible for having picked up and flung the stone, inasmuch as the moving principle of this action was within you. In like manner, as the unjust or profligate man had it originally in his power to avoid becoming such a character, he is unjust or profligate voluntarily; although now that he has become so, it is no longer possible for him to be otherwise.

Not only the vices of the soul, but sometimes those of the body too are voluntary, and are accordingly censured. While we never blame a man for having been born ugly, we do blame those who become so from lack of exercise and carelessness of their appearance. It is the same way with weakness and infirmities: we should all be inclined rather to pity than to reproach a man for having been born blind, or for having become so through disease or accident; but if his blindness were the result of drunkenness or other debauchery, he would be universally blamed. In short, such bodily vices as depend upon ourselves are subject to censure, others not. And this being so, we may infer that other forms of vice too, when they are objects of censure, must be such as depend upon ourselves.

But suppose it were argued: "All men desire what appears to them good, but they cannot help how it appears to them: rather it is in each case the individual's character, whatever that happens to be, that determines what will appear to him as the proper end." In reply we may point out that if an individual is somehow responsible for his 'moral disposition' (*hexis*), he will also be in a sense responsible for the 'manner in which [moral questions] present themselves to him' (*phantasia*). If, on the contrary, we deny that the individual is responsible for his disposition, we must at the same time deny his responsibility for his own original wrongdoing; which means we shall have to suppose that when a man does wrong it is because he is ignorant of his proper end and believes that wrongdoing will procure him his greatest good. On this hypothesis, aspiration toward the goal will depend not on an individual's own choice, but on whether he happens to have been born with a kind of special intuition that enables him to discriminate properly and to choose that which is truly good. Anyone so endowed would be, presumably, a 'natural born aristocrat' (*eu-phy-ês*); for if a quality is at once the greatest and noblest of gifts, and also such as cannot be acquired or learnt from anyone else but can only be possessed in the form implanted by nature, then surely to be well and nobly endowed with such a quality would constitute 'noble birth' (*euphyia*) in the full and true meaning of the word.

But assuming this theory to be true, how will virtue be any more voluntary than vice? To good and bad men alike the end will be an appearance determined by nature, or something of the sort; and both alike will refer whatever actions they undertake to the end as thus determined. Hence, whether we suppose that a man's view of the end, whatever it may be, is not simply given by nature but depends partly on himself; or, on the contrary, that while his view of the end is given by nature, yet virtue is voluntary, in the sense that a good man will voluntarily adopt the means to the given end: in either case vice will be every bit as voluntary as virtue; for in the bad man, no less than in the good, there will be a power of his own to choose, if not ends, at least actions. Granting, then, that the virtues are, as they are asserted to be, voluntary (for we surely must be in some way partly responsible for our own characters, and the characters we possess determine what ends we will set up), we must conclude that vices too are voluntary, for the same argument applies to them.

We have now described in outline the 'general nature' (*genos*) which all the virtues share: viz., that each of them is a certain disposition to achieve a mean between contrary vices; that they naturally tend to issue in the same kind of actions as produced them; that they are in our own power and voluntary; and that they do as right principle prescribes. We have added that actions and the dispositions to which they give rise are not voluntary in quite the same sense. An action can be known in its various phases [8] and is under our control from start to finish; we have control only over the beginning of our habits, the particular stages of their growth being as imperceptible as the progress of a disease. Yet inasmuch as it lay originally in our power to choose how we would or would not act, the resulting dispositions are voluntary.

[8] Or possibly: "*When* (or *so far as*) an action can be known in its various phases, it is under our control. . . ." Andronicus' explanation is helpful: "When we perform our actions we know their bearings in every particular, and consequently we have control over them in the purest sense of the term—to do them or not, as we will, from beginning to end. On the other hand, the 'habit' is not known to the full extent: it is known not through itself, but through the actions by which it is formed. We thoroughly understand the actions by which the habit is formed, but we cease to understand our actions when consolidated into habit." (Hatch, *op. cit.*)

BOOK IV

PARTICULAR VIRTUES

ii. Munificence

OUR NEXT TOPIC, in the logical order of discussion,[1] would seem to be munificence (*megaloprepeia*); for this, too, is evidently a virtue that has to do with wealth. It does not, however, like liberality, apply to all actions pertaining to wealth, but only to such as involve large expenditure; and where a question of large expenditure is involved munificence outdoes liberality in scale, for, as the name itself connotes,[2] munificence is suitable expenditure on a large scale. But the scale is relative to the occasion: suitable expenditure is not the same for the captain of a trireme and for the head of a sacred embassy.[3] Suitability, then, must be relative to the person, the circumstances, and the object. But in any case the term 'munificent' is not applied to one who spends the right amount of money upon small or indifferent occasions—as in the boast, "I gave to many a wandering beggar"; [4] but only to one who does so upon great occasions. In short, the munificent man is liberal, but it does not follow that a liberal man need be munificent.

The corresponding deficiency in character may be called mean-

---

[1] Liberality having been discussed in Chapter i of this Book, it is logical that munificence, being a species of liberality, should be discussed next.

[2] The word *megaloprepeia* is derived from megalos, 'large,' and the impersonal verb *prepei,* 'it is fitting.'

[3] Although a trireme was equipped by the Athenian state, the captain took pride in spending out of pocket to increase its splendor and efficiency. A sacred embassy might be an "embassy sent by the state to the Great Games, or to consult the oracle at Delphi, or to assist at the celebration of the Delia —the solemn festival of the Ionian confederacy." (J. A. Stewart.)

[4] Spoken by Odysseus in *Odyssey*, xvii, 420.

216

ness. The excess is called by such names as 'vulgar display' (*banausia*),[5] tastelessness, and the like; which connote lavish expenditure on wrong objects, not right ones, and in a wrong manner.

The munificent man is like a connoisseur (*epistêmôn*): he can discern what is fitting and spend large sums with good taste. For, as we remarked at the outset, a state of character is defined by the activities (*energeia*) in which it finds expression and by the objects with which it is concerned. That is to say, the munificent man's outlays will be at once large and fitting. Such, too, will be his results, for a great expenditure is fitting only if it produces great and fitting results. And if the result ought to be worthy of the expenditure, it is even more important that the expenditure be worthy of the result. Moreover, the munificent man will make such expenditures purely with a view to what is noble (*kalos*); this motive, indeed, being present in all the virtues. And he will spend cheerfully and lavishly, for careful calculation is a shabby thing. In other words, he will consider how a work can be carried out most nobly and splendidly, rather than how much it will cost or what economies can be practiced. . . .

Munificence pertains to the kinds of expenditure which we call honorable: on the one hand such as are devoted to the worship of the gods (through votive offerings, public buildings, and sacrifices) and of all 'lesser divine beings' (*daimonion*); on the other hand such as express an ambition that is commendably public-spirited, as when someone here or there thinks it his duty to handsomely equip a tragic chorus or a trireme or to give a public banquet. But in all such cases, as we have said, the propriety of the expenditure must be judged with reference to the status and resources of the person spending; that is to say, the expenditure

---

[5] Etymologically *banausia* connotes the life and habits of one whose life is moulded by being engaged in a mechanical occupation. English affords no word corresponding to *mikroprepeia*—the deficiency of which *megaloprepeia* is the sufficiency. Whatever word is chosen—stinginess, meanness, niggardliness, miserliness, or the like—must be understood as connoting deficiency with respect to operations *projected on a grand scale*.

should be proportionate not only to the occasion but to the giver. Hence a poor man cannot be munificent, not having the means to make great outlays fittingly; and if he attempts munificence he is a fool, for he spends more than he can and ought, whereas an action is virtuous only when it is done in the right way. [Lavish expenditure] is proper only for those who possess adequate means, whether acquired by their own exertions or by inheritance or from some present connection, and who enjoy high birth or prestige or some other such mark of greatness and distinction.

Such, then, are the principal traits of the munificent man, and such are the kinds of expenditure—the greatest and most honored —by which munificence is chiefly expressed. But munificence may display itself also on certain private occasions which happen only once, such as a wedding or the like; and in celebrations that interest the entire city or its most eminent citizens; and in welcoming and taking leave of foreign guests and in the formal exchange of presents [with them]. In such expenditures the munificent man regards the public weal rather than his own, and his gifts have something of the character of votive offerings. Moreover, he will furnish his own house in a manner suitable to his wealth, for a fine domestic establishment is likewise a kind of 'public ornament' (*kosmos*). His preference will always be to spend on such objects as are lasting, for it is they that are noblest; and he will make his expenditures appropriate to their occasions, for the same [gifts] are not suitable for gods as for men, nor in a temple as in a tomb. . . .

In contrast to the munificent man, such as we have described him, there stands, on the side of excess (*hyperballein*), the 'vulgar parvenu' (*banausos*), who 'overshoots the mark' (*hyperballein*) by spending more than is fitting. He spends large sums upon trifling occasions and in a tasteless manner: as when he entertains fellow club members on a scale suited to a wedding banquet, or when in furnishing the chorus for a comedy he decks it out in costumes of [royal] purple, as they do in Megara. His motive in all this is nothing noble but merely to show off his wealth, hoping thereby to win admiration. He spends little where he ought to spend much, and much where he ought to spend little.

The stingy man, on the other hand, will always fall short [at some point in an undertaking]. Even when spending a great amount he will spoil the final effect for a trifle, and will always be stopping to think how he can economize and grumbling that he has to spend so much.

Both these states of character, then, [showy vulgarity and stinginess,] are vices; yet not such as we should strongly condemn, for they do not hurt other persons nor are they marks of real depravity.

iii. Aristocratic pride

'Aristocratic pride' (*megalopsychia*), as its very name indicates,[6] has to do with what is great. In examining the nature of this greatness it is immaterial whether we look at the 'moral quality' (*hexis*) itself or at the individual who displays it.

A man is called 'proud' [in the sense here intended] when he is conscious of a superior worth that he really possesses; for only fools rate themselves more highly than they deserve, and to be a fool or dolt is no part of being virtuous. One whose worth is little and who knows it to be little, on the other hand, has the virtue of temperance [or modesty] but not of aristocratic pride; for pride implies greatness, just as personal beauty requires a body of ample size—small people, however elegant and shapely, not being really beautiful.

Those [who err on the one side by] claiming a superior worth which they do not possess are vain. Those, on the other hand,

[6] The word *megalo-psychia*, broken into components, means 'great-souledness.' 'Magn-animity' carries over the parallel components from Latin. But the one epithet has too vague, the other too narrow a meaning in modern English. 'Aristocratic pride' seems to be our closest connotative approximation to the Greek word; and the corresponding adjective will be rendered either 'proud' or 'aristocratic,' according as one or the other connotation appears uppermost in a given context.

who estimate their own worth too meanly have a false humility.[7]
This is the case with all who undervalue themselves, whether their
actual worth be much, moderate, or little, but the fault shows up
most prominently in a man of high worth, for how would such a
man regard himself, we tend to wonder, if his worth were less?
As between these extremes of overrating and underrating oneself,
the proud man—although he stands at an extreme in one sense,
[namely with respect to his high valuation of himself]—stands at
a middle point with respect to the relation between his self-valua-
tion and his actual worth.

Now since the proud man is one who both is and thinks himself
worthy of great things, and of the greatest things most of all, there
is one thing that will interest him especially. 'Worthy' implies a relation to something external to oneself, of which one is
worthy; and the chief object of worthiness is that which we offer
to the gods when we worship them, and which is most coveted by
men of position, and which is awarded as a prize for the noblest
deeds: namely, honor (*timê*), which accordingly is the greatest of
external goods. It follows from this that the proud man is he who
stands in the right relation to honor and dishonor. Indeed, we need
no argument to see that a suitable degree of honor is what proud
men actually do both deserve and expect. . . .

Aristocratic pride, or 'great-souledness,' would seem to involve
something of the greatness belonging to each of the other virtues.
We can hardly imagine a proud man fleeing in panic from battle
or cheating someone. For what motive could he have for base
conduct when its rewards seem paltry in his eyes? Aristocratic
pride is thus the 'crowning perfection' (*kosmos*) of the virtues: it
enhances them, while at the same time it cannot exist apart from
them. Hence to be truly proud is a hard thing, and is impossible
without an 'ingrained beauty of character' (*kalo-k'-agathia*).

Honor and dishonor, then, are of preëminent concern to the
proud man. When great honors are conferred upon him by men

---

[7] Lit., 'are small-souled.'

of worth he will be moderately pleased, regarding them as his due, or even less than his due, since no honor can be worthy of a virtue that is perfect; yet he will accept such honors, as being the best that worthy people can offer. But honor that is bestowed by ordinary people and on trivial grounds he will utterly despise, knowing that this is not what he deserves. Dishonor he will despise also, knowing that it cannot attach to him justly.

Still, external prosperity does seem to contribute something to the formation of aristocratic pride. Men who enjoy the advantages of high birth, power, or wealth are regarded as worthy of honor because their preëminence in any of these respects seems to make them more proudly aristocratic, and there are those who honor them on this account. Strictly, to be sure, it is only the man of moral worth who deserves to be honored. But a man who combines external advantages with high personal excellence is honored even more.

Those who have nothing but external goods like wealth and family as their title to esteem are apt to become supercilious and insolent, for without virtue it is not easy to bear good fortune becomingly. Such people, therefore, regard themselves as superior, treat others with disdain, and behave pretty much as they please. They imitate the truly proud man without being really like him, for whereas he, when he condemns others, does so justly, on the basis of a correct estimation, most people condemn quite at random.

The proud man does not expose himself to trifling dangers, nor is he fond of running risks at all, since there are few things that he values highly enough to make the risk worth while. Great dangers, however, he is willing to face, and when he does so he is unsparing of his life, knowing that it is not worth keeping at the cost of honor. . . .

It is characteristic of the proud man that he seldom or never asks a favor, but is always ready to render aid. He is haughty toward other men of rank and affluence, but unassuming toward those of the middle class; because it is more difficult and [therefore] more dignified to assert one's superiority over the former, but easy over the latter. There is nothing ignoble in showing one's dignity among the great, but to do so among the humble is like displaying physical strength against a cripple. . . .

The proud man will of course be open in his hatreds and friendships, for concealment in these respects is cowardly. Caring more for truth than reputation he is frank in word and deed, for his very disdain leads him to speak boldly. Consequently he is truthful, except so far as he speaks with 'light irony' (*eirôneia*)—an attitude that he will adopt in dealing with 'the masses' (*hoi polloi*). . . . But he never bears grudges, for it is incompatible with his proud nature to brood on the past, especially on past injuries; he will prefer to overlook them.

Again, he is no gossip: he will not chatter about either himself or others, since it is no concern of his to receive compliments or to bestow either compliments or blame. He speaks no evil of others unless by way of deliberate insult to an enemy.

On encountering misfortunes that are either unavoidable or trifling he neither complains nor calls for help; for only those who think such things important behave thus.

He is the kind of man who would rather possess beautiful and profitless things than things that have merely cost and utility to recommend them; such preference being a mark of his self-sufficiency.

Finally, the character of the proud man would seem to require that his gait should be slow, his voice low-pitched, and his diction measured. For a man is not likely to be in a hurry if he takes few things seriously, nor vehement if he considers nothing important. Excessive concern is what produces a shrill voice and a rapid gait.

So much, then, for our account of the aristocratically proud man.

BOOK VI

THE INTELLECTUAL VIRTUES

i. Introduction

. . . WE HAVE already distinguished the virtues of the soul according as they are virtues of character (*êthos*) or virtues of intellect (*dianoia*). As the moral (*êthikos*) virtues have been fully discussed, we may now, after a few preliminary remarks about the soul, pass on to a discussion of the intellectual virtues.

We have said [1] that there are two parts of the soul: the one of which possesses reason [or grasps a rational principle],[2] while the other is irrational. Let us now draw a similar distinction within that part of the soul which possesses reason. Of this part we may postulate two subdivisions: one by which we think about (*theôrein*) things whose moving principles are invariable, the other by which we think about variable things; for where the objects differ in kind, the parts or aspects of the soul corresponding to each must likewise differ in kind, one of the conditions of knowledge being a certain likeness and kinship between the knower and the thing known. We may call one of these subdivisions cognitive (*epistêmonikos*), the other calculative (*logistikos*). To calculate is the same as to deliberate (*boulouesthai*), and as no one ever deliberates about what is invariable, we must distinguish the calculative faculty from the rational aspect of the soul generally. Our next task is to discover what is the best disposition of the cognitive and

---

[1] Bk. I, Chaps. vii and xiii.
[2] Lit., 'has *logos*': connoting both possession of the power of reason in general and a grasp of the 'right principle' (*orthos logos*).

calculative faculties respectively; for this will be the 'virtue, or specific excellence' (*aretê*) appropriate to each.

ii. Intellectual virtue distinguished from moral

There are three forces in the soul by which action as well as truth is governed: sensation (*aesthêsis*), intelligence (*nous*), and desire (*orexis*). Of these, sensation is never the 'moving principle' (*archê*) of 'moral conduct' (*praxis*), as is clear from the fact that brutes, although they enjoy sensation, are incapable of acting morally. What affirmation and negation are to thinking (*dianoia*), pursuit and avoidance are to desire. Accordingly, since moral virtue is a disposition involving choice, and choice is deliberate desire, it follows, if the choice is to be a worthy one, that the reasoning (*logos*) must be true, that the desire must be right, and that the direction of the latter must accord with what the former asserts. Such is the practical type of thinking and of truth. Of the thinking that is theoretical (*theôrêtikos*) rather than practical (*praktikos*) or productive (*poiêtikos*), the good and bad state are respectively truth and falsity, the determination of which is the function of every intellectual activity. But where intellectual activity has a practical character, the good state is truth in harmony with right desire.

The originating principle of action—i.e., the source of its movement, not its telic principle—is choice; while that of choice, in turn, is desire and reasoning with a view to an end. Choice thus presupposes both 'apperceptive intelligence' (*nous*) and thinking (*dianoia*) on the one hand, and a moral disposition on the other; for good and bad conduct achieve active expression only when intellect (*dianoia*) and character (*êthos*) are combined. Intellect in the abstract moves nothing, but only so far as it aims at some end and is practical; and in this sense it controls the productive faculty too, because in making anything we always make it with a view to some end. What we make, in other words, is not an end in itself, but a means to or a condition of something further. But what we do is an end in itself; for well-doing (*eu-praxia*) is the end, and is the object of desire. Choice, therefore, may be regarded either as an intelligence that desires or as a desire that reasons, and this combination makes the moving principle that is man.

The object of choice cannot be something past. No one can choose to have sacked Troy, because no one can deliberate about the past, but only about what is at once in the future and capable of being altered. It is obvious that what has once occurred cannot be made *not* to have occurred. Agathon was right in saying:

> There is just one power denied even to God:
> Of undoing what has been done.

To sum up: the proper task of both of the rational aspects of the soul is truth. Accordingly, the disposition of each in which it best attains truth will be its own 'specific virtue' (*aretê*).

iii. The soul's five faculties for attaining truth

Let us now approach the subject from a fresh point of view. We may assume that the faculties by virtue of which the soul reaches truth by affirming or denying are five in number: viz., 'practical technique' (*technê*), 'scientific understanding' (*epistêmê*), sagacity (*phronêsis*), wisdom (*sophia*), and 'apperceptive intelligence' (*nous*). Guesswork and opinion are left out because they may lead to error.

The nature of 'scientific understanding' (*epistêmê*)—using the word in its strict sense, and not as when its meaning is extended by analogy—may be explained as follows. In the first place, we all take for granted that what we know scientifically is something that fundamentally cannot vary; since in the case of things that can vary, once they have passed beyond the range of our observation, we cannot know whether they exist or not. The objects of scientific understanding must therefore have the character of necessity. This means that they are eternal; for anything that has the character of necessity in an unqualified sense is eternal; which is to say, both ungenerated and imperishable.

In the second place, it is commonly agreed that any scientific knowledge can be communicated by teaching, and that the objects of scientific knowledge are such as can be learned. Now all teaching, as we have already remarked in the *Analytics*,[3] starts from what is already known, proceeding sometimes by induction and sometimes by the syllogism. Induction is the starting-point (*archê*) even of the universal, while the syllogism, in turn, sets out from universal propositions already established. Thus there are principles from which the syllogism proceeds, and which are not themselves established by syllogism but by induction.

Scientific understanding, then, is a 'trained ability' (*hexis*) to demonstrate; its more particular characteristics having been stated in the *Analytics*. To have scientific knowledge is to possess a certain degree of conviction together with a sure knowledge of the principles on which it rests; for unless these principles are better known to us than the conclusions that we derive from them, our knowledge will be merely accidental.[4]

Let this serve as our account of scientific understanding.

iv. The nature of technique (art)

That which is variable includes what can be made and what can be done. Production and action are not the same: a point that has been emphasized in our public discourses. Hence a rationally developed disposition to act is one thing; a rationally developed disposition to produce is another. Neither of them, then, is a species of the other: action is not a kind of production, nor is production a kind of action.

Since architecture is a technique (*technê*) and may be described as a 'trained disposition' (*hexis*) to produce in accordance with

---

[3] The *Posterior Analytics* opens with a statement of this principle.

[4] I.e., as Peters observes, "We may know the truths of science, but unless we know these in their necessary connection, we have not scientific knowledge."

correct calculation (*logos*), and since there is no technique that is not a disposition of this kind, nor any disposition of this kind that is not a technique, we may define a technique as *a trained disposition to make in accordance with correct calculation*. Every technique aims at bringing something into existence. In practicing a technique we must study how to bring into existence a thing whose nature admits both of existence and non-existence, and whose moving cause lies in the maker and not in the thing made. A technique does not deal with what exists or comes into existence either by 'mechanical necessity' (*anangkê*) or by 'organic development' (*physis*), for in either of these cases the 'creative principle' (*archê*) is inherent in the nature of the object. Nor does a technique have to do with action (*praxis*), but with production; these being different, as we have said. The domain of technique is in a sense the same as that of luck (*tychê*), for as Agathon declares, "Art (*technê*) and chance (*tychê*) are lovers." A technique, then, we repeat, is a trained disposition to produce in accordance with true calculations; while 'bad technique' (*atechnia*), on the contrary, is a trained disposition to produce in accordance with false calculations. Both deal with such objects as are variable, i.e., as can be made other than they are.

vii. Wisdom

. . . The wise man (*sophos*) must not only be able to draw deductions from first principles, but must also have a true knowledge of the first principles themselves. Hence wisdom (*sophia*) is evidently a combination of 'apperceptive intelligence' (*nous*) and 'scientific understanding' (*epistêmê*): it is a fully consummated understanding [5] of the most exalted matters. The last phrase is important, for it would be absurd to suppose that political or personal sagacity is the highest form of wisdom, unless indeed man were the best of all things in the universe. As the terms healthy and good have one meaning for men and another for fishes but the

---

[5] Lit., 'understanding with a head on.'

meaning of white and straight is always the same, so in like manner wise has the same meaning for everybody but sagacious has not. Those who have a keen eye to their own interests we call sagacious and deem them competent to handle practical affairs. In some cases we even speak of the lower animals as sagacious, if they appear to have a power of foresight with regard to their own lives.

Wisdom must not be confused with statesmanship, since if we were to extend the term wisdom to include knowledge of what is advantageous, we should have to postulate a plurality of wisdoms, one for each species; for there is not one wisdom embracing the good of every species of animal, any more than there is one art of medicine applicable to them all. To argue that man is superior to the other animals is beside the point; for there are other things more divine in the universe even than man: e.g., the celestial bodies, to name only the most conspicuous.

From these considerations, then, it is plain that wisdom is a combination of apperceptive intelligence and scientific understanding concerned with matters of the most exalted nature. That is why, when we see men like Anaxagoras and Thales ignoring their own interests, we call them wise but not sagacious; and we describe the knowledge they have attained as rare, astounding, difficult, and even half-divine, but still useless, because it is no human good that they seek.

Sagacity, on the other hand, is concerned with human affairs and more particularly with such matters as admit of deliberation. We regard it as the chief function of a sagacious man to deliberate well. No one, however, deliberates about what cannot be altered, nor about things that are not a means to an end—i.e., to an end that is at once good and attainable by action. Hence a good deliberator may be described in general terms as one who can arrive by calculation (*logismos*) at the best of human goods attainable by action.

Nor is sagacity concerned only with general propositions. It must take account also of particular facts; for it issues in action, and action has to do with particulars. This explains why those who are wanting in formal knowledge are sometimes, especially if they are men of wide experience, more effective from a practical stand-point than those who possess it. A man who knows that light meat is digestible and wholesome without knowing what sorts of meat are light, will be less apt to produce health than a man who knows only that, say, chicken is light and wholesome. . . .

viii. Sagacity lacking in young men

. . . What has been said is further confirmed by the generally accepted fact that young men, although they may become expert (*sophos*) in geometry, mathematics, and kindred subjects, can hardly become sagacious. The reason for this is that sagacity in-volves a knowledge of particular facts, which can only be acquired by experience; whereas a young man is necessarily inexperienced, since experience comes only with time. So, too, if it be asked why a boy can become a mathematician but not a philosopher (*sophos*) nor a natural scientist, the answer doubtless is that mathematics is concerned with abstractions, whereas the first principles of philosophy and natural science are built up from experience; and that consequently while a young man may learn to repeat philo-sophical and natural truths he will do so without full conviction, whereas the essential truths of mathematics can be plainly under-stood.

xiii. Sagacity distinguished from cleverness

We must now consider once again the question of virtue. An analogy is offered by the relation between sagacity and mere cleverness. Cleverness is like sagacity but not identical with it; and natural virtue is analogously related to virtue in the strict sense. It is universally agreed that the various types of character are in a manner inborn. We are just, temperate, courageous, and endowed with the other virtues from the moment of birth. But goodness in the strict sense, which is the object of our quest, is not a matter of natural endowment, and the virtues in which such goodness consists are present in us in a quite different way. The innate dispositions are present even in children and beasts, but when unguided by reason they are likely to be hurtful. This much at least, however, seems evident: that as a strong (*ischyros*) —bodied creature without sight will be caused by its want of sight to stumble heavily (*ischyrôs*) when it starts to move about, so it is with natural virtue. But once a man of good natural disposition acquires reason (*nous*), there comes to be a difference in his conduct: the disposition that formerly resembled virtue has now come to be virtue in the strict sense. Just as with regard to the power of forming opinions [6] we have differentiated between [natural] cleverness and [developed] sagacity, so likewise the moral part of the soul assumes two forms, natural virtue and virtue in the strict sense; and the latter of these is impossible without sagacity. Consequently some maintain that all the virtues are merely so many expressions of sagacity; and Socrates was partly right in his inquiry, although partly wrong too: he was wrong in thinking that all the virtues are merely so many expressions of sagacity,[7] but right in saying that they are impossible without it. In corroboration we may point out that even today anyone who defines virtue will not merely characterize it as an 'habitual disposition' (*hexis*) with respect to certain specified types of situation, but will add that it must function in accordance with 'right principle' (*orthos logos*)—'right' meaning as discriminated by the agent's sagacity. Thus everyone evidently has some inkling that virtue is an habitual disposition of the sort described, i.e., guided by sagacity. A slight correction, however, is wanted. Virtue is an habitual disposition not merely *in accordance with* right principle, but *implying the presence of* right principle; and the presence

[6] The faculty of forming opinions is what was termed in Chap. i the calculative faculty.

[7] In Plato's dialogues Socrates habitually identifies virtue with understanding (*epistêmê*), not with sagacity (*phronêsis*).

of right principle is what constitutes sagacity in moral matters. Accordingly, whereas Socrates regarded the virtues as identical with 'rational principles' (*logos*), i.e., with the different forms of 'rational knowledge' (*epistêmê*); we, on the other hand, regard them rather as implying the presence of rational principle.

It is clear, then, from what has been said, that it is impossible either to be good, in the strict sense of the word, without sagacity, or to be truly sagacious without moral virtue. Moreover, we are now in a position to refute a certain dialectical objection which might crop up. The virtues, it might be claimed, can exist in isolation from each other; for as a man will have a stronger natural predisposition toward some virtues than toward others, there seems to be no reason why he cannot already have attained one virtue while remaining deficient in another. We reply that although this is possible in the case of natural virtues, it is not possible in the case of those virtues which entitle a man to be called good in the strict sense. For by possessing the one virtue of moral sagacity a man thereby possesses all the others.

We may conclude, then: (1) that even if it had no bearing on conduct, moral sagacity would still be needful as the 'peculiar excellence' (*aretê*) of one of the two intellectual faculties of the soul; and (2) that our choice of actions will not be right either without sagacity or without 'moral virtue' (*aretê*), for while the latter directs us to the end, the former reveals the means of achieving that end.

But we must not interpret this as implying that sagacity is in authority over wisdom (*sophia*), i.e., over the mind's nobler part, any more than the art of healing is in authority over health. Healing does not employ health, but studies how to produce it; it issues orders not to health, but for health's sake. To suppose the contrary would be like supposing that statecraft, because it regulates all public concerns [including the institution of religious worship], is on that account in authority over the gods.

BOOK VII

INCONTINENCE

ii. Socrates' view of incontinence

How, it may be asked, can a man behave incontinently while recognizing that what he is doing is wrong? Some would say that incontinent behavior is impossible to anyone who really understands its wrongness; for it would be strange, Socrates thought, if, when knowledge was present in a man, something else should drag it about like a slave. A man, he argued, never acts contrary to what is best so long as he has a clear conception of what this is, but only through ignorance. As such a view, however, runs obviously counter to the facts of experience, we must inquire into the actual state of mind of an incontinent man; and if we agree that he acts by reason of ignorance, we must ask what sort of ignorance it is. For it is evident, at any rate, that an incontinent man does not, except at those times when his passion has mastered him, judge his incontinent behavior to be right. . . .

iii. Incontinence and knowledge

Our task, then, is to consider whether or not an incontinent man acts knowingly; and if knowingly, in what sense. . . .

(1) There are two senses in which we employ the word 'know' (*epistasthai*). In the one sense we say that a man knows a thing when he possesses but is not actually using the knowledge of it; in the other, when he is actually using such knowledge. Accordingly, when a man does wrong, it is one thing to suppose that he possesses but is not at the moment 'actually contemplating'

(*theôrein*) the knowledge that his action is wrong; quite another to suppose that he both possesses and is actively engaged in contemplating such knowledge. The latter alternative would be quite astounding, but there is nothing astounding about the former.

(2) Again, as there are two kinds of premises [a major premise which is universal and a minor which is particular], there is nothing to prevent a man's knowing both premises, yet acting against his knowledge in that he uses only the universal premise and not the particular; for it is with particulars that action has to do.

Moreover, it may be that two sorts of universal terms are employed, one of which the reasoner predicates of himself, the other of the thing about which he is reasoning. For example, he may be perfectly well aware (*a*) that dry food is beneficial to every man, (*b*) that he himself is a man, and even (*c*) that a certain kind of food is dry; but whether *this* food is of such a kind, he may either not know or not be attending to the knowledge of. In view, then, of the great difference between these two ways of knowing, it should not be thought remarkable that a man may in one sense know that he is acting incontinently, and in another not.

(3) Again, a man may be said to have knowledge in still another sense than the ones just mentioned. The state of having knowledge without using it may be subjected to a further distinction: a man may, in a matter of speaking, both have and not have knowledge, as when he is asleep, mad, or drunk. People under stress of passion are in a similar condition; for it is a recognized fact that outbursts of anger, sexual desire, and the like actually alter our bodily condition and in some cases even bring on madness. Plainly, then, the incontinent man, if he has the knowledge of his condition, has it merely in the way that one might who is asleep, mad, or drunk. To repeat the words that go with knowledge is no sign of its possession, for in those other states, too, men may repeat scientific proofs or verses from Empedocles; and in a similar fashion learners just starting on a subject will

string words together without understanding them, for a subject can be understood only by being made a part of the learner's very nature, and this takes time. Hence we must suppose that men [who moralize while] in a state of incontinence are much like actors reciting their lines.

(4) Again, we may investigate the cause of incontinence 'from a psychological standpoint' (*physikôs*), as follows. We have a universal premise, which expresses a 'general belief' (*doxa*); while our other premise deals with particular facts, which fall within the province of sense-perception. When these two premises, by their combination, give rise to a single conclusion, the mind must not only assent to the truth of this conclusion but, where the question concerns conduct, it must forthwith act. If we accept, for example, the premises, "Everything sweet ought to be tasted," and "This thing before me is sweet," the latter expressing a particular case falling under the general rule; then, if we are able and not hindered, we are obliged at once to act upon the implied conclusion.

Now suppose we have on the one side a universal proposition forbidding us to taste, and as against this the universal proposition that "Everything sweet is pleasant [and ought to be tasted]" coupled with a particular proposition that spurs us to action, "This thing before me is sweet." If this is the logical situation, and if desire also happens to be present, then, although the one train of reasoning bids us shun this thing, our desire impels us to take it, for desire can set in motion the various members of the body. Thus it appears that when people behave incontinently they may be said after a fashion to be acting according to reason (*logos*) and belief (*doxa*); these, however, are not opposed to 'right reason' (*orthos logos*) in themselves, but only accidentally: it is the desire, not the opinion, that is really opposed. This, we may note in passing, explains why it is that brutes are not incontinent: they have not a conception of universals, but only images and memories of particulars.

As to how the oblivion (*agnoia*) of the incontinent man is dissipated and how he regains the use of his knowledge, this phenomenon requires no special kind of explanation, but may be explained in the same way as recovery from drunkenness or sleep —a problem for the physiologists.

Inasmuch as the ultimate minor premise of a practical syllogism, expressing as it does a belief (*doxa*) with regard to an object of sense-perception, is what determines action; the incontinent man either does not possess this belief or else he possesses it in a way in which, as we have seen, possession is not equivalent to active knowledge, but is only a form of words, like the drunkard who spouts Empedocles. And since the minor term is not universal and is not considered an object of scientific knowledge in the same way as a universal term is, it seems that Socrates' contention is really substantiated. For it is not when knowledge in the proper sense of the word is present that passion arises, nor is it knowledge in this proper sense that gets dragged about by passion, but only in the sense of perceptual belief.[1]

So much, then, for the question of whether a man can be knowingly incontinent, and in what sense this is possible.

---

[1] Andronicus gives the following paraphrase of this paragraph: "When the man of weak will finds himself in the toils of passion, he either does not possess at all, and does not know, the minor premise which controls particular actions (the premise which would tell him that 'Such and such a thing is evil'), or because he possesses it after the manner in which men who are drunk or raving utter verses or demonstrations; more particularly for the reason that the minor premise is not, in fact, scientific by itself in the sense in which the universal and major premise is. Hence it seems that the solution which Socrates tried to present is the real one. The moral temptation does not arise while knowledge (I mean knowledge in the real and recognized sense, i.e., the Universal) is present: desire has no power over this kind of knowledge;—but it does arise in the presence of that kind of knowledge which is concerned with and has control over particular facts, i.e., the minor premise. It is this particular knowledge which is violated by the man who acts under passion—this particular knowledge being concerned with actual conduct; and it is this particular knowledge which is dragged about under temptation, and not the universal knowledge." (Hatch's translation, *op. cit.*)

BOOK VIII

FRIENDSHIP

i. Nature and value of friendship

NEXT we might properly discuss friendship:[1] for it is a sort of virtue, or at any rate involves a sort of virtue;[2] besides which, it is indispensable to human life. No one would choose to live without friends, even though he possessed all other blessings. The rich, indeed, and those in positions of authority and influence, would appear to have especial need of them; for what is the good of prosperity if there is no one with whom to share it? And toward whom is beneficence more often and more admirably displayed than toward friends? Without friends, moreover, how could prosperity be safeguarded and preserved? For generally speaking, the greater it is, the less secure. On the other hand, in poverty and other such adversities friends may serve as our refuge. In our youth they help us to correct our faults, in old age they wait upon us and perform those necessary tasks for which weakness has incapacitated us, and in the prime of life they stir us to noble deeds: "going shoulder to shoulder," [as Homer says,] they inspire us to think and to act.

Friendship is a kind of natural affection, such as exists instinctively in a parent toward its young, and in an offspring toward its parent, not only among men but similarly among birds and a majority of animals. It exists also in creatures of the same race

[1] *Philia* (connected with the verb *philein*, to love) is a stronger word, connoting a greater degree of emotional content, than the word friendship, which however is its closest approximation in English.

[2] Or: ". . . implies virtue as a constituent element in itself"—Hatch.

toward one another, especially of the race of men; whence it happens that we commend those whose disposition is philan-thropic. Even when abroad we can perceive how akin and how dear every man is to his fellow.

Moreover, it seems that friendship is the bond that holds states together, and that lawgivers are more anxious to secure it than justice. For concord bears a certain resemblance to friendship, and it is concord that they try especially to promote, expelling faction as something inimical. Where men are friends there is no need of justice, but men may be just and still need friendship besides. In its highest form, indeed, justice would seem to contain an element of friendship.

Apart from its supreme utility, friendship is also something 'in-trinsically noble' (*kalos*). We commend those who love their friends, and it is accounted a noble thing to have a wide circle of friends. Some even think that to be a good man and to be a good friend are one and the same.

But there are numerous differences of opinion about the mat-ter. Some think of friendship as a kind of likeness, and persons who are alike as essentially friends: by which they account for such sayings as "Like seeks like," "Birds of a feather," [3] and so on. Others, on the contrary, declare that men who are alike behave as quarrelsome potters to one another: [4] and they seek an explana-tion for this in the original nature of things, Euripides, for example, observing that

> Parched Earth loves the rain.
> And high Heaven, rain-filled,
> Loves to fall earthward.

Heraclitus, in a similar vein, says that "opposites tend to unite," that "discordant elements produce the fairest harmony," and that "all things are brought to birth through strife." Others, such as

[3] Lit., "jackdaw to jackdaw."
[4] Alluding to Hesiod's line, "Potter quarrels with potter, and carpenter with carpenter."

Empedocles, take the opposite view, declaring that like aims at like.

But we may put aside the physical aspects of these disputes, as not being germane to the present inquiry. Let us inquire rather into the human aspects, involving character and feeling: as, for instance, whether friendship can arise in all people, or whether it is impossible that men should be friends when they are evil; and whether there is a single kind of friendship or many. To suppose that all friendship must be of one kind simply because it admits of degrees of more and less is unwarranted; for differences in degree do not exclude differences in kind.

ii. *The three objects of liking*

Doubtless these questions can be cleared up by ascertaining what it is that is the object of friendship and love. For it seems that not everything is loved, but only the lovable, which is either good or pleasant or useful. Since we call a thing useful when it is a means to some good or to some pleasure, lovable things may be reduced in the last analysis to what is good and what is pleasant.

But which is it that we love, the good as such or the good relatively to ourselves? The two are often at variance. And the question applies with equal force to the pleasant. The answer seems to be that each man loves what is good in relation to himself: that as a thing absolutely good is lovable without qualification, so a thing that is good in relation to a particular man is lovable by that man. If it is objected that a man loves not what is really good in relation to himself but only what appears to be so, no matter: 'the lovable,' on that interpretation, becomes 'the apparently lovable.'

While there are in general the three above-mentioned grounds on which people love, the love of inanimate objects is not called friendship; for such love is not requited, nor does it involve a wish for the good of the object concerned. It would be absurd, after all, to wish the good of a bottle of wine. We wish, if anything, that the wine may keep so that we can enjoy it. But the good of a friend it is generally supposed that we wish for his own sake. One who thus wishes the good of another is said to bear him goodwill—unless the wish is reciprocated, in which case goodwill is raised to the status of friendship.

Or ought we perhaps to add that the goodwill must be recognized by its recipient? Many of us feel goodwill toward persons whom we have never seen but suppose to be worthy and useful, and one of those persons might conceivably bear us a similar feeling in return. In that case there would be two persons bearing goodwill to each other but how could they be called friends if each were unaware of the other's feelings? To be friends, therefore, men must not only, on one of the three grounds mentioned, bear goodwill toward each other and wish each other's good, but in addition be mutually known to do so.

iii. The corresponding types of friendship

As the three qualities that make for friendship differ in kind, so there will be different kinds of affection (*philêsis*) and friendship. Accordingly, the kinds of friendship are three, equal in number to the kinds of lovable object; each one of which may provide a basis for a reciprocal affection mutually recognized. Those who 'are friends' (*philein*) wish each other's good in respect of the quality on which their friendship is based. If they are friends for utility's sake, each likes the other not for what he is but only for some benefit that he can supply. Similarly with friendships based on pleasure. We like witty people not for what they are in themselves, but merely because they amuse us. . . . Both these types of friendship, then, are friendship 'in a secondary sense' (*kata symbebêkos*), involving as they do no love of the friend for his own sake but simply as affording advantage or amusement. That is why such friendships are readily dissolved: as the relation of the parties becomes altered and they are no longer pleasurable or useful to one another, they cease to be friends. Utility is nothing permanent, but varies from time to time; and when the motive of the friendship is destroyed, the friendship, since it has existed only with a view to that, is dissolved likewise. . . .

Perfect (*teleios*) friendship is such as is found between good men, whose respective virtues serve as a common bond. Such men reciprocally wish each other's good solely by reason of each other's goodness; and the goodness of each of them belongs to his essential character. Now, wishing good to one's friend for his own sake is what constitutes friendship in the truest sense—where each loves the other for what he is in himself, not in some secondary respect. Good men's friendship, therefore, lasts as long as they remain good, and their virtue is an enduring quality. Moreover, each of them besides being good absolutely, is good relatively to his friend; for good men are at once good in themselves and of service to one another. They are pleasant, too, in the same double sense—both in themselves and relatively to one another—for every man finds pleasure in his own actions or in others that resemble them, and to the good man the actions of other good men will be identical with or similar to his own. . . .

Such friendships, of course, are rare, for good men are few. Moreover, time and intimacy are required; for, as the saying goes, people cannot know one another before consuming the proverbial salt together. Neither can they accept each other as friends nor really be friends until each has been found lovable and worthy of confidence by the other. Those who strike up friendships quickly wish to be friends no doubt, but they are not really friends unless they are proper objects of affection and know each other to be so.

iv. *Noble and inferior friendships*

. . . The friendship of good men is the only kind that can withstand calumny, for we do not readily believe another's gossip about someone whom we ourselves have put to the test over a long period of time. Besides, such friendship involves mutual confidence, a sense that the friend would never wrong us, and whatever else belongs to true friendship; while in the inferior types of friendship there is no such security.

As the word 'friends' is frequently applied also to those whose motive is utility (just as we speak of friendships between states, where expediency is generally recognized as the only ground of alliance) and to those whose motive is pleasure (as in the case of children), perhaps we too ought to call such people friends, distinguishing as a consequence the several kinds of friendship— first, in the primary and strict sense, the friendship of good men in so far as it is an expression of their goodness; next, the other kinds of friendship, so-called because of their resemblance to true friendship. For in these latter types of friendship, people are really friends to the extent that their relation involves some good, by virtue of which it resembles true friendship; and pleasure is a good to those who are fond of it. But these two secondary forms of friendship do not altogether coincide, nor do the same people become friends for the sake of utility and of pleasure, for accidental qualities of that sort are not usually found in combination.

Having distinguished friendship into these several species, we may say that bad men will be friends for the sake of pleasure or profit, in so far as they happen to agree in one of these respects; but that good men, when they are friends, love each other for their own sakes—that is, as good men. These, then, we call friends 'without qualification' (*haplôs*); the others 'in a derivative sense' (*kata symbebêkos*), and because of their resemblance to these.

v. Friendship vs. mere fondness

Just as in the case of the virtues some men are called good because of their general character, others because of their actual conduct, so too in the case of friendship. Friends who spend their time together delight in each other's society and render each other services; while those who are asleep or separated, though not actively performing, are yet *disposed* to perform the functions of friendship. Hence distance does not destroy friendship itself, but only its active exercise. If the absence lasts too long, however, it may obliterate the friendship too; whence the saying, "Lack of converse has broken many a friendship." . . .

Fondness (*philêsis*) resembles an emotion (*pathos*), friendship a 'state of character' (*hexis*). Fondness can be displayed just as well toward inanimate things; but the love between friends involves 'purposeful choice' (*proairesis*), and purposeful choice proceeds from a state of character. When we wish the good of anyone for his own sake, our goodwill depends not on emotion but on a state of character. Moreover, in loving one who is genuinely a friend we love what is good in ourselves; for when a good man becomes our friend he thereby becomes a part of our own good. Thus each party to a friendship loves what is a good to himself, while at the same time he returns an amount of goodwill and pleasure equivalent to what he gets; for the saying, "Friendship is equality," holds particularly true of friendships between good men.

vii. Unequal friendships

There is, in the next place, another kind of friendship, such as involves superiority of one of the parties: the friendship, for example, of a father for a son, and in general of an older for a younger person; and likewise of a man for his wife, and of any ruler for his subject. These friendships differ among themselves: the affection of parents for their children is not the same as that of rulers for their subjects; nor is the affection [5] of a father for his son the same as that of a son for his father, nor that of a husband for his wife the same as that of a wife for her husband. For as these differ in type of excellence and in function, the grounds of their affection differ; and so their feelings of love and habits of friendship differ also. What each does for the other is not the same, nor should they expect it to be the same; but when children render to parents what is due to those who begat them, and when parents

[5] The same word, *philia*, is here translated 'friendship,' 'affection,' or 'love,' according as the context and the English usage require.

render what is due to their children in return, then the friendship (or love) between them will be enduring and right. In all these unequal friendships the love on either side should be proportional: that is to say, the one who is better should receive more love than he bestows; and so should the one who is more useful or superior in some other way. For when love is in proportion to merit; there is a sort of equality established, which seems to be an essential element of friendship.

There is an evident difference between equality in justice and equality in friendship. In questions of justice the primary meaning of equal, or fair (*isos*) is 'proportionate to merit,' while 'equal in quantity' is only a secondary meaning; but in questions of friendship 'equal in quantity' is the primary meaning, and 'proportionate to merit' only secondary. This is evident from cases where there is a wide disparity between two persons in respect of virtue or vice or wealth or anything else; for such persons neither are nor expect to be friends. It is most clearly seen in our relations with the gods, for they enjoy the greatest superiority in all good things; but it is evident also in the case of princes, for persons of very inferior station do not claim their friendship, nor do persons of no account claim the friendship of the best and wisest men. We cannot of course define the exact limit to which friendship may go in such cases: much can be taken away and the friendship still remain; but where the difference between two individuals is exceptionally great, as it is between God and man, friendship ceases. This suggests the query, whether we do not, after all, really fail to wish our friends the greatest of all goods, namely that they shall become gods. For if they were to become so, we should lose them as friends, and therein we should lose something good— friends being something good. Consequently, if we were right in saying that a friend wishes good to his friend for the latter's own sake, this can only be upon condition that the second friend remain essentially what he is. What we really wish our friend is the greatest of goods compatible with his remaining a man. And perhaps not even all these goods shall we wish him, for each of us wishes good things most of all to himself.

ix. Friendship and the political community

It appears, as we said at the outset of the present discussion, that friendship and justice are concerned with the same objects and exhibited in the same circumstances. For every community contains some element both of justice and of friendship: thus fellow-voyagers and fellow-soldiers accost each other as friends, and so do fellow-members in other forms of association. But their friendship goes only so far as their common enterprise requires, and to that extent too there is justice among them. The saying, "Friends share what they possess," is true, for community is the essence of friendship. Brothers and comrades have all things in common; other friends share particular things—some more, some fewer, according as the friendships differ in degree. What is just also differs in different relationships: it is not the same between parent and child as between brothers, nor between comrades as between fellow-citizens, and so of other kinds of friendship. What is unjust in each of these relationships differs correspondingly; the wrong becoming greater in proportion as it is done to a nearer friend. It is more wicked to cheat a comrade than a fellow-citizen, more wicked to refuse help to a brother than to a stranger, or to strike one's own father than to strike some other man. The claims of justice increase in proportion to the nearness of the friendship, since both apply to the same situations and are coextensive in range.

All forms of community are, in a sense, parts or aspects of the political community. Thus, men undertake a journey together with a view to some common advantage or other, perhaps in order to procure some necessary supplies. It is likewise for the sake of a common advantage that the political community is believed to have been originally instituted and to continue; that being what legislators aim at, and what is called just.

All non-political forms of association aim at some piecemeal advantage; as when sailors work together at seafaring in order to make money or the like, or when soldiers join forces for the sake of plunder or victory or the capture of a city; and similarly the members of a tribe or of a deme [6] perform sacrifices and carry out the attendant ceremonies, thereby at once paying tribute to the gods and providing pleasurable relaxation for themselves. For it appears that the ancient sacrifices and ceremonies have come to take place after harvest as a festival for the dedicating of first-fruits, because it used to be at these seasons that people had most leisure. Thus we see that all these forms of association are parts of the political community; and the several kinds of friendship that we have been discussing will correspond to the several forms of association.

x. Types of political constitution

There are three kinds of 'political constitution' (*politeia*), and an equal number of variations—or rather, corruptions—of these. The constitutions proper are monarchy, aristocracy, and a third kind, which, as it is based on a property qualification, may appropriately be called timocratic, although most people speak of it simply as 'constitutional government.' [7] The best of these is monarchy, the worst timocracy. The variant of monarchy is tyranny: both are a kind of monarchy, but there is a wide difference between them, the tyrant looking to his own advantage, the king to that of his subjects. For no one is truly a king who is not self-sufficient

---

[6] In the Greek text the following passage (apparently an interpolation) occurs at this point: "Sometimes, too, associations are formed on the basis of pleasure, as religious guilds and amusement clubs, which exist for the sake of sacrifice and good fellowship respectively. But all such associations must be regarded as subordinate to the political community, which aims not at the interests of the moment, but at the interests of life as a whole."

[7] Aristotle uses the same word for constitutions in general, and for the particular kind of commonwealth that is here distinguished from monarchy and aristocracy. In its most general sense the word *politeia* means "the relation in which a citizen stands to the state" (Liddell & Scott); hence, the constitution of a state; hence, the administration of a state; hence, a well-ordered state, free community, or republic.

and superior to his subjects in good qualities; and if he is such, there is nothing more that he needs; so that he will aim at his subjects' advantage rather than at his own. A king of any other sort will be a mere titular king. But tyranny is the direct opposite in this respect, the tyrant pursuing only his own good; and it is pretty clear that this is the worst type of government, inasmuch as the worst is the direct opposite of the best. Monarchy passes over into tyranny; for as both are forms of autocratic rule, the bad king becomes a tyrant. Aristocracy passes into oligarchy through the fault of the rulers who distribute political honors unfairly, taking all or most of the good things for themselves, and keeping political offices always in the same hands, principally for the sake of gain. The result is a small number of bad men in power, instead of the best men. And finally, timocracy passes into democracy: they are, in fact, closely connected; for timocracy also purports to be a government by the masses, and lets all who have the property qualification count as equal. There is least corruption in the shift from timocracy to democracy, for the deviation here is least. These, then, are the ways in which the form of government is most readily altered; for in each of them a minimum of change is involved, and hence can take place with least difficulty.

Analogies and, so to speak, models for the several forms of government may be found in the structure of households. A father's association with his son has the form of a monarchy, since a father cares for his children's welfare. That is why Homer addresses Zeus as father; for monarchy tends to be a paternal rule. Among the Persians, however, the paternal relation is tyrannical, for the fathers there use their sons as slaves. The association of master and slave [8] is also tyrannical, for it is the master's interest that is secured by it. But whereas this seems to be a legitimate kind of tyranny, that of the Persian father appears wrong, for different types of persons require different sorts of rule. The relation of man

[8] This association is also, of course, a part of the Greek household.

and wife may be regarded as aristocratic; for the degree to which the husband rules depends upon his worth and is confined to his proper sphere, while to his wife he assigns what properly pertains to her. When the husband takes command of everything, he transforms the relation into an oligarchy, for he therein acts without reference to the principle of individual worth, and is not ruling by virtue of his superiority. Sometimes, on the other hand, the wife rules, being an heiress. In these cases also authority is not a question of merit, but is based on wealth and influence, as in oligarchies. Finally, the association of brothers resembles a timocracy: for they are equals, save as they may differ in age; and when they differ very widely in age, the friendship between them is no longer what we should call fraternal. Democracy is reflected chiefly in those households which have no master (for here everybody is on an equal footing), or where the head of the house is weak, and lets everybody do as he likes.

xi. *Friendship in perverted forms of commonwealth*

. . . In the perverted forms of commonwealth, as there is little room for justice, so there is little room for friendship; and in the most perverted form there is least, tyranny allowing of scarcely any friendship at all. For when ruler and ruled have nothing in common friendship is no more possible than justice; as may be seen in the relation of a craftsman to his tools, of the soul to the body and of master to slave. While the instruments may be in each case benefited by their users, there is no friendship in one's relations with inanimate objects, any more than with a horse or an ox, or with a slave quâ slave. We have nothing in common with them: for the slave is a living tool, the tool a lifeless slave. Quâ slave, therefore, there can be no friendship with him; quâ man, however, there can: for there is held to be a sort of justice in our relations with any man who can participate in law and contract; consequently, so far as the slave can be considered a man, there is friendship too. But while even tryannies will thus admit of friendship and justice to a slight degree, these qualities are present in democracies more fully [than in any of the other corrupt forms]; for where people are equal they have much in common.

BOOK IX

FURTHER PROBLEMS OF FRIENDSHIP

ix. *Are friends necessary for happiness?*

ANOTHER disputed question is whether or not friends are necessary for happiness. On the one hand it is argued that those who are in felicitous circumstances and sufficient unto themselves have no need of friends; for they already possess the good things of life, and therefore, being sufficient unto themselves, they need nothing more; whereas the office of a friend, as a second self, is to furnish us with things that we cannot procure by our own efforts; whence the saying, "When fortune is kind, what need of friends?"

On the other hand it seems strange, while endowing the happy man with all good things, to deny him friends, which are thought to be the greatest of external goods. Besides, if it is more the mark of a friend to give than to receive benefits, and if beneficence is the mark of a good man and of virtue, and if it is nobler to confer benefits on friends than on strangers, it follows that the good man will have need of friends, as objects of his beneficence. That is why people ask whether friends are more needed in prosperity or in adversity; for in adversity we want someone who will help us, and in prosperity someone whom we may help.

In any case it is ridiculous to suppose that the happy and fortunate man is a recluse. No one would choose to have every conceivable good thing on condition that he remain solitary, for man is a political creature, designed by nature to live with others. The happy man, then, since he will possess all naturally good things, must have social intercourse. But obviously it is better to live with friends and 'decent people' (*epieikês*) than with strangers and chance companions. Therefore the happy man must have friends.

If we look a little deeper into the nature of things, a virtuous friend appears to be naturally desirable for a virtuous man. For that which is good in its own nature is also, as we have previously remarked, intrinsically good and pleasant to the good man. And life, while defined in the case of animals by the capacity for sensation, is defined in the case of man by the capacity for sensation and thought. But a capacity involves a reference to its active exercise, and in this its full reality consists. Life, therefore, seems to be essentially the act of perceiving or thinking. Now, life is one of the things that are good and pleasant in themselves; for it has the character of definiteness,[1] which belongs to the nature of the good: and as that which is good in its own nature is good for the virtuous man, it follows that life, as something naturally good, will seem pleasant to all men. But by life we must understand not an evil and corrupt life, or a life of pain; for such a life is formless, as are its attributes [vice and pain]. (The nature of pain will be clarified presently.[2])

But if life in itself is good and pleasant (as it seems to be from the fact that it is desired by everyone, and most of all by the virtuous and happily circumstanced, since to them life is preëminently desirable and their own existence is most completely blessed), and if, further, he who sees is conscious that he sees, and he who hears is conscious that he hears, and he who walks is conscious that he walks, and similarly in the case of all other forms of activity there is something in us that is conscious of how we are active, so that when we perceive or think we are conscious of perceiving or thinking; and if to be conscious of perceiving or thinking is

---

[1] Cf. the Pythagorean doctrine that 'definiteness' or 'limitation' is a characteristic of the good.

[2] The nature of pleasure is clarified in Bk. X, chiefly Chaps. iv and v. The nature of pain is left to be inferred from the statement that it is pleasure's opposite.

to be conscious that we exist (for our existence, as we found, consists in perceiving or thinking); and if, again, to be conscious that we are alive is a thing pleasant in itself (for life is something good in its own nature, and to be conscious of the presence of something good is pleasant); and if life is desirable, and especially so to good men, since existence is good to them and pleasant as well (for they take pleasure in the consciousness of what is intrinsically good); and if, finally, a virtuous man feels toward his friend just as he does toward himself (for a friend is a second self):—we conclude from all this that as a man's own existence is desirable for him, so (or in much the same manner) his friend's existence is also desirable. But existence is desirable, we found, because of the consciousness that one's self is good, and such consciousness is intrinsically pleasant. [To achieve happiness], therefore, a man must also share his friend's consciousness of his existence; which will be attained by their living together and by communicating and sharing each other's thoughts; for that is the meaning of living together when applied to men, and not, as in the case of cattle, merely feeding in the same place.

If, then, to 'the man blessed with complete happiness' (*makarios*) existence is desirable in itself, being good and pleasant in its very nature, and if his friend's existence is held in pretty much the same regard, it follows that a friend is one of the things that are choiceworthy. But whatever is choiceworthy to him he must have, lest he be deficient in that particular. Therefore the man who is to be happy needs virtuous friends.

BOOK X

PLEASURE AND HAPPINESS

i. Current opinions about pleasure

THE NEXT SUBJECT for us to discuss, perhaps, is pleasure (*hêdonê*). It is generally held that pleasure is bound up in a most intimate way with the human race; which is the reason why in educating the young we use pleasure and pain as rudders to steer their course. Moreover, delight and aversion toward the proper objects are supposed to be of greatest importance in the formation of character; for, inasmuch as we choose the pleasant and avoid the painful, these feelings pervade the whole of life, exerting a powerful influence toward virtue and happiness. The whole subject, then, is one that we should by no means pass over, especially as it admits of much dispute.

Some [philosophers] maintain that pleasure is the supreme good,[1] others that it is unqualifiedly bad.[2] Of this latter group, although there are probably some who speak from a sincere conviction, others suppose that they are serving the interests of morality by declaring pleasure to be an evil even though it is not: the majority of men, they argue, incline toward pleasure and are slaves to it; for which reason they ought to be driven in an opposite direction, in order thus to be set in a middle course.

The view is open to criticism, however. Assertions about matters of feeling and conduct are less persuasive than deeds; hence, when

[1] Principally Eudoxus, discussed in the following chapter. Possibly Aristippus also is meant.

[2] E.g., probably Speusippus, Plato's successor in the Academy; also the earlier Cynic philosophers, Antisthenes and Diogenes.

such assertions clash with palpable facts they are despised, and truth is discredited along with them. Let a man but speak ill of pleasure who is observed now and then to desire it, and his lapses will be taken to mean that he really inclines toward it as something altogether good; for the masses cannot discriminate. It would seem, then, that arguments based on truth are the most useful for conduct as well as for theoretical knowledge; because, being in harmony with the facts, they gain credence, and so encourage those who understand them to be guided by them.

But enough of this. Let us now review the current theories about pleasure.

ii. Eudoxus' arguments for hedonism

Eudoxus used to say that pleasure was the chief good, on the grounds: (1) that he observed all creatures, rational and irrational alike, striving to obtain it; and in every case, he argued, that which is desirable (*hairetos*) [3] is excellent, and that which is most desirable is most excellent. The fact that all creatures are impelled toward one and the same goal—namely pleasure—shows that goal to be the best for all; inasmuch as it lies in the nature of each creature to find out its own particular good, no less than its own particular kind of nourishment. And surely that which is good for all, and which all strive after, is the chief good. (These arguments have found acceptance more because of Eudoxus' splendid character than for any intrinsic value of their own. As he was reputed to be a man of exemplary temperance, and could not be suspected of pleading as a mere votary of pleasure, his views were for that reason accredited.) He argued further (2) that the goodness of pleasure could be proved by considering the nature of its opposite; for as pain is intrinsically an object of universal avoidance, its opposite, pleasure, must be correspondingly desirable. Again, (3) he

---

[3] Elsewhere usually translated 'choiceworthy.' The word has the double connotation of: (1) desired, or an actual object of choice, and (2) desirable, or worthy of choice.

argued, those things are most desirable which are chosen not as a means to or for the sake of anything else, but for their own sake; and this is acknowledged to be the case with pleasure, forasmuch as we never ask a man with what motive he indulges in pleasure, but assume it to be desirable in itself. Finally, (4) he pointed out that any good thing—e.g., just or temperate conduct—is made more desirable by the addition of pleasure; and that it is only by the good that the good can be increased.

This last of Eudoxus' arguments, although it proves that pleasure must be numbered among the good things of life, does not prove that it is superior to other good things. Every good, as a matter of fact, becomes more choiceworthy when joined with another good than when it stands alone. Indeed, Plato uses just such an argument to refute the theory that pleasure is identical with the good: the pleasant life, he argues, is more desirable with wisdom than without; and if pleasure combined with something else is better than pleasure alone, it follows that pleasure cannot in itself be the supreme good; for that which is supremely good in itself cannot be made more choiceworthy by the addition of anything else. The same principle, obviously, can be applied to things other than pleasure: generally speaking, nothing can be the supreme good if it is made more choiceworthy by the addition of anything that has a goodness of its own. What is there, then, that satisfies these requirements and is at the same time a good in which we mortals can have a share? This is the sort of good that we are looking for.

On the other hand, those who declare that what all things aim at is not necessarily any good at all, are talking nonsense. Whatever appears true to everybody must be accepted as such; and he who denies the validity of universal opinion can hardly produce any more valid criterion of his own. If it were merely irrational creatures that strove to obtain the thing in question, there would be some point to the objection, but as intelligent beings strive after it too, on what possible grounds can the objection rest? As a matter of fact, there is perhaps even in inferior creatures an instinctive principle superior to their actual selves, which aims at their proper good.

Nor does the objection to Eudoxus' argument about the opposite of pleasure appear any more tenable. It is objected against him that although pain is bad, it does not follow that pleasure is necessarily good, inasmuch as an evil can just as well be opposed to an evil, and both of the opposed evils opposed to a neutral state. While this contention is true in general, it is not rightly applied to the present discussion. For if both pleasure and pain were evil, both ought to be shunned; and if they were both morally neutral, there would be no reason to shun either of them more than the other. As it is, however, we see men shunning pain as an evil and seeking pleasure as a good: it must therefore be as good and evil that they are opposed.

iii. Criticism of the view that pleasure is evil

Nor again does it follow that because pleasure is not a quality it is therefore not a good; for the exercise of virtue is not a quality either, nor is happiness (*eudaimonia*).

It is argued, however, that the good is something determinate, while pleasure, because it admits of a more and a less, is indeterminate.[4] If this means that it is our actual enjoyment of pleasure that partakes of a more and a less, then the same criticism will apply equally well to justice and the other virtues, the possessors of which we distinguish as possessing them to a greater or less degree, and as acting more or less virtuously; for surely some men are more just and braver than others, and it is possible for a man to act with varying degrees of justice and temperance. If, on the other hand, the reference is to the pleasures themselves, then the objectors are evidently not stating the true cause of the variations within pleasures, for they overlook the fact that same pleasures are unmixed and others mixed. What is to prevent pleasure from being like health, which, though determinate, admits of a more and a less?

[4] See Plato, *Philebus*, 24E, ff.

Health does not require the same proportion of elements in all persons, nor the same proportion always in the same person: to a certain extent it may be diminished without wholly losing its character, and it may vary in degree. The case may be the same with pleasure.

Again, starting with the assumption that the good is something 'final and complete' (*teleios*) while movements and processes of generation are incomplete, the opponents of pleasure try to show that pleasure is a movement and a process of generation. But their contention that it is a movement may be challenged; for every movement must evidently be quick or slow, whether absolutely, like the movement of the universe, or relatively; but pleasure is neither quick nor slow. We can, of course, become quickly pleased or quickly angered, but the feeling itself cannot be quick—not even relatively; whereas walking, growing, and other such movements can partake of quickness. In other words, while it is true that the passage to a state of pleasure can be quick or slow, quickness cannot be attributed to the actual functioning—i.e., to the pleasurable state itself. Besides, in what sense can pleasure be a process of generation? It seems clear that a thing is not generated out of any chance thing at random, but that it is resolved into that out of which it was generated. Pain must therefore be the destruction of that whose generation was pleasure.

The opponents of pleasure further declare that pain is a falling short of the natural state, and that pleasure is the corresponding replenishment. But this deficiency and replenishment are bodily experiences. Accordingly, if pleasure is a replenishment of the natural state, that in which the replenishment takes place, viz. the body, must be the thing that feels pleasure. But few would accept this consequence. It follows, therefore, that pleasure is not a replenishment; but rather that we may feel pleasure while the replenishment is going on, just as pain accompanies [but is not identified with] the process of cutting. The view in question has evidently been suggested by the pleasures and pains connected with nutrition; for in that respect it is true that we first suffer pain from lack of food and afterward find pleasure in replenishment. But this is not the case with all pleasures: neither the pleasure of acquiring knowledge, nor the sensuous pleasures of smell, nor many sights and sounds, memories and hopes, imply any preëxistent pain. Out of what, then, can such pleasures have been generated? There has been no lack in anything of which they can be the replenishment.

As for those who bring forward disgraceful kinds of pleasure, we may say in reply that such things are not pleasurable. While they may be pleasurable to badly conditioned people, they need not be so to anyone else. We do not base our judgments on what appears wholesome, sweet, or bitter to a sick man, nor on what appears white to a man with diseased eyes. Or we might reply thus: that these pleasures may be desirable and choiceworthy, but not when they are derived from such sources; just as it is desirable to be rich though not at the cost of treachery, and to be healthy though not always at the cost of eating what may be prescribed. Or we might argue that pleasures differ in kind: that those derived from noble sources are different from those whose sources are base, and that we cannot experience the pleasures of the just man without being ourselves just, nor the pleasures of the cultured man without being cultured. That pleasures do differ in kind seems clear from the distinction we draw between the true friend and the flatterer. The one looks to the good of his fellows, the other to their pleasure; and while we censure the flatterer, we praise the friend because his motives in associating with us are different. Again, no one would choose to live on condition of having a child's intellect all his life, even though he were to enjoy the pleasures of a child to the highest degree; nor to delight in some abominable deed, even though he were to suffer no pain from it. Conversely, there are many things that we should still care for even though they brought no pleasure: as, for instance, sight, memory, knowledge, moral and intellectual excellence. Even supposing that pleasure necessarily accompanies them, that is beside the point: we would still choose them even though no pleasure resulted.

We conclude, then, that pleasure is not identical with good, and that not all pleasures are choiceworthy; but that there are nevertheless some pleasures, distinguished from others either in kind or by their sources, that are worthy of being chosen for their own sakes. So much for current opinions about pleasure and pain.

iv. The true nature of pleasure

The nature or quality of pleasure will be clarified if we take up the question again from the beginning.

As an act of vision is regarded as complete (*teleios*) at every moment of its duration, since it lacks nothing that could later be added to make its nature (*eidos*) more complete; so pleasure seems in this respect to resemble vision: there is a certain wholeness about each moment of it, which would not be any more fully consummated by being protracted in time. Pleasure, therefore, is not a movement (*kinêsis*); for every movement (such as that of building) is of a temporal nature and moves toward a goal, becoming complete only when what it aims at has been produced. Thus its completion is achieved only either in the whole period of its duration or in the final moment. During the progress of the work all of the individual movements are incomplete, besides being different in kind from the whole movement and from each other. The fitting together of the stones, for example, is different from the fluting of the column, as both are different from the building of the temple. The building of the temple itself is a complete operation, since nothing more is required for the execution of the plan; but the operations of laying the foundation and constructing the triglyph are incomplete, since each is the building of only a part. These movements, accordingly, are specifically different from one another. There is no movement that at any moment can be complete in itself: it will be complete, if at all, only with respect to the whole period in which the operation takes place. . . .

Pleasure, on the other hand, has at every moment a specific quality that is complete in itself. Clearly, therefore, pleasure and movement must be distinct from each other, pleasure belonging to the class of whole and complete things. . . .

Each of the senses acts in relation to its proper object, and when in good condition it acts most perfectly in relation to the finest of the objects that pertain to it; for this is what is supposed principally to constitute the complete 'exercise of a faculty' (*energeia*). The distinction between the faculty itself and the organ in which it resides may be disregarded for the present.[5] In any case the activity proper to each sense goes on best when the sense organ is in the most excellent condition and is acting in relation to the finest of its objects. This sort of activity, being the most perfect, will also be the most pleasant. For there is a pleasure corresponding to every sense, just as there are pleasures corresponding to thought and contemplation, and the pleasure is greatest when the corresponding activity has achieved the highest perfection—which depends both on the good condition of the organ or faculty and on the worthiness of its object. Pleasure makes this activity complete, although not in the same way that the object and the faculty of sense do so—just as health and the physician are both, but in different respects, the causes of our being healthy.

That pleasure is produced with respect to each sense is evident from the fact that we speak of pleasant sights and pleasant sounds. That it is greatest when both the faculty and its object have the highest degree of excellence is evident too: when both the object and the perceiver fulfill this condition there will always be pleasure, so long as there is a subject to act and an object to be acted upon.

Pleasure makes the activity complete not in the way that an activity is made complete by being the expression of a fixed disposition already present in the agent, but as a sort of added perfection —like the bloom of youth to those in their prime.

[5] Cf., however, *Psychology,* Bk. II, Chap. xii, pp. 134–136.

So long, then, as both the object of thought or of sense and the subject that contemplates or perceives are as they ought to be, there will be pleasure involved in their activity; for when both the passive and the active factor remain unchanged in themselves and in their relations to each other, the same result must naturally follow. . . .

v. Pleasure as an accompaniment of activity

Another consequence of the foregoing considerations is that pleasures differ in kind. For we hold that things different in kind must reach perfection through what is correspondingly different in kind—a characteristic which we may note in products both of nature and of art, e.g., animals, trees, a painting, a statue, a house, a piece of furniture. Similarly with regard to activities: those that differ in kind we declare can be completed only by what likewise differs in kind. Since, therefore, the activities of thought differ in kind from those of the senses, and those of the senses from one another, the pleasures that respectively complete them must also be different.

The same conclusion is suggested by the way in which each pleasure is bound up with the particular activity which it completes. An activity is augmented by the pleasure that accompanies it; as shown by the fact that people are better able to judge of a matter and grasp it in detail when they approach it with pleasure. It is those who take delight in geometry, for instance, who become geometers and have a superior grasp of its principles; as similarly, those who are fond of music or architecture or anything else make progress in their particular line because of the delight they take in it. Pleasures, then, augment the activities with which they are connected, and whatever thus augments a thing must be akin to it. But things that are akin to things different in kind must themselves be different in kind.

The conclusion follows perhaps even more clearly from the fact that activities are hindered by pleasures arising from other sorts of activity. Lovers of the flute, for example, are incapable of attending to rational discussions when they hear someone playing that instrument, for they take more delight in flute-playing than in the competing activity: the pleasure connected with flute-playing destroys for them the activity concerned with reasoning. Similarly in all other cases where a man is active with respect to two things at once: the more pleasant activity drives out the other, and if it is considerably more pleasant it does so to a correspondingly greater extent—even to the point of banishing it altogether. That is why, when something gives us intense delight, we cannot engage in anything else at all; and conversely when we turn to something else it is because our original activity entertains us but mildly—as those who eat sweets in the theatre do so most of all when the actors are bad. Since, then, our activities are sharpened, prolonged, and improved by their proper pleasures, but spoiled by pleasures of an alien sort, it is plain that there must be a wide difference between pleasures. . . .

As our activities differ in goodness and badness, some being objects of choice, others of avoidance, while still others are neutral, so pleasures differ likewise; for there is a pleasure corresponding to each activity. While the pleasure that goes with a good activity is good, that which goes with a bad activity is evil; for it is praiseworthy to desire what is noble, but reprehensible to desire what is base. Pleasures have a more intimate connection than desires with the activities that they accompany; for desires are separate from the activities both in time and in their natural basis, whereas the pleasures are closely linked to the activities, and indeed so hard to distinguish from them that it is sometimes asked whether the activity and its pleasure are not one and the same. Absurd as it may appear to identify pleasure with thought or perception, the fact that it is inseparable from them has led some people to regard them as identical. However this may be, it is evident from what has been said that pleasures may be differentiated according to the differences of the activities that they accompany. Sight excels touch in

purity; hearing and smell excel taste. There is therefore a corresponding difference between the pleasures attached to them. So
too, the pleasures of the intellect are superior to any of these pleasures of sense, and of the pleasures within each class some are
superior to others.

Every animal organism is thought to have its own special type
of pleasure, just as it has its own special function; for its pleasure
consists in the exercise of that function. This is clear from a review
of the different species: horse, dog, and man have each its own
form of pleasure, and as Heraclitus says, an ass prefers hay to gold
—for an ass gets more pleasure from fodder than from gold. Thus
the pleasures that go with the activities of the different animal
species (*eidos*) show corresponding differences of form (*eidos*),
while those that go with activities of a single species presumably
are similar. Yet some differences can be observed even within a
single species—at any rate in the case of man. What delights one
man causes pain to another, and what is painful and odious to some
is pleasant and attractive to others. Pleasure is analogous in this
respect to sweetness: the same things do not appear sweet to a
feverish man as to one who is in good health, and what appears
warm to a robust man does not always appear so to an invalid.
Further such discrepancies may be noted in the experience of other
qualities.

Now in all matters of this kind it may be laid down that a thing's
real nature is identical with how it appears to the 'virtuous man'
(*spoudaios*). If this opinion, which is the generally current one,
be correct, i.e. if excellence and the good man quâ good are in
every case to serve as our standard (*metron*),[6] then whatever appears to him a pleasure must really be one, and whatever he delights in will be pleasant. Nor need we be astonished if the things

---

[6] Protagoras the Sophist had taught and popularized the doctrine that
"Man is the measure (*metron*) of all things"—i.e., that good and evil are
merely a matter of how anyone happens to evaluate. Aristotle modifies the
dictum by substituting for 'man' a more determinate standard: 'the good man
quâ good.'

that strike him as disagreeable appear pleasant to someone else, considering the many ways in which men are corrupted and perverted; such things, however, are not pleasant in themselves, but only to those particular individuals who have acquired perverted dispositions. It is clear, then, that we are not to regard admittedly base pleasures as pleasures at all, except to those who are corrupt.

But of the pleasures that are accepted as decent, which or what kind shall be considered proper to man? The answer is supplied by the nature of man's distinctive activities, for these have their own peculiar form of pleasure. It is the pleasures accompanying the activities of the complete (*teleios*) and 'supremely happy' (*makarios*) man, whether they be of one sort or of many, that should be regarded as the pleasures of man properly speaking. Other pleasures can be called human only in a secondary and partial sense, like the activities which they accompany.

vi. Definition of happiness

Having now discussed the various types of virtue, of friendship, and of pleasure, we pass on to a summary account of the nature of happiness (*eudaimonia*), which we may take to be the end and aim of human life. Our discussion will be shortened if we begin by recapitulating certain of the conclusions already arrived at.

Happiness, we have said, is not merely a 'disposition or state of character' (*hexis*): if it were, it could be possessed by a person whose whole life was spent in sleep like a vegetable, or by one afflicted with the direst misfortunes. If we agree that this consequence is inadmissible, we must (as previously stated) describe happiness as an activity. And since activities are distinguishable into those that should be chosen only as necessary means to the furtherance of something else and those that are choiceworthy in themselves, it is clear that happiness must be placed rather with those that are choiceworthy in themselves. For happiness wants nothing; it is self-sufficient. By an activity choiceworthy in itself is meant one from which nothing is sought beyond its actual exercise. Conduct in accordance with 'virtue or excellence' (*aretê*) evidently answers to this description, for the doing of fine and noble deeds is worth choosing for itself.

'Trifling amusements' (*paidia*), when they are pleasant, are also chosen for their own sakes, rather than for any ulterior purpose: indeed, we are more likely to be injured than benefited by them, through neglect of health and fortunes. Most so-called happy persons have recourse to such pastimes (*di-agôgê*); which explains why those who are clever at providing them are apt to find favor with despots: they make themselves agreeable by supplying just the sort of thing the despot wants. Thus it comes about that trivial amusements, because princes devote their leisure to them, are thought to be of the nature of happiness.

But princes are no sure criterion. Virtue and intelligence, which are the sources of noble activity, are not a corollary of despotic power. Merely because despots, never having tasted pure and generous pleasure, take refuge in the pleasures of the body, it does not follow that such pleasures are therefore to be accounted more choiceworthy. Children,[7] too, suppose that the things they value are better than anything else. Little wonder, then, that as children differ from men in their valuations, so bad men differ from good. But let us again repeat: those things are truly valuable and pleasant which appear to be so to the good man. The most desirable (*hairetos*) [8] thing for any man is activity in accordance with his own developed character, and this in the good man will be activity in accordance with virtue.

Happiness, then, does not consist in amusement. To take amusement as our goal and undergo lifelong trouble and hardship just in order to amuse ourselves would be scarcely reasonable. Amusement is, in a sense, like practically everything else, chosen for the

---

[7] *Paidia*, 'trifling amusement, childish game,' is from the same root as *pais* (gen., *paidos*), 'child.' Not to be confused with *paideia*, 'education,' discussed in *On Statecraft*, Bk. VIII.

[8] See note on p. 253.

sake of something beyond itself; in the last analysis it is happiness alone that is chosen for its own sake, since this is man's proper goal. It would be silly and quite childish (*paidikos*) to work and slave for the sake of amusement. But to indulge in amusing pastimes in order, as Anarcharsis recommends, that we may thereafter more effectively exert ourselves, is admittedly right. Amusement is a sort of relaxation, and it is owing to our inability to work continuously that relaxation is needed. Obviously then relaxation, since we use it as a means to further activity, cannot be our final goal. . . . Besides, anyone at all, even a slave, can enjoy bodily pleasures, quite as well as a man of highest excellence; but no one supposes that a slave can participate in happiness, any more than in purposeful life. Happiness, then, does not consist in pleasant pastimes but, we repeat, in virtuous activities.

vii. Happiness and contemplation

If happiness is activity in accordance with virtue, we may reasonably suppose that it must be in accordance with the highest type of virtue—i.e., with such virtue as is distinctive of the best part of us. This best part of us (call it reason or what you will), which seems by nature disposed to rule and guide us and to take thought of noble and divine objects (whether it be a divine principle residing in us or only the most nearly divine part of our nature), is the thing whose activity, when in accordance with its own proper virtue, constitutes happiness. Such activity, as already stated, consists in contemplation.

Our present conclusion seems to agree both with our previous deductions and with known truths. (1) To contemplate is the noblest of activities; for our reason is the noblest part of us, and the objects of reason are the best of all knowable things. Again, (2) contemplation exhibits continuity in the highest degree, for we can 'contemplate truth' (*theôrein*) more continuously than we can do anything else whatever. Again, (3) we hold that happiness ought to contain an admixture of pleasure; and activity in accordance with wisdom (*sophia*) is the most pleasant of all virtuous activities—at any rate, the 'pursuit of wisdom' (*philosophia*) admittedly offers pleasures of remarkable purity and duration, and it is reasonable to assume that those who know are more pleasantly occupied than those who merely inquire.[9] Again, (4) the activity of contemplation is peculiarly characterized by what is called self-sufficiency (*autarkeia*). That is not to say, of course, that possession of wisdom, any more than possession of justice, will enable a man to dispense with the necessaries of life. Nevertheless, when these have been supplied, the just man will still need persons toward whom and in whose company he may behave justly; so, too, the man who is temperate, or brave, or the like. The wise man, on the contrary, will be able to contemplate truth quite alone, and the wiser he is the better able he will be. Doubtless his speculations would be improved if he had other persons with whom to share them; but at any rate he is more truly self-sufficient than anyone else. Again, (5) the activity of contemplation seems to be the only one that is loved for its own sake: it yields no result apart from the contemplating. From practical activities, on the contrary, we expect to achieve some result, whether great or small, beyond the activities themselves.

Finally, (6) happiness is thought to involve leisure; for we toil in order to get leisure, as we make war in order to get peace. But the activity of the practical virtues has to do either with the ordinary affairs of state or with war, and activities concerned with either of these must be accounted unleisurely. Particularly is this true of war: no one chooses to be at war or provokes a war for the sake of war alone; indeed, we should call a man downright bloodthirsty who made enemies of friends in order to bring about battles and slaughter. But it is true also of a statesman's peacetime activities. The statesman aims at something more than the practice of statecraft itself: at despotic powers and honors, perhaps, or else at the happiness of himself and his fellow-citizens. That the hap-

[9] I.e., *a fortiori* the *sophos* is more pleasantly occupied than the *philosophos*.

piness at which he aims is something over and above the art of statecraft which he practices is shown by the fact that we investigate the two fields independently. Inasmuch, then, as politics and war, while surpassing in nobility and grandeur all other practical expressions of human excellence, are unleisurely and aim at an ulterior end instead of being chosen for their own sakes, while the activity of reason is acknowledged to be superior in seriousness (since it is contemplative), to aim at nothing beyond itself, to entail a peculiar pleasure of its own (which in turn promotes the activity), and to be characterized by self-sufficiency, leisureliness, and as much unwearied diligence as is possible to mankind, together with whatever other attributes are ascribed to the 'supremely happy' (*makarios*) man: it evidently follows that complete human happiness will consist in the exercise of reason—provided that we postulate also a complete term of life, for happiness admits of nothing incomplete.

Such a life as this would be superior to anything merely human. He who leads such a life will do so not in his strictly human capacity, but only so far as there is in him an element of the divine. To just the extent that this divine element is superior to our composite human nature, its proper activity will be superior to ordinary virtuous conduct. In short, if reason is divine as compared with the whole man, then the life of reason is divine as compared with ordinary human life. Instead of listening to those who advise us to express our human and mortal nature by giving our attention to human and mortal things, we ought, so far as we can, to become immortal by making every effort to live in accordance with the best that is in us; for though this best part of us be small in bulk, it surpasses all the rest in power and worth. It may even be designated a man's real self, since it is his sovereign and better part. And it would be strange, surely, if one were to prefer some other way of life to the life of his real self.

We may apply here, too, the principle already laid down, that whatever is proper to the nature of each thing is best and pleasantest for that thing. Since it is reason that is most truly man, a life according to reason must be at once best and pleasantest for man. Such a life, therefore, will be the most truly happy.

viii. Argument for the contemplative life

. . . That perfect happiness is some form of contemplative activity appears also from the following consideration. We suppose the gods to be the most blessed and happy of all beings; but what sort of actions shall we ascribe to them? Acts of justice? It would be ridiculous to think of the gods as making contracts, returning deposits, and the like. Courageous acts? Do they, then, endure terrors and nobly face dangers? Acts of liberality? To whom in that case, would they give? Besides, to imagine them dispensing anything material like money would be absurd. As for temperance, what meaning could that have for the gods? Surely it would be an impertinence to praise them for not having evil desires. In short, though we were to run through the whole catalogue of virtues, we would find that all such forms of action are petty and unworthy of godhood. Yet we take for granted that the gods are living and therefore active; we can hardly suppose them to be lying asleep like Endymion. Now if we conceive a living being apart from 'overt deeds' (*prattein*), and more particularly apart from productivity (*poiein*), what remains to him but contemplation (*theôria*)? It follows that the activity (*energeia*) of God, which surpasses all other activities in blessedness, consists in contemplation; and that among human activities, that which is most akin to God's activity will partake most truly of the nature of happiness. . . .

In our mortal state, however, there will be need of external prosperity as well. Human nature is not self-sufficient for contemplation: it is necessary that the body should be in health, and supplied with food, and otherwise cared for. Yet, while 'complete happiness' (*makarios*, adj.) presupposes certain external benefits, that does not mean that in order to be happy a man will require many or great possessions. Excessive abundance is not a condition either of self-sufficiency or of 'moral action' (*praxis*). A man can perform noble deeds without being ruler of earth and sea. Moderate advantages are enough to permit virtuous action; and in fact upright conduct tends to be not less but more widespread among private individuals than among princes. Moderate advantages, then, will suffice; and a man's life will be happy if [having these] he acts in accordance with virtue. . . .

The man who pursues intellectual activity and who cultivates his reason and keeps it in the best condition, is in addition [to being happiest on other grounds] presumably most loved by the gods. For if the gods have any concern with human affairs (as we suppose them to) it is natural that they should delight in what is at once best and most akin to themselves, namely reason (*nous*), and that they should reward those who most greatly love and reverence it, because such men not only care for what is dear to the gods but at the same time are acting rightly and nobly. This whole description applies preëminently to the philosopher (*sophos*). He, therefore, is the most loved by the gods, and is accordingly the most truly happy of mortals.

ix. How ethics leads to statecraft

Now that we have given an adequate outline of these matters, as well as of the virtues, of friendship, and of pleasure, are we to suppose that our program is complete? On the contrary, ought we not rather to accept the maxim that in practical matters it is needful not only to survey and recognize the various things to be done, but also to do them? Applying the principle to the question of virtue, we may declare that understanding alone is not enough; we must endeavor also to possess virtue and use it, and to take whatever other means there may be of achieving actual goodness.

If theories sufficed to make men good, philosophers, as Theognis rightly remarks [of physicians], would have won many fine rewards, and to give such rewards would have been our duty. But the truth is that while theories seem to have power to encourage and stimulate young men of generous minds, and while they may make a finely tempered character, when it is combined with a genuine love of what is noble, more susceptible to the influence of virtue, they are quite powerless to turn the mass of men to goodness and nobility. Most men have an inherent tendency to be swayed by fear rather than by reverence, and to be deterred from base deeds not by the wickedness of them, but by the threat of punishment. Guided only by passion, they pursue, by whatever means may be necessary, such pleasures as are suited to their natures, and shun the corresponding pains. Never having tasted pleasure of a noble sort, they lack even the faintest notion of what it is. How could mere theory be the remaking of such men? It is hard if not impossible to remove by argument traits that have long been engrained in the character. Ordinarily we shall have to be content if, even when all the influences making for goodness are present, a modicum of virtue results.

Some attribute man's goodness to nature, others to the acquisition of certain habits, others to teaching. As for the goodness that comes by nature, it evidently does not depend on ourselves, but is a result of divine causes which bestow it on certain truly fortunate individuals. As for theory and instruction, it is to be feared they will scarcely avail much with all men; rather, the student's soul must first have been cultivated by good habits to feel delights and aversions of the proper kinds, just as the soil must previously have been cultivated if the seed is to thrive. He who lives under the sway of his passions will not listen to dissuasive arguments, nor even understand them; and how can we hope by argument to change the mind of anyone in such a state? As a general rule, it seems that passion yields only to force, not to argument. Accordingly we may conclude that before theory or instruction can be effective the character must originally possess a sort of natural kinship to virtue, loving what is noble and hating what is base.

But unless men have been reared under the proper sort of laws

It is no easy matter to be rightly trained in virtue from youth up. Most people find it unpleasant to live temperately and hardily, especially when they are young. For this reason the education and pursuits of the young should be prescribed by law: once they have been made habitual, they will no longer be painful. Nor is it enough, probably, that people should receive the right sort of education and direction merely when young. To follow sound teachings and infix them as habits is no less important after we are grown up. Hence there should be laws governing adulthood too, and in short every period of life; for the mass of men are swayed more by compulsion than by argument, and by threat of punishment than by a sense of what is noble. Consequently the theory has been advanced that legislators should encourage and exhort people to be virtuous on moral grounds, so as to reach the ear of those who have had a virtuous moral upbringing; while at the same time punishing and exacting penalties from those who are badly disposed and disobedient, and banishing ruthlessly the incorrigibles. The good man, it is argued, being guided by a sense of what is noble will submit to reason; whereas the inferior man, whose desire is for pleasure, must be corrected by pain, like a beast of burden. On the same ground it is declared that the pains inflicted on a transgressor should be such as are most completely opposed to the pleasures he loves.

If then, as we have said, a man in order to be good must have been well nurtured and well trained, and must subsequently pursue an upright way of life, and must never, either willingly or unwillingly, be guilty of shoddy conduct; this can be effected only if men live subject to some kind of intelligence (*nous*) that goes hand in hand with right order (*taxis*), backed by force. Merely paternal authority lacks the compulsive power to achieve such an end; so does the authority of any one man, unless he be a king or something equivalent. The law, on the other hand, does possess this compelling force, while at the same time it is a set of principles based on moral insight and sound reason. And while we take offense at individuals who, however rightly, oppose our impulses, we do not feel aggrieved against the law for enjoining virtuous conduct. Yet Sparta is practically the only state where the legislator has apparently paid much attention to the upbringing and daily pursuits of its citizens. In most states such matters have been neglected, and each man lives as he likes, ruling his wife and children in the manner of the Cyclops.

Thus although the best arrangement would be for the regulation of moral matters to be taken over and properly administered by the community, yet inasmuch as the community neglects them it is rightly considered the duty of each of us to help his own children and friends along the road to virtue—or at least to have the will, even though we lack the power, to do this. Such aid, as the foregoing discussion shows, can be administered most effectively by one who has become versed in legislation. For public regulation can be effected only by means of laws, and good regulation only by means of good laws.[10] As legal statutes and national customs are what exert authority in states, so in households the injunctions and habits of the father exert a like authority—perhaps an even greater one, considering the ties of kinship and obligation, for the members of a family have at the outset a natural disposition to love and obey.

Individual treatment is preferable to mass treatment no less in education than in medicine. While it is generally true, for instance, that repose and fasting are good for a man with a fever, they are not always so in a particular case. Nor, presumably, does a boxing instructor recommend the same style of fighting to all his pupils. Thus it appears that a more exact education is provided under a system of instruction adapted to individuals, since each will then be more likely to get what suits his particular case.

Now a physician or an athletic trainer or any other such person can best administer treatment to the individual if he knows what

[10] Aristotle's gloss, inserted in the Greek text at this point: "Whether the laws are written or unwritten, and whether they pertain to the education of individuals or of groups, makes no appreciable difference, any more than in the case of cultural education, gymnastics, or any other such discipline."

as a general rule is good for all men of the same type: for science is correctly said to deal with what is common to a number of individuals. It sometimes happens, of course, that a particular individual can be cured by a person with no scientific knowledge, who by accurate empirical observations has worked out the details of the treatment required in that one individual's case; just as some people are apparently their own best doctors, although they would be quite unable to prescribe for anyone else. Nevertheless, we shall doubtless agree that if a man wishes to become master of any art, or of any science, he must advance to general principles, and get to know them by the proper method: for it is with them, we repeat, that the sciences are concerned. Accordingly, he who wishes to improve other persons by discipline (whether they be many or few) must try to become expert at legislation—at any rate, so far as moral improvement can really be effected by law. To take any and every person that happens along and mould his character rightly, is not a task for the first chance comer; but as in medicine and all other matters involving delicacy and sound judgment, it can be done, if at all, only by the man with knowledge.

Should not our next task, then, be to inquire from whom and by what means we can learn to legislate? Legislation, as we have seen, is a branch of statecraft (*politikê*): are we to conclude, then, drawing an analogy from the other arts, that we must learn lawmaking from statesmen? Or is there a significant difference between statecraft and the other arts and sciences? In them, at any rate, we find instruction being offered by actual practitioners—by physicians and painters, for instance—whereas in the case of statecraft the sophists, who profess to teach it, are never found practicing it, while the politicians, who practice it, appear to rely less on reasoning (*dianoia*) than on a certain 'natural ability' (*dynamis*) combined with experience (*empeiria*). This seems clear from the fact that they never talk or write about their art; although to do so were doubtless worthier employment than to make speeches in courts and assemblies. Nor do they ever make statesmen of their own sons and friends—a thing which they presumably would have done had they been able, for apart from the invaluable legacy they would thereby confer on their city governments, there is no art whose possession they would have chosen for themselves, and consequently for their dearest friends, in preference to statecraft. At the same time, a statesman's natural ability must be supplemented by experience; for otherwise we would not see men becoming statesmen by familiarity with practical statecraft. Anyone, therefore, who aims at a knowledge of statecraft will require practical experience as well.

Those of the sophists who prefess to teach statecraft seem to be very far from doing anything of the kind: generally speaking, they scarcely know even the rudiments of the subject. If they did, they would not treat it as something identical with or even inferior to oratory, nor would they imagine it a simple matter to frame a system of laws by collecting whatever existing laws happen to be in good repute. In assuming that they can pick out whatever laws are best they forget that such selection presupposes sound understanding, and that it is every bit as hard to judge correctly in these matters as, say, in music. For while those who are well experienced in any department will pass valid judgments upon the particular results produced in it, and understand the means and method of their production, and know what combinations are harmonious; those, on the other hand, who are not well experienced must be content if they can perceive whether the general result produced is good or bad—as we may see also in the case of painting. Accordingly, since laws are, in a manner of speaking, the products of statecraft, how could anyone learn from the laws alone to become a legislator, or to judge which laws are best? Even physicians, it appears, are not made by the study of textbooks. It is true that the writers of medical textbooks undertake to describe not only the remedies but how to apply them in curing particular types of patient, classified according to their bodily dispositions. But all that information, however serviceable it may be to those who have had experience, is useless to those who have had none. Similarly, then, while compilations of laws and constitutions are no doubt very serviceable to those who know how to examine them critically, to judge what is good or bad in them and what enactments suit what circumstances; yet when people without a 'trained faculty' (*hexis*) plod through such compilations, they cannot frame valid judgments (unless they chance to do so by instinct)—although they may, to be sure, acquire a certain amount of political discernment in the process.

As our predecessors have left the subject of legislation virtually unexamined, it will perhaps be well for us to inquire into it ourselves—together with the whole question of 'administering a state' (*politeia*),[11] in order that our philosophy of human nature may be made as complete as possible. Our program will be: first, to review whatever valid utterances any of our predecessors may have made upon this or that branch of the subject; next, on the basis of our collection of constitutions,[12] to consider what factors tend to preserve or destroy states in general, what factors tend to preserve or destroy the different particular 'forms of constitution' (*politeia*), and to what causes it is due that some states are well and others ill governed. After we have examined these questions we shall perhaps be in a better position to discern what kind of constitution is to be preferred, how each must be ordered, and what laws and customs are best suited to each. Let us, then, begin.[13]

[11] See note on p. 245.
[12] Of 158 Greek states. Only one, *The Constitution of Athens*, survives.
[13] This concluding paragraph of the *Ethics* forms a preface to Aristotle's treatise on Statecraft (*Politikē*), familiarly known as 'the Politics.'

On Statecraft

On Statecraft

BOOK I

THE STATE

i. State and community

EVERY STATE (*polis*) being a kind of community (*koinônia*), and every community being established with a view to some good (for men always act in order to obtain what appears good to them), it plainly follows from this that the state or political community, which of all communities is the highest and most inclusive, will aim at the good more distinctively than the others, and at the highest good. . . .

ii. Natural origin of the state

The state can be studied best if we proceed here as we have done elsewhere and investigate first its origin and early development. Let us start by observing that wherever there are two things which cannot exist without each other, they must necessarily combine. This applies first of all to the relation of male and female, who unite for the sake of procreation—not by 'deliberate intent' (*proairesis*) of course, but by a natural drive, shared with other animals and plants, to leave a likeness of themselves behind. It applies also to the relation of ruler and subject, who unite in order that both may be preserved. For he who has the 'practical reason' (*dianoia*) to foresee [what should be done] is suited by nature to be lord and master, while he who is endowed with the bodily power to carry out [such plans] is by nature a subject and slave. There is a sense, then, in which master and slave have an identity of interest. . . .

Out of these two elementary community-relationships (*koinônia*)—between man and woman, and between master and slave—the 'family household' (*oikia*) first arises. Hesiod was right when he sang:

> First a house (*oikon*), and a wife, and an ox for the plough;

for the ox is the poor man's substitute for household slaves. The family household, then, is the form of association (*koinônia*) set up by nature to supply men's everyday wants. . . . When several households combine into a larger community-relationship, and for the satisfaction of something more than daily needs, the immediate result is the village (*kômê*). . . . Finally, out of the union of several villages there now grows that perfected (*teleios*) and self-sufficing type of community which is the city-state (*polis*). It originates that life may be possible, but it exists that life may be good. Therefore, if the earlier forms of community-relationship are natural, the city-state must be so; for by the nature of anything—whether of a man or a horse or a family household—we mean what it is in its full development. [And as a further proof that the city-state exists naturally]: The end or essential aim of anything is its highest good, and to be self-sufficing is an end, [therefore] a highest good, [and therefore natural].

From these considerations it is clear that the state, or *polis*, is a part of the natural order, and that man is by nature a political animal. . . . That man is more truly a political animal than the bee or any other gregarious creature is evident when we consider that nature, as we agree, makes nothing in vain, and that man is the only animal endowed with speech. Since pleasure and pain can be indicated by simple sounds, the power of uttering these is common to all animals: their natures being developed only to the point where they can have perceptions of pleasure and pain and signify them to one another. But 'rational speech' (*logos*) is able to declare what is advantageous or disadvantageous, and therefore also what is just or unjust. For what especially distinguishes man from the other animals is that he alone has a sense of good and evil, just and unjust, and this is what makes possible the kind of association that constitutes both a household and a state. . . .

The state is prior in the order of nature [though not in the order of time] to the family household and the individual. For the whole is necessarily prior to the part. If the whole body be destroyed there will be no foot or hand, except in the equivocal sense in which we apply the word 'hand' to that part of a stone statue, for a man's hand will be much like this when his body is destroyed. It is the 'function and capacity' (*dynamis*) of things that makes them what they are, and so when this is lost they should no longer be spoken of as the same but as 'different things designated by the same word' (*homonymos*).

Thus we see that the state exists by nature and is 'prior' to the individual. For if the individual is not self-sufficient when separated from a larger whole he must be like a part in relation to that whole. [And it is a fact that he is not self-sufficient when separated, for] he who is unable to share in community life or who in his self-sufficiency has no need of it must be either a beast or a god.

There is, then, a natural impulse (*hormê*) in all men toward 'community living' (*koinônia*); nevertheless he who first established a community was mankind's greatest benefactor. For as man when perfected is the noblest of animals, so apart from law and justice he is the worst of all; because injustice is most dangerous when it is armed, and man is equipped at birth with weapons intended to serve the cause of moral intelligence and virtue but capable of being put to opposite uses. Hence, where man is without virtue he is the most unscrupulous and bestial of animals, outdoing all the rest in lust and gluttony. By living in a politically ordered community, on the other hand, he learns justice, for justice is the ordering principle of such a community.

BOOK III

JUSTICE

ix. *Justice essential to the state*

LET US now turn to . . . the conceptions of justice held by advocates of oligarchy and of democracy. Oligarchs and democrats all cling to some idea of justice or other, but their thinking does not go far enough to grasp the true concept of justice in its entirety. The democrats believe that justice implies equality—and so it does, but only for those who are equal, not for everybody. The oligarchs, on the other hand, believe that justice implies inequality—and so it does, but only for those who are unequal, not for everybody. Both sides judge erroneously because they do not specify the class of persons to which their principles apply. That is because such judgments affect their own interests, and most men are rather bad judges where their own interests are involved. For justice involves persons—a just distribution being one in which [the value of] the things distributed corresponds to [the worth of] the persons receiving them, as has already been said in the *Ethics;* and although the two parties agree on what constitutes equality in things, they are at odds on what constitutes equality in persons. The main reason for such disagreement is the one here stated, namely that both parties judge badly of what most nearly concerns them; but there is also another reason, that because each party is espousing some limited conception of justice, each thinks of itself as espousing justice absolutely. The oligarchs think that because they are superior in one respect—say wealth—they are superior in all; while the democrats think that because they are equal with others in one respect—say in being [born] free—they are equal in all. Both sides ignore, however, the really cardinal question [of the end for which the state exists].

Now if men came together and formed a [political] association for the sake of wealth alone, then their shares in the state would be proportionate to the amounts they possessed, and the oligarchical argument would be valid—viz., that it is not right for a person who contributes the hundredth of an investment to receive the same returns, either in principal or in profits, as he who has contributed the other ninety-nine one-hundredths. The state exists, however, not merely that men may live but that they may live well; were it not so, then slaves and the lower animals might form a state—an impossibility, since they share neither in 'true felicity' (*eudaimonia*) nor in life guided by 'moral purpose' (*proairesis*).

Nor again does a state exist merely as a defensive alliance to secure its members against all injury, nor yet for the sake of exchange and economic intercourse; otherwise the Tyrrhenians and Carthaginians and all other nations having such relations with one another could be regarded as citizens of one inclusive state. It is true that they have customs agreements, compacts against mutual injury, and written articles of defensive alliance. But there are no common law-enforcing bodies to uphold such agreements; the power of enforcement being limited to the internal affairs of each state. Moreover, neither of the contracting states cares about the moral character of the citizens of the other—about ridding them of all unjust and evil tendencies—but cares only about preventing violations of the compact. Those who really think in terms of good government, on the other hand, have a concern for [the more fundamental issue of] virtue and vice in individuals. Whence it is plain that a state which is truly and not superficially so called must be concerned with virtue: for where this concern is lacking, a political community degenerates into a mere alliance, differing only in spatial extent from those alliances whose members [are states and] live apart; while law degenerates into a mere compact—"a guarantor of mutual rights," in Lycophron the Sophist's phrase—without any power to produce goodness and justice in its citizens.

BOOK VIII

EDUCATION

ii. Avoidance of 'banausic' studies

THAT EDUCATION (*paideia*) should be subject to legislation and regarded as an affair of the entire community is now evident.[1] But we must not overlook the question of what this education is, and how it should be practiced. . . .

Granted that useful studies should be taught so far as they are really necessary, this is not to say that *all* useful studies should be taught. There is a difference between liberal and illiberal occupations [i.e., those fit and those unfit for a freeman], and we should impart to our youth only such useful knowledge as they may learn without becoming 'utility-minded, or banausic' (*banausos*).[2] Any occupation, art, or study must be regarded as 'banausic' if it makes the body or soul or mind of a freeman less fit for the practice and exercise of virtue. Accordingly we call those arts that tend to deform the body banausic, and likewise all employments that are followed for the sake of gain, since they make the mind unleisurely and mean. Even among the liberal studies, indeed, there are some in which a freeman may properly engage up to a certain point but

[1] I.e., from the argument of Book VII. In some editions and in Welldon's translation Books VII and VIII are given as IV and V.

[2] See note on p. 217. Barker renders *banausos* 'mechanically minded'; Jowett uses forms of the verb 'vulgarize.' An English word is lacking that will carry both of these connotations and be equally applicable to an occupation and to the person practicing it. Because the idea is so pertinent to our technological era it might be well to incorporate the word *banausic* into our language—signifying the character and prevalent attitude of one whose principal energies are given to a somewhat mechanical way of life.

which if pursued too assiduously and with a desire for perfect mastery produce the evil effects just mentioned. A man's purpose makes considerable difference: if he does or learns something for its own sake or for the sake of his friends or as a means to virtue, it will not be taken as illiberal, but if he does the same thing repeatedly at the instance of others his behavior comes to be regarded as menial and servile.

iii. Role of music in a liberal education

The studies of which present-day education consists are ambiguous in implication.[8] They are usually regarded as four in number: 'reading and writing' (*grammata*), gymnastic, music, and drawing—although the last is sometimes omitted. Reading and writing on the one hand and drawing on the other are included because of their manifold utility for the everyday purposes of life. Gymnastic is regarded as tending to promote courage. The educational purpose of music is a matter of current dispute. For while it is studied nowadays mainly for the pleasure it affords, it was originally included in education for a different reason: because, as is often remarked, we fulfill our nature not only when we work well but when we use leisure well. For I must repeat what I have said before: that leisure (*scholê*)[4] is the 'initiating principle' (*archê*) of all [achievements]. Granted that work and leisure are both necessary, yet leisure is the desired end for which work is done; and this raises the question how we ought to employ our leisure. Not by merely amusing ourselves, obviously, for that would be to set up amusement as the chief end of life.

---

[8] "I.e., they may be used in support of the view that useful subjects should be studied, or in support of the view that subjects tending to promote virtue should be studied."—W. L. Newman, *The Politics of Aristotle.* The sentence with which Chapter iii here begins is traditionally placed at the end of Chapter ii.

[4] In this passage, however, Aristotle uses the verb *scholazein.* From its earlier meaning of 'leisure' *scholê* came to mean the kind of work that requires leisure, hence a learned disputation, hence a place where such disputations are held, or school.

And amusement is clearly not the chief end of life. It is used, in fact, primarily in connection with men's business activities; for the busy man needs amusement as a relaxation after the strain of his exertions. We may conclude, then, that amusements should be introduced [into our lives] only at the proper times and so far as they can be used medicinally as restoratives, for the motion of the soul which they produce gives a relief from strain, and its pleasure relaxes us. Leisure, on the other hand, [is not a means but an end; it] offers not only pleasure but happiness and the very joy of living, and these are not available to the busy man but only to the leisurely. For the busy man has in view some end not yet attained, whereas happiness—which, incidentally, everyone admits to carry pleasure along with it, rather than pain—is an end in itself. . . .

It is clear, then, that there are some branches of learning and education that are pursued for the sake of knowing how to guide our leisure, and that such studies are valuable in themselves; whereas those that are pursued for the sake of some practical business have only an extrinsic value, in the sense of being necessary [for some external end]. And so it was that our forefathers introduced music into education, even though it is neither indispensable nor useful. For it is not, like reading and writing, useful in money-making or in household management or in the acquisition of knowledge or in various political activities; nor, like drawing, in improving one's judgment of works of art; nor, like gymnastic, in promoting health and strength. None of these benefits are to be gained from music. What remains, then, is its value for the cultivated enjoyment of leisure; and this is evidently why it was originally brought into education, by those who regarded it as a way in which a freeman's leisure might suitably be employed. . . .

Evidently, then, there is a kind of education in which our sons should be trained not because it is useful or necessary for a specific purpose but because it is liberal [i.e., proper for a freeman] and noble (*kalos*).

The Art of Poetry

The Art of Poetry

i. Mimêsis: its means

IN STUDYING the 'art of poetry' (*poiêtikê*) our task will be to treat of: (1) the intrinsic nature of poetry, (2) its various kinds, (3) the essential 'function and potentiality' (*dynamis*) of each, (4) the kind of plot (*mythos*)-construction requisite to a good poem (*poiêsis*), (5) the number and nature of a poem's constituent parts, and anything else that falls within the scope of the inquiry. Let us follow the natural order, starting with what is most basic.

Epic poetry and tragedy, as well as comedy and dithyrambic poetry, and most flute and lyre playing, all share the general characteristic of being 'modes of mimetic representation' (*mimêsis*). But at the same time they differ from one another in three respects: in the medium which they employ, in the objects represented, and in the manner of representing.

Just as there are persons who—whether by conscious art or by a skill based on habit—represent various objects by making likenesses of them through the medium of color and form or by the voice; so in the arts above mentioned the representing is done through the medium of rhythm, language, and melodic intervals, whether simply or in certain combinations. Flute and lyre playing employ a combination of rhythm and melodic intervals; and this is the case with any other arts that function similarly, like that of the shepherd's pipe. Rhythm alone, without melody, is the dancer's means of representation; for the dancer too represents human characters, feelings, and actions, by the use of rhythmical gestures.

There is also an art which represents by language alone—either in prose or verse, and if in verse either in one meter or in several. This kind of representation has not yet received a name. For there is no common term we could apply to the mimes [1] of Sophron or Xenarchus and to the Socratic discourses; nor would the difficulty be removed if both of these contrasting types of imitative art were couched in, say, [iambic] trimeter or elegiac meter or the like. It is common practice, of course, to attach to the word 'poet' (*poiêtes*) the name of the meter that he makes (*poiein*) and in speaking of elegiac poets and epic poets, to bestow the title not by reason of the principle of mimetic representation embodied in their work but indiscriminately because of the meter they write in. Even when a treatise on medicine or natural science is published in verse the same practice prevails. It would be better, however, when we compare say Homer and Empedocles, who have nothing in common except meter, to distinguish the one as a poet, the other not as a poet but as a natural scientist. . . . Such then are the ways in which arts may be distinguished with respect to *medium.*

ii. The objects of mimêsis

The *objects* which the poet as mimetic artist represents are human beings in action. Such agents must be either good or bad, for the diversities of human character are nearly always secondary to the primary distinction between virtue and vice. Accordingly they must be represented as either better than our everyday selves or as worse or as similar. It is the same with painters: Polygnotus was wont to portray men as better than in real life, Pauson as worse, and Dionysius as they actually are. It is clear that each of the modes of representation that we have mentioned will admit

---

[1] The Greek *mimos* was a sort of burlesqued drama written in rhythmic but colloquial prose.

of these differences in the character of the object, and that each will become a distinct species of art by representing objects that are thus distinct. . . . It is this kind of difference that distinguishes tragedy from comedy: the one aims to represent men as superior, the other as inferior to their actual condition.

iii. The manner of mimêsis

A third difference among the arts under consideration is found in the *manner* in which any of the foregoing types of objects may be represented. Given a certain medium and a certain type of objects to be represented, the poet may represent them [in one of three ways]: he may alternate between narrative and the speeches of individuals as Homer does, or he may speak from the standpoint of a single individual throughout, or he may represent his character as living and acting before our eyes.

So, as we declared at the outset, artistic representation is distinguishable in three ways—in respect of medium, objects, and manner. Accordingly, Sophocles' mimetic art is akin to Homer's in one respect, namely that both portray characters of a worthier sort, and to Aristophanes' in another, namely that both set their characters before us as living and acting. . . .

iv. Origin and early development of poetry

Broadly considered, the origin of poetry may be traced to two causes (*aitia*), each of them inherent in man's nature. On the one hand the desire to 'imitate or represent' is instinctive in man from childhood; in fact one of man's distinguishing marks is that he is the most mimetic of all animals, and it is through his mimetic activity that he first begins to learn. Moreover, such imitating and representing is always a source of delight, as experience plainly shows: for even where the objects themselves are disagreeable to behold—repulsive animals, for instance, or dead bodies—we take delight in artistically exact reproductions of them. The reason for this is that learning gives the keenest pleasure—not only to philosophers but even to the rest of mankind despite the scant attention they bestow on it. Hence the reason why men enjoy seeing a picture is that in contemplating it they are incidentally learning and inferring in their recognition of particulars, as when they exclaim, "Ah, that is so-and-so!" For if they happen not to have seen the original, any pleasure that they get will be due not to the picture in its representational role but to the execution or coloring or some other such cause.

Now since mimetic representation is natural to us on the one hand, and harmonic intervals and rhythms on the other (meters being obviously only special kinds of rhythm), it was through these natural human aptitudes that men originally made rude improvisations, which, as practice gradually improved them, developed into poetry.

Poetry split into two kinds, corresponding to a difference of character in the poets. The more serious poets would represent noble actions performed by noble men, the more trivial ones the actions of the ignoble. Hence the one class of poets took to composing hymns and panegyrics, the other lampoons. . . . Iambic came into use as the meter best suited to the latter style: which explains why even today iambic connotes the meter in which people lampoon or 'iambize' one another.

Homer, who stands supreme among serious poets by reason not only of the literary but of the dramatic qualities of his representations, also established the outlines of comedy by dramatizing the ludicrous instead of merely lampooning. Thus his *Margites* stands in the same relation to later comedies as the *Iliad* and *Odyssey* stand to later tragedies. With the emergence of tragedy and comedy the two types of poet continued to follow their natural bent: instead of lampoons the one type took to the writing of comedy, and instead of epics the other type began to compose tragedies, since these new art forms had wider possibilities and were more highly esteemed than the old.[2]

---

[2] "Whether present-day tragedy has fully realized its formative possibilities

Tragedy arose, as did comedy, from improvisation—as practiced respectively by choral leaders of the dithyramb and of phallic songs such as are still in vogue in many of our cities. Thence tragedy developed little by little as its possibilities were gradually brought to light, and only after a long succession of changes did it reach the end of its development by finding its natural form. Thus, Aeschylus first increased the number of actors from one to two, curtailed the chanting of the chorus, and gave dialogue the leading role. The third actor and the use of painted scenery were introduced by Sophocles. Meanwhile tragedy had been developing beyond the short plots and grotesque diction of the early satyr-plays and attaining to greater magnitude and dignity, while the meter changed from [trochaic] tetrameter to iambic [double trimeter]. Tetrameter was employed in early times as being better suited to the kind of poetry then in vogue, namely the satyr-play, which involved more dancing than plays do now; but as soon as dialogue was introduced, nature herself discovered the proper meter. For iambic is the most conversational of all meters, as evidenced by the fact that it is the one we most readily fall into when talking with one another, whereas meters such as the [dactyllic] hexameter are used rarely and only when we depart from a conversational tone. As for other changes in the development of tragedy—the division into episodes, and the introduction of various embellishments [like masks, costumes, and stage properties]—all this had better be taken as told, for a detailed account would doubtless be a very long task.

v. Comedy, epic

Comedy, as we have said, is a representation of men who are morally inferior—not in the sense of being thoroughly evil, but only in the sense of being ludicrous. For the ludicrous is a sub-

---

is a matter for separate inquiry, and would have to be judged not only on the intrinsic merits of the case but with reference to essential theatrical requirements as well."—Aristotle's gloss.

division of the morally ugly, consisting in some defect or ugliness which does not produce actual harm and hence causes no pain to the beholder: as a comic mask is ugly and distorted without causing pain. . . .

Epic poetry is similar to tragedy in being a representation of serious subjects in stately verse, but differs in being limited to a single meter and by reason of its narrative form. It differs also in respect of length: for whereas tragedy tries to confine itself to a single revolution of the sun or not much more than that, the action of an epic has no fixed time limit. This is a point of difference between them, although originally tragedies had the same freedom as epics in this respect. Finally, they differ in constituent parts, some of which are common to both forms while others are peculiar to tragedy. Therefore, since all the elements of the epic are to be found in tragedy but not all those of tragedy in the epic, it follows that whoever can judge of good and bad in tragedy can do so in the epic also.

vi. Definition of tragedy; its six formative elements

Let us postpone discussion of epic poetry and of comedy till later,[3] and proceed now with a discussion of tragedy, deriving from what has been said a definition of what it essentially is. Tragedy, then, is a representation (*mimêsis*) of an action (*praxis*) that is serious, complete, and of a certain magnitude; in language pleasurably and variously embellished suitably to the different parts of the play; in the form of actions directly presented, not narrated; with incidents arousing pity and fear in such a way as to accomplish a purgation (*katharsis*) of such emotions. By 'language pleasurably embellished' I refer to the use of rhythm, 'harmonic modes' (*harmonia*), and song (*melos*). By 'variously for the different parts' I mean that some parts of the play produce their effects through verse alone, others through song.

---

[3] Epic poetry is discussed in Chaps. xxiii–xxvi. The purposed discussion of comedy was not written.

Since tragic representation consists of showing people in action, it follows that staging (*opsis*) will be one of the necessary aspects of tragedy. Next come song (*melos*) and diction (*lexis*), these being the immediate instruments of representation. By diction I mean simply the metrical arrangement of words; song has its customary signification. Next, since the subject represented is an action, and since actions are performed by agents, each of whom is distinguished by certain traits of character and thought—for it is from such traits that a man's actions and hence his eventual success or failure springs, whether in drama or in real life—it follows that the representation of action in the play will have the form of a 'story or plot' (*mythos*) [and will include character (*êthos*) and thought (*dianoia*) as necessary elements]. By story or plot I mean the way in which the incidents are constructed into a whole; by character, that by which we ascribe certain qualities to the agents or persons of the drama; by thought, that which is expressed when they argue a point or even merely enunciate a general truth.

Every tragedy, therefore, must have six aspects, which make it what it is: story, characters, diction, thought, staging, and song. Two of these elements [diction and song] may be regarded as the media of representation, one of them [the staging] as the manner of representation, and three of them [story, characters, and thought] as the objects of representation. The list is exhaustive. All six of these 'formative elements' (*eidos*) are generally taken account of in writing a tragedy, for all tragedies involve just these elements of staging, character, story, diction, song, and thought.

The most important of the six is the structure of incidents [which form the story]. Tragedy is a representation essentially not of men but of 'human action' (*praxis*): i.e., of human life, its happiness and its misery; for on the stage these must find expression in action, and the proper end [of dramatic representation] therefore is a mode of action, not some sort of quality. [The persons of a drama] will be of one sort or another according to their several characters, but [they must be shown to] achieve happiness or misery according to their actions. What they do, then, is not simply a way of representing their characters; rather, their characters are developed as subsidiary and instrumental to the action. Hence the incidents and the story or plot [which they constitute] are the real end of the tragedy; and the real end is of course our principal concern.

[That plot is more essential than character] is further indicated by the fact that while there cannot be a tragedy without action, there may be one without character. The tragedies of most modern dramatists are lacking in character portrayal—a lack which is to be found among modern poets generally, and which has its counterpart in the paintings of Zeuxis as compared with those of Polygnotus; for whereas Polygnotus is a good character painter, the paintings of Zeuxis offer nothing in the way of character. Moreover, even though a writer string together a number of speeches expressing character in polished style as regards both diction and thought, he may utterly fail to produce the proper tragic effect; whereas he will succeed much better with a tragedy which, however deficient in those respects, yet has a plot consisting of well-arranged incidents. Again, it is in the plot that we find those elements whereby tragedy achieves its most powerful emotional effect, namely 'reversals of the situation' (*peripeteia*) and recognition scenes. Still another indication is found in the fact that novices in the tragic art achieve competence in language and character-portrayal before they are able to construct a good pattern of incidents: as is the case with nearly all the early poets.

The story or plot, then, is the 'initiating principle' (*archê*) and, so to speak, the soul of tragedy; character being in second place. Tragedy is the representation of an action; and it is principally in carrying out this function that it represents agents likewise.

Third [in importance] comes thought; i.e., the faculty of saying what is possible and appropriate [in a given situation]. This element, which is found in the dialogue and speeches of a tragedy [not in the choral parts], belongs to the provinces of statecraft (*politikê*) and oratory (*rhêtorikê*), for the older poets made their personages talk like statesmen, the modern like orators. Character, as distinguished from thought, reveals 'moral purpose' (*proairesis*) —that is, what a dramatic personage will choose or shun in situations where the ground of choice is obscure. Speeches that do not manifest any concern with choice or avoidance are not expressive of character. Thought, on the other hand, finds expression whenever anyone argues for or against some point or enunciates some generalization.

Fourth among the literary [4] elements of tragedy comes diction: by which I mean, as already explained, the interpretive use of language, this being the essential function of diction whether in verse or in prose.

Of the two remaining elements we may say that musical composition holds chief place among the embellishments of tragedy. The 'visual aspect of the staging' (*opsis*), despite its emotional appeal, is the least artistic of all the elements and has least to do with the art of poetry. For the 'essential power' (*dynamis*) of tragedy is independent of a 'stage presentation' (*agôn*) and of actors, and moreover the production of scenic effects lies more in the province of the 'costumer and stage-manager' (*skeuopoios*) than of the poet.

vii. Plot requirements: Proper magnitude

Having thus distinguished the formative elements, let us now discuss the proper arrangement of incidents [into a story or plot], since this is the first and most important aspect of tragedy. According to our definition, tragedy is a representation of an action that is whole, complete, and of a certain magnitude—for a thing might be completely whole and yet lack magnitude. Now a whole in-

---

[4] The first four elements of tragedy—story, character, thought, and diction—belong to it as a work of literature and are shared by the epic; the fifth and sixth elements—music and staging—are accessories, which attach to tragedy only when it is enacted on the stage.

volves having a beginning, a middle, and an end. A beginning is that which does not follow as a necessary consequent upon something else, but which is followed by something else existing or occurring as its own natural result; an end, on the contrary, is that which follows as a natural result, either inevitably or usually, from something else, but has nothing following it in turn; while a middle both follows and is followed by something else. That is to say, a well-constructed plot must neither begin nor end at random, but must observe these distinctions.

Furthermore, any beautiful object, whether a living creature or anything else made up of parts, must not only have its parts well arranged but must also be of an appropriate size, for beauty depends on size and order. Thus, a very minute creature cannot be beautiful to us, for our perception of it is instantaneous without any clear discrimination of its parts; nor, on the other hand, could a monstrously large creature, miles and miles in length, be beautiful to us, for our inability to see it all at once would leave us without any sense of its unity and wholeness. Now just as there is a proper size for living creatures and other physical bodies— a size, namely, which the eye can take in; so there is a proper size for stories and plots—a size, namely, that can be taken in by the memory. . . . The limit must be set by the nature of the case, but in general the greater the length the more beautiful the story will be in this respect, provided it can still be grasped as a whole. In general, a sufficient length will mean one which allows of a development, by steps whose connection [appears] inevitable or at any rate plausible, from misfortune to happiness or from happiness to misfortune.

viii. Plot requirements: Unity

A plot does not have unity, as some believe, merely because it deals with a single hero. The incidents that befall even a single man are numberless, and not all of them will fit into a unified conception of what happens to him; likewise his actions are numerous and cannot all be combined into one action. Whence the mistake of all those poets who have composed a *Heracleid*, a *Theseid*, or the like: they suppose that because Heracles was one individual the story about him must correspondingly be one. Homer, on the other hand, whether by conscious art or instinctive genius, seems to have been well aware of this principle—another evidence of his superiority to other poets. In composing the *Odyssey* he did not introduce all that ever befell his hero. There was the incident of Odysseus' being wounded on Mount Parnassus, for example, and there was the incident of his feigning madness when the army was being mustered,[5] but the two incidents had no necessary or even plausible relation with each other, and Homer was building the *Odyssey*, as he had built the *Iliad*, around a unity of action in the sense here defined. In short, just as in the other mimetic arts the *mimêsis* or representation is one when the object mimed or represented is one, so the plot, being a representation of an action, should represent an action that is single and whole—that is to say, an action whose component parts hang together in such a way that to displace or remove any one of them would disturb and even destroy the whole. For a part that can be present or absent indifferently is no real part of the whole.

ix. Poetry compared with history

The poet's function, then, as appears from the foregoing discussion, is to describe not what has actually happened but the kind of thing that might well happen—i.e., what is [dramatically] possible in the sense of being either plausible or inevitable. The difference between a historian and a poet is not that the one writes in prose and the other in verse. Herodotus' writings, for example,

---

[5] The first of these incidents, as a matter of fact, is briefly narrated in Book XIX, lines 560 ff., but it plays no part in the real action of the *Odyssey*. The second incident occurred at the outset of the Trojan War. To avoid conscription Odysseus feigned madness by ploughing his field with an ox and a horse; but when Palamedes laid the infant Telemachus in the way of the plough, Odysseus stopped, thereby revealing his sanity.

even though they were versified would still be a kind of history, the meter notwithstanding. No, the real difference consists in this, that the one speaks of what has occurred, the other of what might occur. Hence poetry is something more philosophical and more highly serious than history, for poetry tends to express universals, history particulars. By universal is meant what a man of a certain sort will say or do, either probably or inevitably; and this is what poetry aims at, despite the particular names it employs. By particular is meant [some such thing as] what Alcibiades did or had done to him.

The distinction has lately become obvious in the field of comedy; for modern comedy writers—as distinguished from the ancient iambic poets who wrote about particular persons—first construct their plots out of plausible incidents, then affix proper names at random. Writers of tragedy, on the contrary, still adhere to the use of real names. Their reason for doing so is that only the possible has credibility, and we are apt to be unsure of the possibility of what has never actually occurred, whereas when something *has* occurred its very occurrence proves that it must be possible. Nevertheless there are some tragedies that employ only one or two familiar names, the rest being fictitious; and there are some, like Agathon's *The Blossoming*, without even a single familiar name, the names being as fictitious as the incidents, although the play is no whit less effective on that account. It is by no means absolutely essential, then, that a poet confine himself to the traditional stories. Such a restriction would be inconsistent in any case, because the familiar stories are familiar only to a few, yet they give delight to all.

From all this it is manifest that the poet [which is to say, the maker] must be primarily a maker of plots rather than of verses, for he is a poet by virtue of the representing (*mimêsis*) that he does, and the object that he represents is actions. Even though he should happen to take a subject from history, he is none the less a poet on that account; for there is nothing to prevent certain historical events from being plausible and [dramatically] possible, and it is in relation to this aspect of them that he is their proper maker, or poet.

The worst kind of plot and dramatic action is the episodic; by which I mean a plot in which the episodes follow one another in a way that is neither plausible nor inevitable. Bad poets commit this fault through want of skill, while good ones do so through adapting the action to the actors, for in meeting the requirements of a theatrical contest they stretch the plot beyond its natural capacity and thereby, frequently, have to sacrifice dramatic continuity.

Tragedy, however, is a representation of an action that is not only complete but that consists of events inspiring fear and pity; and this effect is best produced when the events are at once unexpected and causally related. For thereby they stir our wonder more than if they happened by themselves or by mere chance. Even coincidences appear most remarkable when they have some appearance of design: when, for instance, the statue of Mitys at Argos toppled over on Mitys' very murderer at a festival, the occurrence did not seem entirely accidental. Accordingly, plots which have this [double aspect of unexpectedness and apparent causal relation] are the best.

x. Simple and complex plots

Some plots are simple, others are complex; for the actions they represent are similarly distinguishable. I call dramatic action simple when (granted that it has the unity and continuity prescribed) the 'change in the hero's fortune' (*metabasis*) is produced without employing either reversal or discovery in the technical sense; complex, when the catastrophe is attended by reversal or discovery or both. These devices should arise out of the very structure of the plot, so that what follows comes to be the result, plausi-

ble or inevitable, of what has preceded. There is a great difference
between happening *because of* something and merely happening
after it.

xi. Reversal and discovery

A reversal (*peripeteia*) is a change of the situation into its opposite [from good fortune to bad or from bad to good], as has been
said, and in a way that is either plausible or inevitable, as has
also been said.[6] In the *Oedipus,* for example, the messenger who
comes to gladden Oedipus and release him from his fears about
his mother, actually produces just the opposite effect through revealing the secret of his birth. . . .

A discovery (*ana-gnôrisis*), as the word itself indicates, is a
change from ignorance to knowledge, and thereby to either friendship or enmity, according as the characters involved are marked
for good or evil fortune. The best kind of discovery is one combined with reversals, like the reversal in the *Oedipus.* There are
no doubt other kinds. It is possible to 'discover,' within our meaning of the word, whether a person has done something or not,
and there may even be discoveries about trivial inanimate things.
But the kind of discovery most intimately connected with the
plot and the dramatic action is such as we have been describing.
This kind of discovery, combined with reversal, will arouse
either pity or fear; and according to our theory, it is actions productive of such effects that are properly represented in tragedy.
Moreover, it is upon situations such as these that good or bad fortune will depend. Confining the term 'discovery,' then, to relations

---

[6] The reference here is presumably to the last sentence of Chap. vii, although reversal was not there mentioned. How technical reversal differs from
simple change of fortune is well stated by Bywater: "Every tragedy, according to Aristotle, describes a transition from happiness to misery or vice
versa; but in the 'complex story' the change, however gradual it may be,
seems to the hero to come upon him all at once, by a sudden reversal of the
state of things; he thinks himself a happy man (let us say) at the beginning
of an [episode], and a miserable man at the end of it." (*Aristotle on the Art
of Poetry,* p. 199.)

between persons, we may distinguish between cases where one person's identity is already known and cases where each must discover the identity of the other. Thus Iphigeneia became known to Orestes through sending the letter, but a separate act of discovery was required to make him known to Iphigeneia.[7]

So much, then, for these two elements of the plot, reversal and discovery, which involve the kind of incident here described. A third element is the 'scene of pathos' (*pathos*), which may be defined as 'dramatic action' (*praxis*) involving destruction or pain, such as deaths on the stage, agonies, woundings, and the like.

xii. The technical divisions of tragedy

The formative elements of tragedy having been discussed, we may now examine the quantitatively distinct parts which it comprises: prologue, episode, and exode on the one hand, and chorus on the other; which last is divided into parode and stasimon, both of which are found in all tragedies, whereas songs by an individual actor and *kommoi* are found in some tragedies and not in others. The prologue is all that portion of a tragedy which precedes the parode [or entrance chant] of the chorus; the episode is all that portion which comes between whole choric songs; the exode is all that part which has no choric song following it. Of the choric portion, the parode is the entire first utterance of the chorus; the stasimon is [any later] choric song; [8] the kommos, a lamentation carried on between the chorus and an actor.

xiii. Aim and proper effect of tragedy

The next points to consider, after the matters just mentioned, are: what should be aimed at and what avoided in the construction

---

[7] Euripides, *Iphigeneia in Tauris*, l. 11.

[8] What Aristotle actually says is, "a choric song without anapests or trochees," but this does not apply to the surviving Greek tragedies. The more usual definition of a stasimon is a 'stationary song' (W. Rhys Roberts), sung after the chorus has taken up its station in the orchestra.

of plots; and by what means the 'proper effect' (*ergon*) of tragedy is to be achieved.

Tragedy at its best, as we have seen, will have not a simple but a complex type of construction, and also it will represent actions arousing pity and fear. Since this latter operation is the distinctive function of tragic *mimêsis*, it evidently follows that there are three types of plot to be avoided. First a [thoroughly] good man should not be shown passing from prosperity to misfortune, for such a situation does not arouse either pity or fear, but merely offends us by its brutality. Nor, on the other hand, should a bad man be shown passing from adversity to prosperity—a situation entirely alien to tragedy, meeting none of its requirements, for it excites neither our pity and fear nor our moral sympathies. Finally, it must not be an utterly wicked man who is shown passing from prosperity to adversity. Such a situation may excite our moral sympathies but it will not arouse our pity nor our fear: pity is aroused by undeserved misfortune, and fear by the misfortune of someone like ourselves, so that an event of the sort described is neither piteous nor fear-inspiring. The remaining case is that of the man who is a mean between these extremes: who, though not outstandingly virtuous and just, yet falls into misfortune not through vice or depravity but through some 'tragic flaw' (*hamartia*); and moreover he should be drawn from the ranks of men who have enjoyed great reputation and prosperity, like Oedipus, Thyestes, and men of equally illustrious families.

Ideally, then, tragedy is at its best when constructed in the way described, and those critics are wrong who censure Euripides for constructing many of his plays on that principle and so giving them unhappy endings. In this respect he was right, as we have said; the best proof of which is that when well produced and performed upon the stage such plays are the most pronouncedly tragic, and Euripides himself, although he sometimes handles his subjects badly, is still the most tragic of poets.

Of second rank, although there are some who put it first, is the double dramatic construction like that of the *Odyssey*, in which there are opposite outcomes for the good characters and the bad. That it passes for the best is owing to the sentimentality of theatre audiences, to whose cravings the dramatist has accommodated his writing. But the pleasure which such dramas produce is not essentially tragic; it belongs rather to comedy, where those whom the story presents as bitter enemies, like Orestes and Aegisthus, quit the stage as good friends, with no slaying or being slain.

xiv. Kinds of action arousing pity and fear

Fear and pity may be aroused by spectacular staging, or they may be aroused by the dramatic construction. The latter method is the one which better poets employ. For the plot ought to be constructed in such a way that anyone, by merely hearing an account of the incidents and without seeing them, will be filled with horror and pity at what occurs. That is how anyone hearing the story of Oedipus would be affected. To rely on spectacular staging is less artistic and makes the production more dependent upon 'financial backing' (*chorêgia*).[9] Those who stage the play in such a way as to produce an effect which is not terrible but merely showy are not really writers of tragedy at all. For what we should expect of tragedy is not any random pleasure, but only such pleasure as is proper to it. And since the dramatist's task is to produce through *mimêsis* the kind of pleasure that comes from responding with pity and fear, it is clear that this effect should be drawn from the incidents themselves.

Let us examine, then, what kinds of incident strike us as terrible and as pitiable. Logically, the persons involved must be either friends or enemies or indifferent to each other. If an enemy per-

[9] The *chorêgos* was a man of wealth who voluntarily assumed responsibility for "assembling and hiring a body of *choreutae*, engaging a trainer to drill them, purchasing or renting costumes for the chorus, employing mute characters, providing showy extras of various kinds, etc. . . . There was no surer method of displaying one's wealth and of currying favor with the populace than by voluntary and lavish assumption of the choregia."—Roy C. Flickinger, *The Greek Theatre and its Drama*.

forms a deed against an enemy, there is nothing to arouse our pity in either the deed or the intention; our pity is confined to the suffering which results. The same will be true when the participants are neither friends nor enemies. But when the 'tragic occurrence' (*pathos*) takes place between friends—when, for instance, some such crime as murder is done or planned by brother against brother, or by son against father, or by son against mother or mother against son—here is the kind of situation that the dramatist should look for. Traditional stories, then, like Orestes' slaying of Clytemnestra and Alcmaeon's of Eriphyle, should not be radically altered; it is left for the poet to show his inventiveness by his skillful handling of the traditional material. What I mean by skillful handling I will next explain.

A dreadful deed may be done in full consciousness of what it involves, as in the older poets and in the scene where Euripides has Medea slay her children. Or it may be done in ignorance of its dreadful nature, which becomes revealed only later when some intimate relationship is discovered, as in Sophocles' *Oedipus*. In that case, to be sure, the deed lies outside the play, but there are other examples where the deed lies within the play itself. Thirdly, a character may be about to do some irreparable deed through ignorance and make the discovery in time to desist. [And lastly, one may be about to act in full knowledge of what is involved and then change his mind.] These exhaust the possibilities, for the deed must either be done or not be done, and either knowingly or unwittingly.

The worst of these situations is where one is about to act in full knowledge and then changes his mind. Such a situation is not tragic but merely revolting, for no tragic feeling is involved. Hence it is rarely employed, the scene between Haemon and Creon in the *Antigone* being one of the few exceptions. Next [in ascending order of merit] comes the doing of the deed [in full knowledge]. Still better is the acting in ignorance and subsequent discovery, for there is nothing revolting about it and the discovery is [effectively] startling. Best of all is the remaining type of situation. In the *Cresphorites* [of Euripides], for example, Merope intends to kill her son but discovers who he is and so spares his life; there is a similar situation in Euripides' *Iphigeneia in Tauris* between sister and brother; and in the *Helle* [10] a son discovers the identity of his mother just as he is about to surrender her.

Thus we see the reason why tragedies, as we said just now, deal with the fortunes of a few [illustrious] families. For it is not technical proficiency but the happy chance [of having discovered suitable situations in the traditional tales about those families] that enabled the tragic poets to embody such incidents in their plots. Accordingly they still feel bound to have recourse to the families in which such tragic occurrences took place.

Enough now has been said about the proper arrangement of incidents and the character of plots.

xv. Requirements of tragic characters

Respecting the characters (*êthos*) in tragedy, there are four things to be aimed at. First and foremost they must be good. The play will have an 'element of character, or ethical element' (*êthos*) if, as has already been remarked, some kind of 'moral purpose' (*proairesis*) is expressed, either in the 'speeches and dialogue' (*logos*) or in the action; and the character will be good if the moral purpose is good. The rule holds for all classes of people—even of women and slaves, although it is doubtless true that the one is an inferior type of person and the other without any personal worth whatever. Secondly, the characters should be appropriate: manly valor, for instance, has its proper place, but manly valor and domination are hardly appropriate in a woman. Thirdly, the characters should resemble [their models], which is something quite distinct from making them good or, in the sense here defined, appropriate. Fourthly, they should be consistent: for even where an inconsistent person is to be represented, he should be consistently repre-

[10] Nothing is known of this play.

sented as inconsistent. Menelaos in the *Orestes* [of Euripides] is an example (*paradeigma*) of unnecessary badness of character; Melanippe's speech [11] exemplifies character that is incongruous; Odysseus' lament in the *Scylla,* character that does not resemble its model; and Iphigeneia in Aulis [in Euripides' play of that name], character that is inconsistent—for Iphigeneia as suppliant is quite unlike her later self. In short, the rule in character drawing, just as in plot construction, is that one should always seek what is [dramatically] inevitable or [at least] dramatically plausible, so that it becomes inevitable or [at least] plausible that a given person should speak or act in a certain way, and inevitable or [at least] plausible that one incident should follow another.

[To digress for a moment.] It is clear from this last point that the 'denouement or resolution' (*lysis*) of a plot should arise out of the plot itself and not be produced by a mechanical device as in the *Medea* [of Euripides] and in the account of the [supernaturally prevented] return of the Greek army in the *Iliad.* The mechanical device [12] should only be employed for what lies outside the drama; that is, in the explaining or foretelling of unfamiliar events that precede or follow the drama itself. [In such cases it is permissible to introduce a god by mechanical device,] for the gods are credited with omniscience. In short, there should be no supernatural elements within the drama proper, but only, if at all, peripheral to it, as in Sophocles' *Oedipus.*

[Returning to the subject of character portrayal] we may remark

[11] In *Melanippe the Wise,* a lost play of Euripides, of which only certain fragments have been preserved. Melanippe, seduced by Neptune, bore him twins and concealed them in her father's stable. Her father, taking them for monstrous offspring of his cows, ordered them burned. Melanippe, in order to save them without exposing her indiscretion, had recourse to a 'masculine' type of argument, based upon the principles of Anaxagoras, to prove that monstrous births are 'natural.' Of the *Scylla* nothing is known.

[12] This epithet appears to have a double and perhaps shifting meaning in the present paragraph: (1) the *deus ex machina,* a mechanical contraption, standard in the Greek theatre, for lowering a god on to the stage; (2) hence, the kind of artificial resolution of plot which the use of the contraption ordinarily involved.

that since tragedy is a representation of men better than ordinary, the example of good portrait painters should be followed. Their method is to produce a likeness of a man's distinctive features and beautify him at the same time. Analogously the poet, when representing a man who is irascible or lazy or otherwise morally defective, should set him forth with these very traits while at the same time ennobling him. This is how both Agathon and Homer have represented Achilles.[13]

Such are the rules to be observed in the writing of tragedy. There is also, of course, the question of theatrical effects to be considered, for there are many ways in which a play can go wrong when it is being presented on the stage; but this subject has been sufficiently treated in our published writings.

xvi. Kinds of 'discovery'

The general nature of 'discovery' has already been explained; let us now distinguish its species.

The first and least artistic kind of discovery, usually a mark of incompetence, is discovery by means of visible signs: whether they be congenital, such as birthmarks, or acquired, such as bodily scars on the one hand and external tokens like necklaces on the other. The treatment of such signs admits of varying degrees of skill: compare, for instance, the way in which Odysseus was recognized by his nurse with the way in which he was recognized by the swineherds.[14] A discovery in which the signs are deliberately shown as a means of proof, or any other such labored contrivance, is artistically inferior to one in which (as in the incident just cited,

---

[13] Professor Jaeger quotes the rhetor Dio of Prusa to similar effect: "Homer praised almost everything—animals and plants, water and earth, weapons and horses. He passed over nothing without somehow honoring and glorifying it. Even the one man whom he abused, Thersites, he called a clear-voiced speaker." (Werner Jaeger, *Paideia*, Vol. I, p. 42; Oxford University Press.)

[14] The old nurse Eurycleia sees Odysseus' scar by a natural accident (*Odyssey*, xix, 386 ff.) whereas Odysseus deliberately shows it to the herdsmen in order to convince them of his identity (*Odyssey*, xxi, 205 ff.). The former of these constitutes a 'dramatic reversal.'

of Odysseus being bathed by the old nurse) they occur as a spontaneous reversal of the situation.

Secondly, there are discoveries arbitrarily invented by the poet: e.g., where Orestes, in the *Iphigeneia* [*in Tauris*], reveals his identity. Whereas Iphigeneia becomes known to Orestes by means of the letter, he becomes known to her by speaking what the poet and not what the plot requires. This second fault, then, comes close to the one already mentioned, for [when Orestes describes things at home in order to prove his identity] it is virtually as if he had brought some tokens to show. Another example is offered by the 'voice of the shuttle' device in Sophocles' *Tereus*.[15]

Thirdly, there is discovery through memory, whereby the sight of something stirs an emotional recollection. Thus when Odysseus heard the minstrel Alcinoüs play the lyre he remembered the past and burst into tears, thereby being recognized.[16]

The fourth kind of discovery comes about through rational inference. An example is [Electra's] reasoning in [Aeschylus'] *Choëphori:* "Someone like myself has come here, no one resembles me but Orestes, therefore Orestes has come." . . .

But of all discoveries the best is that which arises from the action itself, where the shock of surprise is the outcome of a plausible succession of events. Such is the discovery in Sophocles' *Oedipus.* Another example is found in the *Iphigeneia* [*in Tauris*], for it is plausible enough that Iphigeneia should want to send a letter home.

The last type of discovery, being the only one entirely free from artificial contrivances, is best. Second in excellence is the type that depends on inference.

---

[15] A lost play. After Tereus had raped Philomela and cut out her tongue, the wronged girl succeeded in telling her sister Procne what had happened by weaving the story into the embroidery. The shuttle with which she wove thereby had a 'voice.' Aristotle regards such disclosure as too deliberate to be artistically effective.

[16] *Odyssey*, viii, 521 ff.

xvii. Practical advice for the tragic poet

In constructing his plots and elaborating them in language (*lexis*) the poet should keep the scene before his eyes as far as possible. Thereby, seeing everything as vividly as if he were an actual spectator, he will discover what is appropriate and will detect incongruities.

Moreover, he should work out the action even down to gestures. To be entirely convincing he must be able to enter into the emotions of his characters through sharing in their nature. One enacts agitation or anger most convincingly when he is actually feeling them. That is why poetry requires either a natural talent or an enthusiasm that verges on madness: by the one a man is adaptable, by the other ecstatically inspired.

As for the story—whether the poet takes it ready-made or invents it himself—he should first sketch its general outline, then write the episodes and otherwise amplify it. . . . He should take care that the episodes are appropriate: as illustrated by the madness of Orestes, which led to his capture, and the ritual purification which saved him.[17]

The episodes in a drama should be short, whereas in an epic they are used for lengthening out the action. . . .

xviii. On plot construction

Every tragedy falls into two parts—the complication or 'tying up' and the resolution or 'unraveling.' The complication usually contains not only elements within the drama proper but incidents referred to as occurring outside it; the rest is dramatic resolution. In other words, the complication is everything from the beginning of the story up to that crucial point which is followed by a change

[17] This situation, in Euripides' *Iphigeneia in Tauris*, takes place after Orestes has murdered his mother. Although the ritual purification is merely a stratagem by Iphigeneia to 'save' them from their captors, the madness is ethically appropriate in view of Orestes' crime, and the purification and 'saving' (the Greek word *sôtêria* here connotes both escape from captivity and religious salvation) is appropriate symbolically.

from prosperity to adversity; the resolution is all that extends from this turning-point to the end of the play. The soundest basis on which to compare or contrast one tragedy with another is plot—specifically, by comparing them with respect to complication and resolution. Many poets are good at tying the knot but poor at untying it. Both arts should be mastered.

There are four species of tragedy, corresponding to the four elements which have just been discussed: [18] (1) complex tragedy, depending entirely on reversal and discovery, (2) tragedy 'of suffering' (*pathêtikos*), like the various *Ajaxes* and *Ixions*, (3) tragedy 'of character' (*êthikos*), like *The Phthiotides* and *Peleus*, and finally, (4) tragedy depending upon spectacle, exemplified by *The Phorcides*, *Prometheus*, and all those plays whose scene is laid in Hades. A poet should aim to combine all four elements if possible, or at any rate as many of them in as significant a way as he can—especially in these days when there is so much ill-considered criticism of poets. Just because there have been poets who were adept at writing one or another particular species of tragedy, critics now expect a poet to show his superiority by combining all the different excellences of his predecessors into one.

Again, the poet should remember what has been repeatedly said, and not construct a tragedy in the manner of an epic (which comprises a number of stories) by trying to dramatize, for instance, the entire *Iliad*. An epic is long enough to allow of the parts being as long as they need to be, but a drama so constructed will fail of its intended effect. A proof of this is that poets who have dramatized the entire story of Troy's fall, instead of presenting it part by part like Euripides, or the entire story of Niobe instead of selecting a portion of it like Aeschylus, either fail utterly or at any rate come out badly in the competition. . . .

The Chorus should be considered as one of the persons in the

---

[18] The reference is apparently to Chaps. xi ff. In the traditional arrangement this paragraph is introduced three sentences earlier.

drama; it should be an integral part of the whole and have a share in the action—following the practice of Sophocles, not Euripides. The rest [of the moderns] use songs that have no more to do with the plot of the tragedy that contains them than with any other. Hence they come to be sung as mere interludes—a practice which Agathon first began. And yet how is the singing of interludes any better than transferring a speech or an entire scene from one play to another?

xix. *Diction and thought*

The other aspects of tragedy having been discussed, it remains to speak of the diction and the thought. As for thought, we may refer to what has been said about it in our *Rhetoric*, for it is to that field of study that the subject more properly belongs. The 'thought' of a tragedy includes whatever effects are produced by the speeches and dialogues: wherever anyone is engaged in proving or disproving, arousing some emotion (such as pity, fear, anger, and the like), or exaggerating or belittling. Dramatic incidents, to be sure, can have essentially the same effect as speeches, arousing pity or horror or suggesting that something is important or probable. The only difference is that dramatic incident must make its impression without explanation, whereas in the speeches the effect is produced by the speaker, in consequence of what he *says*—the speech being necessary where the thought is not adequately conveyed by incident alone.

[Aristotle next proceeds to discuss diction. Some of what he says— on the Greek letters, syllables, and parts of speech—is of little interest except to a reader of Greek. Only his discussion of metaphor, therefore, is included here.]

xxi. *Metaphor*

Metaphor (*meta-phora*) consists in the transference (*epi-phora*) of a name [from the thing which it properly denotes] to some other thing; the transference being either from genus to species, or from species to genus, or from species to species, or by 'analogy and proportion' (*analogia*). From genus to species is exemplified by "Here stays my ship"; for being at anchor is a species of staying. From species to genus, by "Odysseus wrought ten thousand noble deeds"; where ten thousand, which is a particular large number, is made to stand for the idea of large number in general. From species to species, by "Drawing off his life with a bronze [knife]" and "Cutting off [his life] with a durable bronze [mixing-bowl]"; where the poet says 'draw off' instead of 'cut off' and 'cut off' instead of 'draw off'—both of them being species of removal.[19] Finally, analogy or proportion consists in this, that a second term being related to a first as a fourth is to a third, the poet employs the second for the fourth or the fourth for the second. Sometimes, too, a poet will qualify such a metaphor by adding the word that goes with what it supplants. For instance, since the cup is to Dionysus as the shield is to Ares, he may metaphorically describe the cup as 'Dionysus' shield' or the shield as 'Ares' cup.' Again, since old age is to life as evening is to day, one may describe evening as 'the old age of the day,' somewhat in the manner of Empedocles, or old age as 'the sunset of life.' This type of metaphor can sometimes be used even when there is no word for one of the terms of the proportion. For instance, to scatter seed is called sowing, but there is no single word for the sun's dispersion of his rays. Still, as this process bears to the sunlight the same relation as sowing to the seed, a poet can speak of 'sowing the god-created rays.' There is also another way of using this kind of metaphor. We may give something an alien name and then qualify this negatively by negating some attribute that properly goes with the name: as for instance, if we were to call the shield not simply 'the cup of Ares' but 'the cup that holds no wine.' . . .

[19] In other words, in the description of the total act (of ritual sacrifice?) there is a metaphoric interchange between two equally concrete elements (both 'species')—namely, severing the body with a knife and drawing off the blood into a mixing-bowl. Aristotle ignores the further metaphor, in the first phrase, of substituting 'life' (*psyché*) for blood.

xxii. *The role of poetic diction*

Excellence of diction consists in being lucid without bogging down. The most lucid diction consists of words in common use, but it bogs down. On the other hand, diction is given majesty and distinction by the [judicious] use of unusual forms—by which I mean rare words, metaphors, lengthened words, in short whatever departs from the current idiom. Exclusive reliance on such forms, however, produces either obscurity or jargon—obscurity if there are too many metaphors, jargon if too many rare words. There ought rather to be a judicious admixture of different types of expression. Rare, metaphoric, ornamental, and other such special forms raise language above the commonplace, while the ordinary words which it contains give it clarity. To condemn poetic diction, then, as some do, and blame the poet for resorting to it, is quite unjustified. . . .

While the proper use of all these various poetic devices is important, by far the greatest thing for a poet is to be a master of metaphor. Such mastery is the one thing that cannot be learned from others. It is a mark of genius (*euphuia*), for to be good at metaphor is to be intuitively aware of hidden resemblances.

xxiii. *The epic*

As for [the epic, which is to say] that kind of poetry in which the representation is in narrative form and employs a single kind of meter, it is evidently like tragedy in requiring a plot (*mythos*) constructed on dramatic principles—i.e., which forms one entire action, with a beginning, middle, and end, so that by functioning integrally, like a 'living organism' (*zôon*), it may produce its proper pleasure. Epics, accordingly, should be constructed on a quite different plan from histories. The proper subject-matter of a history is not a single action, but a single period of time, containing any number of fortuitously related happenings as they affect one or more persons. For two events may happen simultaneously, like the naval battle of Salamis and the Carthaginian battle in Sicily, without conducing toward any common end (*telos*), and the same may be true of events that happen consecutively. Most poets, however, write without observing the distinction.

Here again, as in previous connections, we must recognize the incomparable superiority of Homer to other poets. He made no attempt to deal with the Trojan War in its entirety, even though it did have a definite beginning and end: perceiving, no doubt, that the story was too long, or perhaps too complicated in the variety of its events, to be brought into a single perspective. Accordingly he confined himself to one section of the war, diversifying his presentation here and there with episodes such as the catalogue of ships and the like. Other [epic writers] take for their subject [all that happened to] a single hero or within a single period of time, or else an action which even though unified contains too great a diversity of parts—a fault exemplified in the *Cypria* and the so-called *Little Iliad*. As a result, either the *Iliad* or the *Odyssey* will properly furnish the story-material for a single tragedy, or at most two, whereas the *Cypria* furnishes material for several, and the *Little Iliad* for no less than eight. . . .

Now there must be as many species of epic poetry as of tragedy: for an epic, too, must be either simple or complex [in the sense already defined], or 'a tale of character' (*êthikos*) or 'a tale of suffering' (*pathêtikos*).[20] The elements composing the two types are likewise similar, with the exception of music and stage presentation; for reversals and discoveries and scenes of suffering are contained in epic and tragedy alike. Both, moreover, require artistically developed thought and diction. In all these respects Homer supplies the earliest and most satisfactory model. His poems exemplify the different types of construction: the *Iliad* being a 'simple' poem which depends on suffering for its effect, while the *Odyssey* is 'complex' (abounding as it does in dis-

[20] Cf. the second paragraph of Chap. xviii.

coveries) and a tale of character. Moreover they surpass all other poems both in diction and in thought.

Epic poetry differs from tragedy [not only in its use of the narrative form but also] as to the scale on which it is constructed and in its meter. With regard to scale, an adequate criterion has already been stated: it should be such as to allow us to bring the beginning and end within a single perspective—a condition which would be realized if the epic were reduced from its ancient length so as to be no longer than a group of tragedies presented at a single hearing. But there is one feature peculiar to the epic which allows its length to be greatly increased. In a tragedy it is not possible for several lines of action to be presented simultaneously: at any given moment the action is confined to what the actors are performing on the stage. In the epic, on the other hand, thanks to the narrative form, it is possible to present several simultaneous incidents, which, provided they are relevant, give greater substance and grandeur to the poem, as well as variety of interest. Many a tragedy fails because the uniformity of its incidents produces satiety in the audience.

With regard to meter, long experience has established the heroic [i.e., the dactyllic hexameter] as the most proper. The incongruity of any other meter or meters for a narrative poem becomes apparent as soon as it is tried. For of all meters the heroic is at once the stateliest and most permanently satisfying; and this is why narrative poetry goes beyond other forms in its tolerance of rare words and figures of speech. The iambic and trochaic, on the other hand, are meters expressing movement—the one of life and action, the other of the dance. . . . No one, accordingly, has ever written a long narrative in any but heroic meter. Nature herself, as we have said, teaches us the proper kind of verse to select.[21]

[21] The last three paragraphs are traditionally placed at the beginning of Chap. xxiv.

xxiv. Poetry and truth

Homer, in addition to his many other merits, has succeeded in being the only poet who has understood his proper role in relation to the poem. He saw that a poet should speak as little as possible in his own person, for such a method does not constitute 'poetic representation' (*mimêsis*). In contrast to other poets, who are always intruding their own personalities, and whose poetic representations are few and feeble, Homer, after a short preliminary, introduces some specific character—it may be a man or a woman, but in any case someone with distinctive characteristics.

Tragedy should stir our wonder; but the incredible, which is the principal cause of wonder, can be brought more freely into the epic, where the action is not laid right out before our eyes. Achilles' pursuit of Hector [in the *Iliad*] would look ridiculous on the stage —the Greeks standing by and refraining from pursuit as Achilles waves them back; but in the epic the absurdity is overlooked. Such excitations of wonder are pleasurable, as is shown by the way in which we all embellish our stories to make them more entertaining.

Homer more than anyone else has taught other poets the art of poetic fiction. It consists in 'the skilful exploitation of a fallacy' (*paralogismos*). When one thing is observed to be regularly accompanied or followed by another, men are apt to infer from the occurrence of the latter that the former must have occurred. Although the inference is logically invalid, it is [poetically] justifiable to supplement an untrue event with a true event that would normally follow as its consequent; for by knowing the truth of the consequent our mind (*psychê*) is betrayed into accepting the antecedent as likewise true. An illustration is provided by the bathing scene [in the *Odyssey*.] [22]

[22] Odysseus, disguised as a beggar, describes his own clothing in order to convince Penelope that he is alive while at the same time concealing his identity. Now if he *had* seen Odysseus—i.e., as someone other than himself—

In short, a plausible impossibility is always preferable to an implausible possibility. This is not to say that the story should be built out of elements that are incredible; indeed, these should be entirely avoided so far as possible. If unavoidable they should at least be exterior to the action itself, like Oedipus' ignorance of the circumstances surrounding Laius' death; not within the drama, like the [anachronistic] introduction of the Pythian games into the *Electra*. To complain that the removal of such incidents would spoil the plot is ridiculous: a plot of that kind should not have been devised in the first place. But given such a plot, if we see that it could have been developed more plausibly, we may dismiss it as [not only ill-chosen but] inept as well. Thus in the *Odyssey* the unlikely account of the hero's being landed [on the shore of Ithaca while asleep] would have been intolerable in the hands of a lesser poet; Homer, however, has managed the incident so charmingly that the absurdity is overlooked. [This should not be interpreted as a plea for elaborate diction.] In fact, elaborate diction should be confined to passages where the action is suspended—i.e., where there is no development of either character or thought, both of which an over-brilliant diction obscures.

xxv. *Some problems of poetic criticism*

Critical attacks (*problêma*) [23] upon poetry, the number and nature of the 'basic ideas' (*eidos*) on which they rest, and the

---

he would doubtless have been able to describe his clothing. But from the description of the clothing it does not follow logically—although it may well be psychologically and therefore dramatically persuasive—that Odysseus is alive *and* is someone other than the speaker.

[23] It appears to have been a custom in Aristotle's time to express criticisms in the form, or at least under the label, of *problêmata*, which is to say, problems or questions. Many criticisms of Homer were published under the title of *Homeric Problems*.

Thomas Twining remarks: "The scope of this part of Aristotle's work is of more importance to his subject than, at first view, it may appear to be. In teaching how to *answer* criticisms it in fact teaches (as far, I mean, as it goes) possible 'ways of meeting and resolving them' (*lysis*) can be examined in the light of the following considerations.

(1) The poet, being a portrayer (*mimêtês*), like the painter or any other artist, must always portray one of three kinds of object: things as they really were or are, things as they are said or popularly supposed to be, or things as they ought to be.

(2) His portrayal is accomplished by means of diction, and this may be either familiar or literary and figurative, for we concede the poet's right to use the various modifications of which language is susceptible.

(3) Furthermore, what is right in poetry must be judged by a quite different standard from what is right in the political or any other art. Two kinds of fault in a poem should be distinguished: one essential, the other incidental. If a poet has chosen to portray something and fails to do so through want of ability, the fault is inherent in the poetry. But if it was his intention to portray an object according to a certain conception of it and the conception happens to be factually incorrect—if, for instance, he were to represent a horse as throwing forward both his right legs at once, or were to commit some technical inaccuracy in medicine or other special science—such an error is not intrinsic to poetry. These three considerations should be kept in mind when we confront the objections (*problêma*) that are raised against poetry.

Let us consider the last question first, namely of [how far certain factual defects should affect our judgment of] the poetry itself. What if a poem contains incidents that could not possibly be true? This is admittedly a fault. It may be an excusable one, however, provided that the proper end of poetry is thereby more effectively attained, through producing a more striking effect in this or some

---

what the poet should do to avoid giving occasion to them. It seems, indeed, intended as an apology for poetry, and a vindication of its privileges upon true *poetical* principles, at a time when the art and its professors were unfairly attacked on all sides, by the cavils of prosaic philosophers and sophists, and by the puritanical objections of Plato and his followers." (From the Notes to his translation of the *Poetics*, second edition, 1812.)

other part of the poem. The pursuit of Hector is a case in point.[24] If, however, the poetic end might have been served as well or better without violating the canons of literal truth, the error is not justified, for all error should be avoided whenever possible. [Our guiding consideration here should be] whether a given error touches the poetic art in its essentials or only in an incidental way: it is less of an artistic fault, for instance, not to know that a hind has no horns [25] than to fail in portraying a hind [as one conceives it].

Another line of defense when a poem is criticized for factual inaccuracies [is suggested by the first of the three considerations enumerated above]: viz., that it is offered as an expression of things [not as they are or have been but] as they ought to be. This was the answer Sophocles used to give—that he drew men as they ought to be, Euripides as they are. Of course, in judging a character's excellence [26] we must look beyond any particular deed or utterance and consider the person who does or says it, the person affected, the occasion, the manner, and lastly the purpose— whether, for instance, it is for the sake of obtaining a greater good or of avoiding a greater evil.

Where a poem cannot be justified either as true to fact or as true to the ideal, it may still be defended as according with popular belief. Tales about the gods may be considered in this light. Such stories are doubtless neither true to fact nor higher than fact, but have sprung into existence quite fortuitously, as Xenophanes remarks; nevertheless they do accord with what is widely believed.

[Having discussed the first and third ways of meeting critical attacks upon poetry (as enumerated at the beginning of the chapter), Aristotle now takes up the second, which consists in considering the peculiarities

---

[24] Referring to the incident described in the second paragraph of Chap. xxiv. The same justification could be given of Homer's factually improbable account of the landing of Odysseus, mentioned at the end of that chapter.

[25] Possibly Pindar's mention of "a hind with golden horns," in his third Olympian Ode, had been a subject of critical cavil.

[26] Traditionally this sentence has been put after the following paragraph.

of poetic diction. The question is of strong importance for a precise understanding of the nature and function of poetry; Aristotle's treatment of it, however, is too intimately bound up with peculiarities of Greek idiom to be illuminating to an English reader. The chapter ends with an enumeration of five types of critical objection that can be brought against poetry: that it contains elements which cannot be true, or are contrary to good sense, or are morally pernicious, or are inconsistent with one another, or violate the canons of art. The subject of the chapter has been the possible ways of answering one or other of these criticisms.]

xxvi. Epic and tragedy compared

It may be asked which of the two forms of poetic *mimêsis*—epic or tragedy—is the better. [Opponents of tragedy argue that] since the better is the less vulgar (*phortikos*) and since the less vulgar is that which makes its appeal to a select audience, then an art which appeals to everyone is the more vulgar [and hence inferior]. Besides, [it is argued,] actors use too many gestures, as though the audience could not understand the play without their commentary —much as bad flute-players whirl about to represent discus throwing or make passes at the chorus leader when they are playing Scylla. Thus the charge against tragedy in general is much like that which actors of the older school used to bring against their successors: as when Mynniscus would call Callipides 'the ape' because of his overacting. Tragedy, in short, stands in the same relation to epic poetry—so the argument runs—as these later actors in relation to their predecessors: inasmuch as the epic appeals to a cultivated group of readers who have no need of an actor's posturings, while tragedy appeals to the masses—which means that it is a vulgar thing and therefore plainly inferior.

But in the first place, this censure should be directed against the acting rather than the poetry; for in the recital of epic, too, a minstrel can overdo the gestures. And in any case, we should not condemn all stage movements—unless we are ready to rule out dancing—but only those of inept performers. This has been the objection to Callipides, as well as to certain actors of our own day who enact a gentlewoman as though she were a slut.[27] Moreover, tragedy, no less than the epic, may produce its proper effect without being acted: we can judge its quality quite well by reading it. If, then, tragedy is superior in other respects, the fault in question may be dismissed as inessential.

[And tragedy *is* superior in other respects.] It contains everything to be found in the epic—it can even use the epic meter on occasion—and to this it makes its own significant addition of music and staging, which contribute to a more vivid pleasure—a vividness that can be felt whether the play is being acted or read. Moreover, tragic *mimêsis* attains its end in shorter compass than epic; and a concentrated effect is more pleasurable than one that is diffused by being spread out over a long period of time: imagine, for instance, Sophocles' *Oedipus* having as many words as the *Iliad!* Finally, epic *mimêsis* has less unity than tragic. This is proved by the fact that any epic poem will furnish material for a number of tragedies: so much so that if an epic poet limits himself to a single story, he either tells it concisely and so produces a truncated poem or else by stretching it out to the usual epic length produces a diluted one. In other words, an epic is [normally] made up of a number of separate actions, and therein it is deficient in unity. Even the *Iliad* and the *Odyssey* have many such parts, each with a magnitude of its own; yet the construction of those poems is as perfect, and approaches as nearly to the representation of a single action, as possible.

If, then, tragedy is superior to epic poetry in all these respects, and also in the nature of its artistic function (*ergon*)—for a given species of poetry must be regarded as producing, not any random pleasure, but tne pleasure proper to it, as we have said—it plainly follows that tragedy, in attaining the artistic end better than epic can do, is the higher rorm of poetry.

[27] Female roles were played entirely by male actors.

Indices

INDEX OF GREEK WORDS

The circumflex distinguishes long *e* and *o* (*êta* and *ômega*) from short (*epsilon* and *omikron*). A single translation consisting of more than one word is enclosed in single quotes.

Hypolêpsis: judgment, 68; 'rational belief,' 143.

Hypothesis: postulate, 80.

Idea: archetype, xxix, 163, 165; form, 96.

Ischyros: strong, 230; heavy, 230.

Isos: equal, 189, 243; fair, 189n., 243.

Kalos: 'nobly beautiful,' 186; noble, 217, 287; 'intrinsically noble,' 237.

Kalo-k'-agathia: 'ingrained beauty of character,' 220.

Kata physin: see *physis.*

Kata symbebêkos: accidental, xxxvii, 32n.; incidentally, xxxvii, 33, 134; 'in an incidental sense,' 6; 'in an incidental respect,' xl; 'in a derivative sense,' 241; 'in a secondary sense,' 239; indirectly, 129, 134, 137.

Kataphasis: see *phasis.*

Kenon: 'empty space,' 43.

Kinêsis: motion, xxvii, xxviii, xxxiv, 43, 44, 47, 61, 75, 112, 113; movement, 20, 137, 258; change, xxvii, xxxiv. *Kinein:* 'to move or change,' 45n.; 'to produce motion,' 99n. *Akinêtos:* 'immutable, changeless,' 97. Cf. *metabolê.*

Koinônia: society, xii, 279; association, 280; 'community relationship,' 280; 'community livng,' 281.

Kommos: 'lamentation carried on between the chorus and an actor,' 305.

Kosmos: 'public ornament,' 218; 'crowning perfection,' 220.

Krasis: blending, xlv.

Leukos (adj.): 'pallid whiteness,' 6.

Lexis: diction, xliv, 297; language, 313.

Logismos: reasoning, 67; 'reasoning power,' 129; calculating, 152; calculation, 228.

Logos: meaning, xxxv, 42, 45, 103, 120; 'articulable meaning,' xxxi; 'logical meaning,' 4, 23; 'formal meaning,' 79; 'definitive meaning,' 118; 'real meaning,' 121; 'essential meaning,' 131; 'meaning of the whole,' 121; reason, 169, 207, 234; reasoning, 224; 'articulate reason,' 142; 'rational understanding,' 88; 'rational principle,' xxxix, 169, 231; 'rational speech,' 281; 'logical account,' 80; 'logical explanation,' 8; 'set of propositions,' 88; calculation, 227; theory, 68; ratio, 135; proportion, 140; 'proportionate arrangement of parts,' 135; 'speeches and dialogue,' 309. *Logos praktikos:* 'practical reason,' 41. *Eidos kai logos:* see *eidos. Logon echôn:* 'having reason,' 169n. 'Have *logos* of': 'pay heed to,' 179; 'have a rational understanding of,' 179; cf. 223n. *Orthos logos:* 'right principle,' 223n., 230, 234.

Lysis: 'denouement or resolution,' 310; 'ways of meeting and resolving [criticisms],' 322.

Makarios: blessed, 169; 'supremely happy,' 263, 267; 'blessed with supreme happiness,' 177 and n.; 'complete happiness,' 268.

Megaloprepeia: munificence, 216.

Megalopsychia: see *psychê.*

Melas (adj.): 'swarthy blackness,' 6.

Melos: song, xliv, 296, 297.

Meson: 'mean' (noun), 189, 191. *Mesotês:* 'mean' (noun), 149n.; moderation, 191; 'state of tension between opposite qualities,' 135.

Metabasis: 'change in the hero's fortune,' 303.

Metabolê: change, xxxiv, 20, 43, 44 and n., 48, 50, 95; 'process of change,' 60. Cf. *kinêsis.*

Metaphora: metaphor, 315.

Methodos: procedure, 118; 'scientific investigation,' 157; 'type of inquiry,' 170.

Mêtis: wisdom, 141.

Phasis: proposition, 148. *Kataphasis:* affirmation, 148.

Philia: friendship, 236 and n.; 'friendly affection,' 188; 'friendship, affection, or love,' 242n. *Philein:* 'to be friends,' 239. *Philêsis:* affection, 239; fondness, 242.

Philomythos: myth-lover, 72n.

Philosophos: philosopher, 72n. *Philosophia:* 'pursuit of wisdom,' 266. *Protê philosophia:* 'basic philosophy,' xxvii.

Phobos: 'fear, or apprehension,' xlv.

Phonê: 'vocal sound,' 140.

Phora: locomotion, xxxiv, 44 and n., 61; 'spatial movement,' 100.

Phortikos: vulgar, 324.

Phronein: 'to take counsel,' 145; intelligence, 141, 'typically human intelligence,' 141. *Phronêsis:* sagacity, 142, 143, 225; 'moral sagacity,' xli; 'prudent counsel,' 143; thinking, 72.

Phthora: passing - out - of - existence, xxxiv; annihilation, 45; disintegration, 60 and n.

Physei: 'by nature,' 21, 29, 39; naturally, 23. *Kata physin:* 'in accordance with nature,' 21, 22. *Physis kai ousia:* 'real nature,' 22. *Physikê epistêmê:* 'science of nature,' 81.

Physis: nature, xxxii, 20, 21, 22, 95, 117; 'organic nature,' 207; 'organic development,' 227; 'fundamental respect,' 78. *Physikos:* natural, xxxiii; 'of the order of nature,' 97; 'natural scientist,' 24; 'natural philosopher,' 98. *Physikê:* 'natural science,' xxxii, 24. *Physikon:* 'natural basis,' 22.

Pistis: 'trustworthy conviction,' 117.

Poiein: 'to make,' 292; productivity, 218. *Poiêsis:* making, xxvii and n.; poem, 291. *Poiêtikos:* productive, xxvii, 70, 72, 224; creative, 147. *Poiêtikê:* poetics, xxvii; 'art of poetry,' 281. *Poiêtikê epistêmê:* 'productive form of knowledge,' 87. *Poiêtês:* poet, 292.

Pragma: 'situation referred to,' 88.

Prattein (verb): 'overt deeds,' 268.

Praktikos: moral, 82; practical, 224.

Praxis: action, xliv, 157, 200, 202, 227, 296; 'moral action,' xxxix, xl, 34, 183; 'moral conduct,' 224; 'conscious action,' 171; 'human action,' 297; 'dramatic action,' 305. *Eupraxia:* 'well doing,' 34, 225.

Proairesis: choice, 33; 'choice of ends,' 203; 'moral choice,' xl, 81, 'deliberate choice,' 34, 188; 'purposive choice,' xxvii, 157, 205; 'purposeful choice,' xxxix, xli, 242; 'moral purpose,' 283, 299, 309; 'deliberate intent,' 279; will, xli; 'responsible human will,' xliv.

Problêma: [critical] attack, 321 and n.; objection, 322.

Prôtos: basic, 58. *Prôtê hylê, proton hypokeimenon,* etc.: see *hylê, hypokeimenon,* etc.

Psychê: soul, xxxix; life, 117, 316; mind, 320. *Prôtê psychê:* 'rudimentary soul,' 132. *Megalopsycha:* 'proper pride,' 193; 'aristocratic pride,' 219 and n. *Mikropsychia:* pettiness, 193.

Rhetorikê: oratory, xxvii, 158, 299.

Schêma: 'visible form,' 23; 'visible form not capable of reproducing itself,' 23.

Scholê: leisure, 286 and n.

Skeuopoios: 'costumer and stage-manager,' 299.

Sôma: 'physical body,' 55.

Sophos: 'wise man,' 227; philosopher, 229, 269; expert, 229. *Sophia:* wisdom, 70, 225, 227, 231, 266.

Sôtêria: 'escape from captivity, and religious salvation,' 313n.

Spoudaios: 'virtuous man,' 262; 'ideally good man,' 210.

Stasis: rest, 20.

Sterêsis: 'falling short,' xxxiii; 'lack of form,' 14; 'lack of final character,' xxxv; incompleteness, 16, 17; not-

INDEX OF PERSONS MENTIONED BY ARISTOTLE

INDEX OF TOPICS